The Extraordinary Story of

Ann Hasseltine Judson

A Life Beyond Boundaries

ROSALIE HALL HUNT

Foreword by Jerry B. Cain

JUDSON PRESS
PUBLISHERS SINCE 1824

Join our mailing list for updates and special offers.
www.judsonpress.com/mailing_list.cfm

The Extraordinary Story of Ann Hasseltine Judson: A Life Beyond Boundaries

Judson Press has made every effort to trace the ownership of all quotes. In the event of a question arising from the use of a quote, we regret any error made and will be pleased to make the necessary correction in future printings and editions of this book.

Bible quotations in this volume are from the King James Version.

The cover picture is a golden sunset over the Andaman Sea that was captured in Moulmein, Burma, just one block from the Judsons' home. The photo was taken by David Hanna, great-great-grandson of Adoniram Judson.

Library of Congress Cataloging-in-Publication Data
Names: Hunt, Rosalie Hall, author.
Title: The extraordinary story of Ann Hasseltine Judson: a life beyond boundaries Rosalie Hall Hunt. Description: Valley Forge, PA: Judson Press, 2018.| Includes bibliographical references and index. Identifiers: LCCN 2017037432 (print) | LCCN 2017044183 (ebook) | ISBN 9780817081843 (e-book) | ISBN 9780817017934 (pbk.: alk. paper) Subjects: LCSH: Judson, Ann Hasseltine, 1789-1826.| Missionaries—Burma—Biography. | Missionaries—United States—Biography. | Missionaries' spouses—Burma—Biography. Classification: LCC BV3271.J81 (ebook) | LCC BV3271.J81 H86 2018 (print) | DDC 266/.61092 [B]—dc23 LC record available at https://lccn.loc.gov/2017037432

Printed in the U.S.A.
First printing, 2018.

To

Bob — my husband and inspiration

and

Faye Pearson — our missionary hero

CONTENTS

Contents

FOREWORD

"DO WE NEED ANOTHER ONE?" I ASKED MYSELF LAST YEAR WHEN I heard that someone was writing a new Judson biography. When it was explained to me that the someone was Dr. Rosalie Hall Hunt, author of the very popular *Bless God and Take Courage: The Judson History and Legacy* (Judson Press, 2005), and that she was writing about Ann Hasseltine Judson, the first wife of Adoniram and the first female missionary of American Baptists, I immediately exclaimed, "Yes! *That* is a story we need to hear anew!"

I am grateful that Rosalie has invested the past few years researching, writing, and reminding the public of Ann Judson's contribution to history and missiology. She has provided the most intimate account of Ann Judson I have read. This retelling of Ann's heroics as she kept her husband, Adoniram, alive while he was imprisoned describes not only the facts of those twenty-one months of persecution but also the personal anguish of a young mother torn between nursing a new baby and taking food to her husband who is starving while incarcerated. The personal side of Ann's exploits is a riveting addition to the details of her incredible life.

Dr. Hunt reminds us of Ann Hasseltine Judson's work with women and children. In particular, education for girls and women were high priorities for Ann, almost two centuries before Malala Yousafzai brought the cause to the attention of the Nobel Peace Prize committee. Ann Judson's regular writings in missionary periodicals and her captivating *Account of the American Baptist Mission to the Burman Empire* (1827) would inspire the next two generations of missionaries.

With this new biography, we get to laugh with Ann Hasseltine Judson and we get to cry with her in the struggles of missionary life. *The Extraordinary Story* describes the emotional side of this "missionary heroine" (as one nineteenth-century biographer hailed her),[1] adding a perspective on her humanity that is as compelling as the standard picture of her brilliant mind and stubborn tenacity. The empathy that Dr. Hunt adds to the story greatly enhances the saga of this great hero in the faith, and the hero becomes a friend. The facts are enriched with feelings, the exploits enhanced by emotions.

Born in China to missionary parents, author Rosalie Hall Hunt has lived the life of a missionary in eight nations. She understands not only the facts of missionary experience but also the emotional highs and lows, and the emotional power of pioneer missionary Ann Judson comes to life in these pages. Rosalie's previous work on the Judsons, *Bless God and Take Courage*, as well as *Her Way: The Remarkable Story of Hephzibah Jenkins Townsend*, have proven her sagacity in both research and writing. The reading public, especially those interested in missions and women in leadership, will be inspired by the model of Ann Hasseltine Judson and be grateful to Rosalie Hall Hunt for retelling her important saga, combining the facts of the story with the human feelings of a compassionate woman.

In the true missionary spirit of Ann and Rosalie, royalties from the sale of this book will not go into any private purse but will be reinvested in missionary work around the world. Get ready for a great story, and keep a tissue handy.

Jerry B. Cain, Chancellor
Judson University

Note

1. "The Missionary Heroine," in *Queenly Women, Crowned and Uncrowned*, S. W. Williams, ed. (Cincinnati: Cranston and Stowe, 1885).

PREFACE

THIS ACCOUNT OF ANN HASSELTINE JUDSON IS NOT FICTION. IT IS narrative based on fact. Conversations are based on my understanding of the contents of the many letters written by Ann, in addition to the plethora of material recorded about this key figure in American missions history. This narrative is as faithful as possible to the intent of Ann's own thoughts and words, and any errors contained herein are certainly unintentional. Much time these past nineteen years has been spent delving into Ann's legacy and it has been the adventure of a lifetime. Ann Hasseltine Judson has felt like part of my family since early childhood, for my middle name, Ann, is in honor of my maternal grandmother, Ann Judson Fogle Wells.

Dealing with documented facts is quite different from writing fiction. In fiction, the writer has liberty to manipulate the leading characters and their supporting cast and can safely conclude with, "And they lived happily ever after." Had this narrative been make-believe, I would have chosen a different ending. New details of Ann's early years have come to light and shed clarity on how she became a woman of such extraordinary spiritual depth. With her brilliant mind, linguistic aptitude, force of will, and depth of character, Ann managed not only to keep her husband alive but also to leave behind her own splendid translation work and the foundation of women's education. This narrative is *real life*—often an excruciatingly painful, exciting, suspenseful, turbulent, and tragic life. Above all it was a life lived victoriously and courageously, one that left a remarkable legacy that is alive and well more than two hundred years later.

Centuries before missionaries came to clearly understand the importance of training nationals in ministry to reach their own people, it was already the policy and practice of Ann and Adoniram Judson. They identified so closely with the people of Burma that their way of thinking took on the shading of the people they came to love so devotedly and to whom they dedicated their lives and energies.

VIII

Ann's life exemplified the message of Roman's 12:1, to present our bodies a living sacrifice. That is exactly what she did, in an heroic way the world has seldom encountered. Her patience, perseverance, tenacity, and courage were remarkable. She and Adoniram were the first to translate Scripture into Burmese, and in Ann's case, into Siamese as well. She was the pioneer missionary school teacher and women's evangelist. In the absence of her husband, Ann frequently conducted worship services in Burmese and became a universally beloved figure among the believers.

The significance of the Judsons in US missions history continues to unfold more than two hundred years after they lived. Ann Hasseltine Judson was an Ebenezer of courage to whom every generation of believers can look and be inspired. In the last years of his life, her husband was often asked, "Dr. Judson, what do you see as the future of missions?" He would invariably reply, "It is as bright as the promises of God." With that same assurance strong in her heart, Ann never lost sight of God's great call and her own determination to be a "living sacrifice, holy, acceptable unto God" (Romans 12:1). Her extraordinary legacy is very much alive.

ACKNOWLEDGMENTS

THE INFORMATION AND ENCOURAGEMENT FOR THIS BOOK HAVE come over a period of nearly twenty years. I began researching the Judson legacy in 1999 during a month in Burma, teaching and visiting locations that had been part of the Judsons' lives. Material gathered over the years has provided a rich background of Judson family history from which to reconstruct Ann's life. Seven trips to Burma and numerous journeys to New England to visit locations important in the Judsons' early years produced even more information.

I extend deep gratitude to the late Dr. Stanley Hanna, Judson's great-grandson, who made available countless primary sources from the Judson family trunk during the early years of research. Traveling to Burma with Dr. Hanna and his family to visit spots where his great-grandparents served was a moving and unforgettable experience. Special thanks as well to David Hanna, the great-great-grandson of Judson, for his encouragement and photographic expertise.

The American Baptist Historical Society was another repository for primary sources about the lives of the Judsons. Harriet Bain of Rolla, Missouri, gave valuable assistance in translating Burmese phrases and language materials: Harriet's ever-so-great- grandfather was Ah Vong, the Chinese-Burmese printer who printed the first edition of Judson's peerless Burmese Bible translation. The professional expertise of Ella Robinson, who edited the first draft, was indispensable, and Shelley Glassco of Guntersville, Alabama, was tireless in proofreading. Dr. Jerry Cain, chancellor of Judson University in Elgin, Illinois, and noted Judson scholar, was a great source of encouragement and expertise. Special thanks as well to editor Rebecca Irwin-Diehl and the Judson Press staff for their splendid assistance and editing skills.

The support of the Woman's Missionary Union Foundation, Southern Baptist Convention, made the book a reality. The Foundation's aim is to promote the future of missions and missions education worldwide. Their assistance in making this account of Ann Judson a reality will in turn provide resources to continue the vital ministry of the Foundation.

Beginnings in Bradford 1789–1796

The oldest portrait of Ann Hasseltine Judson is this 1811 miniature, carefully preserved in the archives of the American Baptist Historical Society.

DURING CHRISTMAS WEEK OF 1789, the little town of Bradford, Massachusetts, lay under a blanket of soft white snow that was growing deeper by the minute. A quiet stillness filled the evening air. Inside the snug house on Boxford Road, however, lamps blazed in several rooms, and everyone inside the Hasseltine home was wide awake. Rebecca Hasseltine had thought her baby would surely not arrive before Christmas Day, but this little one seemed determined to come on her own schedule. Time would prove that this determination was an inbred part of a remarkable personality.

The four older children had been shooed off to another room for big sister to Becky to read a Christmas tale. Polly, a self-important five-year-old, had a pretty good idea that something momentous was going on that night. Even three-year-old Johnny was old enough to know that something was different. However, the two children listened to Becky read while the fourth child, baby Abigail, slept peacefully in her little trundle bed.

Just before midnight that Tuesday night, December 22, 1789, a tiny girl took her first breath, and Rebecca's heart instantly made room for another child to love. She was fascinated at the way the newborn's black curls, so soft to the touch, would wrap around her finger like the baby was already entwined around her mother's heart.

1

John Hasseltine reached out a gentle finger to touch the baby's delicate hand, and her tiny fingers curved tightly around his. The doting father exclaimed, "Rebecca! See how strong she is! And she looks amazingly like her beautiful mother." Rebecca gave an exhausted smile as she noted the little red face scrunched up as if annoyed by the lights and noise invading her world for the first time. "I do believe she's bound to improve in temperament upon acquaintance, John," she suggested. "And I think she wants a name."

John was partial to "Nancy," but Rebecca was leaning toward "Ann," so they compromised and used both within the family. Rebecca thought back to the eminent Ann Langley, who had become the first bride in the whole Rowley district when she married Robert Hasseltine in 1639. "Maybe our little one will one day be redoubtable like your ancestress as well," she suggested to John. "Mayhap," he responded, "our little mite will someday be both renowned and strong."

Not even in their wildest imaginations could Rebecca and John Hasseltine have dreamed that one day this tiny child would be known as America's "Woman of the Century" or as "An Illuminated Initial Letter" on the pages of missionary history. Who could ever have guessed that the unpretentious little town of Bradford would become a shining star on the map of missions history? The birth of Ann Hasseltine was destined to forever place it squarely in the forefront of America's missions legacy.

Baby Ann became the family Christmas present that year, and friends and neighbors passing along the Boston Road, as Boxford Road was commonly called, stopped by the comfortable Hasseltine home that holiday season to congratulate the family on the new arrival. America had a newly ratified constitution, and a sense of destiny and optimism prevailed in the land. Little Ann had picked a fortuitous time in history and a beautiful spot in which to be born. The Merrimac River flowed nearby, and even in the dead of winter, it was a splendid sight. The settlement dated back to the earliest days of the Old Commonwealth, and Hasseltines had been the first settlers back to 1637, when brothers Robert and John both acquired large tracts of land and began farming. Robert opened the first ferry across the long and winding Merrimac and was the first selectman in the new settlement. He and his wife, Ann, built the first permanent residence in Bradford village, which was a bustling center of community life. That seventeenth-century Ann was a woman of courage and determination. And her namesake, born that snowy December 1789 night, would become a worthy successor.

Life in the two-story Hasseltine home was never dull and seldom quiet. Ann, the baby girl, became a big sister the August before her third birthday when Joseph Hall made his appearance. Little Joseph, the second son, became the center of attention, and John Hasseltine was delighted to think that they had a quiver full of six healthy, intelligent little ones.

Rebecca Hasseltine was thirty that year of 1791, and although never strong, she had learned how to deal with the undiagnosed condition that sapped her energy. Friends in the neighborhood never fully realized that most of the time she was also in pain. Rebecca had been a great beauty and still displayed a bone-deep loveliness that time would never be able to erase. The fragile young mother learned to pace herself and demonstrated a keen ability to train and direct her little ones to participate in all the household duties. She was never one to complain but instead managed to appear to the unobserving eye as a strong, healthy woman. Rebecca adroitly managed to make even the most mundane chore appear like fun to her brood. She knew how to engage the older children to guide the younger ones in their tasks.

Rebecca had a reputation in Bradford for reading more books in a month than any other woman in the district read in a full year. John was aware of Rebecca's fragile health as well as her voracious appetite for reading. It was his pleasure to be sure she got a new supply of books each month from the social library in nearby Salem, as well as from the Salem Philosophical Library. She was one of their most consistent patrons. When Ann was about seven years old, nearby Haverhill opened a lending library, and it was like a Christmas present to Rebecca. She loved to sit in her favorite rocking chair at the bay window of the east parlor, with a fire glowing in the fireplace, and read about adventures and places far away. From this vantage point, she could gently direct the work of the household.

Rebecca loved the special wallpaper John had purchased when they built their house the year of their wedding. The lovely pink blossoms with their intertwined leaves were complimented by delicate yellow flowers that seemed to nod and smile. Rebecca's window seat was the heart of the family circle, and the first place John came when returning from a day's work supervising those who labored in Hasseltine fields. The bay window looked out on Boxford Road, and Rebecca could see at a glance when John was on his way home.

John Hasseltine was a favorite employer in the area—always affable, and always a man of his word. He was a favorite with his children as well, for they had learned how to wrap him around their small fingers, especially young Ann, who instinctively knew the quickest route to her Papa's heart, whether with her winsome smile or a fervent kiss on his cheek. It did not take family and friends long to realize that John and his youngest daughter were strikingly alike in their outgoing personalities and love of people.

Ann could wield a handy broom by the time she was three years old, and sister Becky, at ten, was a patient teacher, although sometimes exasperated by the way Ann would manage to slip away on some venture that had captured her mind. Mama would shake her head as the contrite young Ann stood in front of her, hanging her head in seeming repentance at another unexplained disappearance.

"Ah, Ann! Dear, dear daughter mine," Rebecca would give a smiling sigh. "I wonder if you'll ever get over your strong tendency to ramble from place to place?" Ann would give her roguish little grin and explain, "But Mama, it is just something that I *need* to do!" Ann was also adept at changing the subject and would often respond with, "Mama, what are you reading now? Where are you dreaming of going in this book?" Her dark curls would nod as she earnestly asked: "Is it a pretty place? Would I like to go there, too?"

4

Then Rebecca would take her little one onto her lap and tell her tales of faraway places with strange-sounding names. Ann never tired of Mama's stories, and this early thirst for adventure and the exotic lasted a lifetime.

Ann loved helping take care of baby Joseph. Her dimple-cheeked younger brother had stolen her heart immediately, and she instinctively knew how to be gentle with him. By the time Joseph was born, the older children were already in the little red schoolhouse that offered a basic education for the more fortunate village children. Both John and Rebecca Hasseltine were quite revolutionary in thinking that an education was as important for girls as for boys. Many of their neighbors thought them a bit radical in their thinking. After all, weren't girls going to grow up to be wives and mothers who follow their husbands' instructions just as they had listened to their fathers? Maybe John Hasseltine was ahead of his time, but in his mind each child was gifted with the ability to learn and to make a difference in the world. Small wonder, with two such forward-thinking parents, that the Hasseltine offspring would one day make such significant contributions to the world.

John, the family patriarch, was the most outgoing family member, and a favorite in the town and district. However, certain of the town fathers were rather perturbed that this successful and upstanding member of the community was not involved in the church. First Congregational Church of Bradford was the center of life in the town and just a stone's throw from the Hasseltine's home. The family attended services sporadically, although they were firm believers in the Ten Commandments. They carefully instilled good morals in their offspring but not the need for a living faith. It was a puzzle to many because John's own father, Deacon Hasseltine, had been a pillar of the church, and John had grown up attending regularly. There was no rebellion there, but neither was there any real involvement. It was perplexing.

Rebecca, the matriarch, had been a dreamer since her childhood in Sutton and had always had a thirst for travel, new sights, new adventures. Of all the children, Ann was most attuned to her mother's heart and shared the same sense of wanderlust. John loved each of his children with all his heart, but it was plain to see that Ann was John's favorite. Thankfully, she did not attempt to take advantage, which might have caused her siblings to resent her influence.

Rebecca, the oldest and named after her mother, was always called Becky. Gentle by nature, she was a little mother to her younger siblings, and like all the Hasseltine brood, bright as a newly minted penny.

Next came Mary, who was called Polly. She was ever the pragmatist who enjoyed action more than books, so anyone who was a dreamer or an idealist found faint favor with Polly.

John, the oldest son, had a lifelong fascination with the sea and could scarcely wait until he was old enough to join the crew of one of the ships that sailed in and out of Salem Harbor. The Hasseltines had several relatives living in Salem, and young John loved to spend days at a time with them, roaming the wharves and talking to sea captains who often came ashore. Papa insisted that he go to school first, so John impatiently bided his time. All the land around town had once belonged to Great-Great-Great-Grandfather Robert, and John, in turn, had given it to the town of Bradford, but it appeared young John was not interested in farming like his father.

Abigail was the shy one in the family. While the other Hasseltine siblings displayed outgoing personalities, Abby appeared content to sit back and let her siblings take the lead in an activity, sitting with her thumb tucked firmly in her mouth, quietly observing all that went on around her.

Joseph Hall was the second son and followed Ann in the Hasseltine brood. He idolized his closest older sister, Ann, and tried to emulate her behavior.

July 13, 1796, was a red-letter day in the mind of six-year-old Ann, for that was the day Bille was born. William, always lovingly known at Bille (pronounced Billy), was the third son and the youngest of all the Hasseltine children. Ann doted on baby Bille, who looked uncannily like her, with large brown eyes and shiny dark curls. By the time he was a few weeks old, Ann could not imagine life without him. Each new ability he developed was like a milestone to big sister, and she loved carrying him from room to room and explaining everything to him, as if he could understand. While Mama nursed Bille, Ann would sit at her feet and dream out loud about the adventures the two of them would have one day. "Oh dear," Rebecca would smile, "do you think he will be a rambler, too?" "Of course," Ann replied, "I'm sure of it. I will personally train him!" Rebecca's mind immediately jumped to thoughts of how she could keep up with two ramblers in one household, especially if the second displayed the same innovative ability for rambling as did the first.

All the Hasseltine family was anticipating the splendor of Christmas, with the children caught up in the excitement of the season, even little Bille. Ann delighted in having her baby brother help celebrate her seventh birthday just three days before Christmas. The baby's eyes were wide with wonder at all the sights and fragrances of the season on display in the Hasseltine home. But then the totally unexpected occurred. Bille developed a high fever on Christmas Eve, prompting a worried John to call in Dr. Walker to see what was wrong. The fever was puzzling, and their efforts to cool down Bille were ineffective. They tried cooling cloths, and Dr. Walker even tried using a fever-reducing powder, but nothing availed.

Christmas Day was fraught with worry in the Hasseltine household, and everyone took turns walking with the fretting infant and trying to soothe his cries. A cloud of anxiety engulfed the normally buoyant household. Worried eyes looked into other worried eyes, seeking an answer that didn't seem to be out there, no matter how hard each one tried to find it.

Bradford's Kimball Tavern, circa 1692, is the site where Bradford Academy was voted into existence in 1803.

KIMBALL
TAVERN
1692
BRADFORD COLLEGE
FOUNDED HERE
MARCH 7, 1803

An Academy Is Contemplated
1796–1803

CHRISTMAS 1796 WAS ONE THE HASSELTINE FAMILY WOULD NEVER FORget, and certainly one they hoped never to repeat. Despite all their efforts, the mysterious fever overcame little Bille, and the day after Christmas, he lost his grasp on life. The family dissolved in sorrow, and forever after, the memory of that beautiful baby was starkly imprinted on the heart of his big sister. In her ramblings now, Ann often walked to the burying ground and stood beside the little marker, lovingly tracing his engraved name, William Hasseltine, with her fingers, her mind searching for an answer. She would sit on her mother's lap and ask again and again, "Why, Mama, why is Bille gone?" knowing even as she asked that Mama had no answer.

John and Rebecca worked hard to swallow their own grief in order to help their other children. Infant deaths were common in the New

England of their day, but that did not make the loss any easier. The Hasseltines had escaped death's cold finger until now. It helped a bit that Ann was now old enough to attend school with her older siblings, as she needed to keep her sorrowing mind busy. Bradford was considered quite a forward-thinking community to have a school available for a good number of the village children, with even the young girls learning to read, to write, and to cipher along with the boys.

The days passed slowly after Bille's tragic death, and of course the remaining children still required love and nurture. Ann slowly switched her attachment from Bille to her older but shyer sister, Abby, and watched over her. And big sister Becky, ever the little mother, seemed born to her role as the oldest. Any problem that confronted the younger ones during the school day was taken immediately to Becky, who always found a way to effect a good compromise. Becky was not only a competent big sister but also loved passing on her reading skills to her younger siblings.

In contrast to Ann and her other siblings, the ever-shy Abigail seemed both diffident and uncertain in her grasp of new information. John and Rebecca were growing a trifle worried; all their other children appeared to be exceptionally bright, but Abby's development seemed delayed. Until age four, she never uttered a complete sentence, whereas toddler Ann was constantly talking. Perhaps that was part of why Abby was so deeply attached to Ann, usually depending on her talkative little sister to be the vocal one. However, as Ann quickly picked up on Becky's instruction, it seemed to become contagious for Abby. And then a light came on. One evening when John returned from the fields, little Abby ran to clutch his trouser leg and said, "Daddy, come see what I made today!" The entire family was astonished to hear Abby suddenly speaking in whole sentences.

Who would have guessed then that shy Abigail Hasseltine would one day become the commanding, queenly principal of Bradford Academy, one of New England's premier institutions for the education of women? Perhaps her own struggle with language made her keenly sympathetic to those who learned slowly. Whatever the case,

9

while each Hasseltine child was bright, Abigail soon exhibited an ability to teach. Miss Kimball, their instructor at the schoolhouse down by the frog pond and alder swamp, was thankful for this child who loved explaining how to do their numbers to the youngest ones in the one-room school.

As for Ann, by the time she was four she already knew her letters and could read simple words. She was amazingly quick in her understanding, absorbing new information with the same ease with which she dug into a good bowl of porridge. Johnny, however, presented something of a problem. School was not his favorite pastime; he would rather be out walking alongside the blue-flowing Merrimac, dreaming of those waters reaching the sea and rolling on to those faraway places of which he yearned. School was awfully dull and restrictive to a child with wanderlust. Practical Polly simply could not understand the attraction of anything exotic, far preferring what she could see and touch and control as she wished. Of all her siblings, Ann seemed most sympathetic to Johnny—but then she would be, since her own small feet took her exploring every chance they got.

Ann quickly became known as "the rambler." Following recess on many a warm spring day, Miss Kimball would ring the bell for students to return to their desks, and as frequently as not, the last one to slip back in was Ann. She was forever finding some new and interesting spot to explore or some new wonder of nature to examine. At first her teacher had been exasperated, but she soon learned that a genuine curiosity called to Ann's inquiring mind. Ann would invariably return to her assigned lesson, albeit a trifle breathless or disheveled, but always sweetly repentant. Miss Kimball would shake her head in resignation, inwardly smiling at the clever creativity of Ann Hasseltine in offering a sound reason for the necessity of her rambles. Thankfully, her mind was as facile as her feet, and she managed to curb some of that restless spirit by having adventures through the stories she absorbed with such rapidity.

Often in the late evenings after their children had said their prayers, listened to a bedtime story, and been tucked into their beds, John and

Rebecca would discuss how to further their children's education. Rebecca sat in her favorite rocking chair by the bay window, while their gray tabby cat, Ulysses, slept purring by the fire. She always lent an aura of peace to any place she could be found. Here in her favorite room, John liked to wind down after a busy day in the fields and in the town. John himself had had little opportunity for learning beyond the basics, although he had become a surveyor of both highways and timber for Bradford, and had held as many as seventeen different positions, indicative of his breadth knowledge as well as the high respect in which he was held. Nevertheless, he longed for his children to have opportunities that he had never known.

Few communities in the state of Massachusetts, nor in any state in the new nation, for that matter, had much to offer in the way of education beyond the basics. Unless families were wealthy enough to hire private tutors, only a handful of their sons could think of going away to Harvard or a bit further north to Brown College in Providence. Even fewer families contemplated further education for their daughters. The opportunity to learn reading, writing, and arithmetic was available to only a small minority of girls, since so many citizens did not see any need for schooling females. John and Rebecca Hasseltine were not of that number, however, and they intended to do something to further the education of all their children, regardless of gender. John was particularly proud of Rebecca's keen and inquiring mind and of her influence on their children. He believed that the education of mothers was vital to developing children who would grow up to make a difference in the world, and that women were the true civilizing influence.

By the time she was thirteen, Ann had plumbed the depths of learning available at the local schoolhouse. Furthermore, school only met a few months of the year. That was not enough for the Hasseltines. Rebecca was spending as much time as she could helping the children expand their depth of knowledge, so John decided the time had come to take matters into his own hands. He began talking with other fathers in Bradford, many of whom had children the same age as the

Hasseltines'. He and Rebecca were pleased to find a general desire for advanced learning for the children of Bradford. John set into motion plans for interested men in the town to gather at Kimball Tavern, on the village green, just a stone's throw from both the church and the Hasseltine home.

John was pleased to find interest in starting an academy from all the men in attendance. The several Kimball families of Bradford were also descendants of Robert Hasseltine of founding lore. Moses Kimball (who ran the tavern and inn), Colonel James Kimball, and Ed Kimball all had children who were cousins and playmates with the Hasseltine brood, and the three Kimball men thought an academy was a splendid idea. Other supporters included Dr. Benjamin Walker, the Bartletts, the Chadwicks, Squire Thurston, and several other prominent families.

The idea caught on quickly, and John Hasseltine discovered a leading supporter in Parson Jonathan Allen, whose fifteen-year-old Betsey was a good friend of the Hasseltine girls. Parson Allen, the town's well-respected minister of First Congregational Church, had overseen the spiritual life of the parish for some eleven years. He had often wished that John was as interested in spiritual matters as he was in community affairs; the talents and people skills Hasseltine possessed would mean a lot to the parish church. He frequently prayed for the day when he would see John Hasseltine leading in the church as well as in the town. A solid supporter of the idea of an academy, Parson Allen soon became a key figure in helping John get the word out and in bringing the idea of an academy to life.

Word spread, and on a rather blustery March 4, 1803, well over a dozen leaders of Bradford's first parish gathered in the warm confines of Kimball Tavern, a venerable building dating back to 1668. Moses Kimball was a genial host, and his tavern had a well-deserved reputation for a warm welcome and plenty of good Jamaican rum. The presence of Pastor Allen—always looking groomed to the inch, from his powdered wig to his cocked hat, short breeches, and polished boots with their shiny silver buckles—lent weight to John Hasseltine's proposal.

John Hasseltine, not as finely adorned though always neat and trim in appearance, opened the gathering with a look at their common purpose: providing the best education available for their children. It was an easy sell for such a group of community leaders, and those especially gifted in financial matters began to discuss how much they would need to get started. Several chimed in with ideas for a convenient location and even for possible instructors. Hasseltine was warmed to the heart by such response, and before the meeting ended, those assembled had voted to organize and subscribe to underwriting the costs of such an undertaking. Parson Allen noted, a bit tongue-in-cheek, that if the good men of Bradford spent as much on education as they did in the taprooms of the tavern, school finances would certainly be no problem.

The assembled men decided that an initial $1,500, quite a vast sum in the early 1800s, would be necessary to make their academy a reality. Each man volunteered the amount he would contribute, with a single share being $100. Most were able to pledge $100, but John Hasseltine and a few others, such as Squire Thurston and Dr. Walker, contributed a double pledge, thus expressing their serious intent about a quality education for their young ones.

Once the town fathers took action, things moved rapidly. An ideal location was the property adjacent to the Greenleaf house, next to which stood the large Hasseltine home, only rods (a rod was five yards) from Kimball Inn. This spot was the crossroads of the thriving little town of some fourteen hundred residents. Right on the corner of Boxford Road and Salem Street stood the inn, to which post riders delivered the town's mail two or three times a week, and the First Parish Church stood a short distance away.

No one wasted time, and work proceeded apace. Within two months the new school was complete. Bradford's new academy had one main story with two departments—one for young men, one for young ladies. The gleaming white structure was topped by a two-story steeple, surmounted by a circular belfry in which hung a beautiful new bell. Excitement mounted as the youth of Bradford realized that by the first of June 1803, they would be in their new academy, with two brand-new teachers.

Thirteen-year-old Ann Hasseltine was breathless with excitement when that Wednesday morning arrived. She and her siblings, upon hearing the school bell toll, stepped out their front door and, within a minute, entered their new school. John and Joseph were among the fourteen boys who constituted the boy's class, to be instructed by the academy's first preceptor, Samuel Walker, a recent Dartmouth graduate. Harriet Swan was preceptor for the thirty-seven young ladies who comprised the girls' opening class, including three Hasseltines, Ann Bartlett, and the Chadwick sisters. Fanny Woodbury came from Beverly to stay as a boarding student with a neighboring family, and she and Ann bonded from the first day. Ann's good friend Betsey Allen took possession of the desk next to Ann's, and the younger Harriet Atwood, who idolized her older friend Ann, sat in the same row as well. The young ladies were more than double the number of their male counterparts, and the two groups developed something of a good-natured competition in academic prowess, several of the more motivated being challenged by the idea of excelling.

From the cradle, the Hasseltine children had been taught by a strict moral code, liberally laced with warmth and love. Regular church attendance had not been the norm for their young lives, but school brought a new discipline in relation to Bible teaching, for each day began with Scripture reading and prayer, as did the afternoon session as well. Initially it seemed excessive to these children who were not used to so much "religion." However, constant exposure began to make an impression on their way of thinking. Little did they realize that the years just ahead would bring about an extraordinary change in the life of the Hasseltine family, and that this immense change would be led by the youngest daughter.

CHAPTER 3

A Growing Mind
1803–1805

Hasseltine House, circa 1781, Bradford, Massachusetts, was the birthplace of Ann Hasseltine Judson.

ANN LOVED BEING PART OF BRADFORD ACADEMY. EVER THE SOCIAL pacesetter, she relished being with classmates and having the stimulation of countless friends. Just as important to her were the numerous books through which her mind could encompass new ideas and fresh challenges on a daily basis. She found it quite boring to sit and listen to several chapters of the Bible each morning, however. What's more, the teachers, Mr. Walker and Miss Swan, seemed overly fond of long prayers, during which her facile mind would ramble to faraway places while the interminable prayers droned on. Despite herself, Ann would occasionally be caught up in some biblical story and wonder about the lives and characters of those long-ago children of Israel. She was wont to reflect that human nature had not changed a great deal since then.

Even for a rapidly maturing young lady, recess was still a favorite time of day for thirteen-year-old Ann Hasseltine. It meant a chance to ramble and to think long thoughts if she wished. It was also a time to have a bit of fun. Young Rufus Anderson was her junior by several years and especially enjoyed teasing the girls if he thought it would aggravate them sufficiently. One day he irritated Ann to the point that she went after him with a long stick, and Rufus prudently decided to tone down his teasing.

Quiet Harriet Atwood, who was several years younger than Ann, idolized the charming and quick-witted Ann. The more mature Ann was gentle with Harriet and sensed in her a need for companionship and encouragement. Harriet's father, only in his mid-forties, was rapidly failing with consumption, and she greatly feared losing this vital figure in her life. Ann's presence and understanding were a constant comfort to the shy girl. No matter how confident and carefree Ann felt within herself, she displayed a ready sense of compassion and depth of understanding of human nature that went far beyond her years.

As the days progressed at Bradford Academy, learning was a constant delight to an eager mind that absorbed knowledge so retentively. Ann had trouble deciding which was her preferred subject. The academy's curriculum was quite varied, and the stronger students were able to absorb a prodigious amount of information. Grammar, physics, history, and literature classes all captured Ann's interest. She enjoyed parsing Pope's *Essay on Man,* even when her classmates groaned about the tedious work. Milton's *Paradise Lost* and Bunyan's *Pilgrim's Progress,* which were both considered proper Sabbath reading, spoke to her keen mind, and she constantly found some new concept within their pages. *The Vicar of Wakefield* was one of her favorite books, and she never tired of reading and rereading the popular novel. The more she read, the more she suspected that it was written as satire, a thought that made the contemplative side of Ann wonder just what values were being extolled.

Some of the young ladies complained about chemistry, math, and botany, but Ann's ready mind had room for all the disciplines.

History ranked right up there with geography among her favorite subjects. Surely she was her mother's daughter, as she reveled in learning of those faraway places about which most women could only dream. Ann could have had no idea that one day she would blaze a trail as a pioneer woman in travel and would journey to a world far distant from the crystal-blue waters of the Merrimac that drifted by so near.

While ancient history held great lure for Miss Hasseltine, current events also captured her fancy. The same year Bradford Academy was founded, the United States acquired the vast Louisiana Purchase, and Ann thought how lovely it would be to explore that vast unknown territory.

Young ladies at the academy also received instruction in drawing, painting, and fine embroidery, but each Hasseltine daughter had a head start in needlework, having learned at the feet of their talented mother how to do the most intricate stitching. Ann felt time spent in such subjects was time that could be more profitably invested in the search for knowledge within the pages of all the books that beckoned her to learn about people and places heretofore unknown. Hers was an active mind, always on the go, and a book could entice her more quickly than just about anything.

Concurrent with beginning her teen years at Bradford Academy, Ann began her lifelong habit of journaling. She recorded her impressions and feelings, sensing that this was a safe outlet for expressing her innermost thoughts, thoughts she would not be likely to share even with her closest friend. Again, Ann had no way of foreseeing that this habit would someday prove a blessing to thousands of others, that her insights would make a vast difference in the lives of many far beyond her own lifetime. To Ann, her journal was merely a means for expressing the convictions of her heart, an outlet for her feelings— sometimes of joy, other times of frustration.

Nevertheless, Ann was never too absorbed in her thirst for knowledge to neglect her social life. The youngest Hasseltine daughter had a strong relish for social amusements; whatever she did, she did with ardent feeling. John Hasseltine was frequently quoted as saying, "Where Ann is, no one can be gloomy or unhappy." The outgoing John, who enjoyed seeing his children happy and thriving, fell upon the idea of a "frolic room" for the Hasseltine dwelling. Ann and her siblings were caught up in excitement as a large second-floor room was added to the back of the house. The other students at Bradford Academy felt a similar excitement, for the Hasseltines lived right next to the academy, and the dwelling quickly became the social center of their young lives. The Hasseltine frolic room was often ablaze with lights and music. Ann was in her element there, loving the music, the singing, the dancing, and the opportunity to enjoy the evenings with so many friends. The captivating Ann Hasseltine, with her shiny black curls and enchanting dark eyes, was the acknowledged Belle of Bradford. Not one to vaunt herself, however, Ann happily included all her friends in the fun.

The frolic room caused more than a few of the village spinsters to criticize Mr. Hasseltine for allowing, as they put it, "festivities in the Hasseltine dance hall." Surely this was a departure from the prim traditions of respectable New England citizens. Because Parson Allen was often part of the group gathering in the scandalous room, he could not escape the gossipers' needle-sharp tongues. Several Bradford dowagers commented on what they ascertained was his need to pay more attention to spiritual matters and less time condoning such frivolity in the youth of Bradford. Furthermore, it was said that possibly Parson Allen was embracing Arminianism, something shocking indeed to their firmly Puritan minds.

When John Hasseltine managed to obtain one of the new pianos made by John Behrent, the immigrant German piano maker, Bradford's students delighted in performing the gavotte and the minuet. Often the dancing and games would continue until midnight, but criticize as they might, the village gossips were not able to discover a lessening of learning among the youth of Bradford. The evenings in the Hasseltine home were actually beneficial in strengthening the bond among students, many of whom would remain friends for a lifetime.

One of Ann's favorite personalities at Bradford Academy was the school janitor, Joel Chadwick. Joel had been born a slave but was given his freedom by Colonel Chadwick even before Massachusetts passed a law in 1783 that freed all slaves in the state. Joel loved to show his manumission papers and cherished the thought that, although once a slave, he was now free. Joel never took that blessing for granted. Ann often slipped him a piece of her mother's favorite pound cake and was invariably rewarded with his flashing smile of appreciation.

Each summer the academy had a twelve-week break, and Ann spent much of her free time reading, thankful for all the books her mother received from the Salem and Haverhill libraries. Nothing pleased the girl more than to plop her lithe figure down in an easy chair in Mama's room and discuss those books with her well-read mother. Rebecca Hasseltine recognized in Ann an incisive ability to understand the inner workings of the human mind.

During the Academy's winter session, only the male class met, but young women who wished to attend could avail themselves of this instruction. This suited Ann to a T, for this kind of challenge was just what she thrived on. She took special delight in learning Latin and Greek, little realizing their value to her future contributions in teaching others. Ann enjoyed the sense of competition in the classroom during the winter session, which sparked her to even greater effort. A new master had come the winter Ann was fifteen, Mr. Samuel Greele from Harvard, and Ann responded especially well to his brand of instruction. Her friends Harriet Webster and Betsey Allen attended during the winter months as well, and in time, those two young women became apprentice teachers.

For a young woman in the early nineteenth century, few other options were open. The goal of the average female was simply to marry and become a mother. After all, it was the only way of life most of them had ever observed. Some might marry a clergyman and, hence, have the good fortune of opportunities for special community involvement. A favored few might become teachers like Miss

Kimball, but very little else was available for females. Ann found this highly frustrating, and she already felt the strictures of nineteenth-century society, with its rigid limitations on women. No wonder Mama loved to visit distant and exotic lands by wandering through the pages of books. She had no other way to travel. What woman did? Ann frequently compared the lot of women with that of men. Her brother John was already excited about leaving soon to sail the seven seas and see the world beyond their shores. For her part, that option wasn't open. How could this be fair?

No matter how much she enjoyed the stimulation of classes, as she grew older, recess time remained important to Ann. Often she would spend the break from class walking with particular friends, talking about the great issues of life and where they thought life itself might one day take them. Choice among these friends were Fanny Woodbury and cousin Lydia Kimball of Salem and, of course, Harriet Atwood, who over the years maintained a special spot in Ann's heart. Ann Bartlett and Betsey Allen were boon companions as well. Often they would stroll along the Merrimac, and Ann might comment on the meaning of the beautiful river's name—"the place of strong currents." If she were feeling especially philosophical that day, she might allude to how that name might be a reflection of how life really was— a place of strong currents. Little could she have envisioned how incredibly true that would be of her own life in just a few short years. The present was a time for dreaming, however, and that Ann did with the same ardent skill she threw into any activity.

Bradford Academy days were a time of blooming, growing, and learning for Ann Hasseltine. Her spirit of enterprise found full sway in devising plans to attain her wishes. Her parents had come to realize that when Ann caught on to an idea, she was not likely to let it go until she had accomplished her purpose. This tenacity would one day be tried to its fullest and prove itself in the crucible of unimaginable danger and suffering. Those innate traits of her personality would be used by her Creator to save lives and impact more than one nation.

Much as Ann relished companionship and loved social functions, she also craved periods of silence and the space in which to reflect and dream. As she matured and her mind developed and expanded, she seemed to need more and more time to herself. Friends and family, fun and frolic—each delighted the beautiful young woman, yet she sensed a growing need to simply think, contemplate, and ponder on the true purpose of life. No matter how much fun it was to sing and dance and laugh with friends, the gaiety began to seem a bit superficial to Ann. It was fun for the moment—but moments always proved transient.

A sense of disquiet invaded Ann's thinking, and occasionally she would throw herself even further into the social pleasures around her in order to find more satisfaction. Rebecca observed that sometimes her effervescent daughter would come running in the door, bubbling over with excitement about some anticipated party just around the corner— often declaring, "Mama, I think I am the happiest creature on earth!" At the same time, the ever-perceptive Rebecca noticed the new pensiveness in her daughter and wondered at its source. A tentative anxiety was building in her daughter's heart and emotions, as though Ann realized that something was lacking in her life. As mothers do, Rebecca fretted a bit about those times when she could do nothing but hope Ann would somehow find a solution to her own inner uncertainties.

Neither Ann nor her mother could have known that a profound change was about to occur, not only for sixteen-year-old Ann but for the entire community as well. This change began with the arrival of a new teaching master at Bradford Academy, Mr. Abraham Burnham. Mr. Burnham, at thirty, was a bit older than the average college graduate, but this young man from a poor New England farm had paid his own way through Dartmouth College and came to Bradford Academy as a teaching master in order to earn the necessary funds to pay his expenses at seminary. Mr. Burnham had felt the call of God to serve as a minister, but the financial responsibility for the necessary training was his alone. Burnham's arrival in Bradford marked the beginning of a transformation in that town, a change that touched the Hasseltine household directly, beginning with Ann herself.

Enduring Change 1805–1807

Bradford Parish Church where Ann Hasseltine was baptized in 1806.

ANN WAS WORRIED. THE HOUSE WAS unusually quiet. All the other family members were out for one reason or another, so she sat in the easy chair in Mama's special room and tried to enjoy the opportunity for some uninterrupted solitude. She needed peace and quiet in which to puzzle through the troubling thoughts that nagged at her mind like a persistent itch that refused to go away. Had Rebecca been present, she would have recognized the telltale sign of Ann: gnawing at the corner of her lip, as if trying to get to the issue that was preying on her mind.

Ann was highly disappointed with herself. For months now, she had been the gayest of the gay, always ready for a new lark, constantly planning some new party or new frock with which to impress her friends and all the young men who were drawn to the sparkle of Ann's winsome personality and arresting beauty. In her heart of hearts, however, Ann confessed to the duplicity with which she was trying to fool others.

All around her, Ann had been observing changes in a number of her friends. Mr. Burnham was influencing so many of them. This earnest young man was quite clear in what he knew to be the redemptive need of every human heart. There *was* a heaven and a hell. If you did not know Christ personally, you would be eternally lost. Shocking. From childhood, Ann and her siblings had been taught: be good, do not tell falsehoods, never steal, and if you are a good child, you will escape the horrors of hell. Now here she was, confronted with a stark new truth: goodness was not enough. Ann flung herself out of the easy chair and headed to her room to find her journal. Maybe she and her journal could talk it through.

Here at her desk was a place where she could safely reveal her heart. For several years now she had been pushing away these disquieting thoughts and instead throwing herself into being the life of the party. Occasionally Ann's conscience would prod her, and she would resolve to reform, to occupy herself instead with important matters and spend no more time on frivolity. These resolutions would last about two or three days at best. Then, at the earliest announcement of a party or dance, Ann Hasseltine was the first to participate.

In later years, Ann would read back over early portions of her daily journal and sometimes smile at the recollection of that ardent young girl who had struggled so mightily over the condition of her soul. Late in 1805 the younger Ann had written, *"One Sabbath morning . . . I accidentally took up Hannah More's* Strictures on Female Education *and the first words that caught my eye were, 'She that liveth in pleasure, is dead while she liveth.' They were written in italics . . . and they struck me to the heart."* No matter how feverishly Ann threw herself into the pursuit of pleasure, events seemed to conspire to force her to consider the condition of her soul.

The following summer of 1806 was glorious, with an abundance of flowers blooming in garden beds throughout Bradford. But Ann's soul was too disquieted to appreciate such natural perfection. She wasn't even sleeping well at night, which had never happened to her before. A series of conference meetings were being held at the parish church, and Ann, not usually one to participate in such sessions on her own, attended several evenings in a row, slipping into one of the pews at the back of the sanctuary and listening with keen ears to the messages.

What's more, Mr. Burnham was a frequent visitor in the Hasseltine home. After all, the academy was right next door, John Hasseltine was a congenial host, Rebecca was ever kind and welcoming, and the four charming young women in the home were always scintillating conversationalists. One evening, the conversation became serious, as the subject turned to the insidious temptations of Satan. The teaching master remarked that Satan tempts some to extreme gaiety in order to "conceal their true feelings from others lest their religious convictions should increase." The comment struck Ann to the core, and she quietly stole out of the room. Going to the solitude of her bedroom, Ann sank to her knees beside the bed, her body wracked by sobs. To God she acknowledged that she was indeed enthralled by Satan, but she was fearful about letting anyone discover these gnawing inner anxieties.

The week following Mr. Burnham's unsettling visit, Ann went with several friends to a nearby village and decided to visit Aunt Elizabeth, Mama's older sister who lived near the edge of town. Everybody in the family knew that Aunt Elizabeth was a devout lady, one who had a special air of peace and comfort. Maybe she could provide some balm for her niece's increasingly troubled soul. Upon arriving, Ann found Aunt Elizabeth reading a religious magazine. Ann was determined that her aunt not discern the distress in her mind, hoping instead that, by listening carefully, she might discern something of why her aunt always seemed so serene. As Ann later recorded in her journal:

> I had not been with her long, before she asked me to read to her. I began, but could not govern my feelings and burst into tears. She kindly begged to know what thus affected me. I then, for the first time in my life, communicated feelings which I had determined should be known to none but myself. She urged the importance of my cherishing those feelings, and of devoting myself entirely to seeing an interest in Christ, before it should be too late. She told me, that if I trifled with impressions which were evidently made by the Holy Spirit, I should be left to hardness of heart and blindness of mind. Her words penetrated my heart.

Ann returned home with her heart roiling in turmoil. The very next morning, following a night with little sleep, she sought out Mr. Burnham to ask him what to do about the condition of her soul. She noted in her journal, *"He told me to pray for mercy and submit myself to God."* Ann next recorded the impressions on her mind and spirit as she read Scripture and the religious magazines Abraham Burnham had given her. She detailed how the truth of salvation began to penetrate her heart, and as she put it:

> *I began to discover a beauty in the way of salvation by Christ. . . . I felt a disposition to commit myself unreservedly into His hands, and leave it with Him to save me. . . . I now began to hope that I had passed from death unto life. . . . My chief happiness now consisted in contemplating the moral perfections of the glorious God. . . . Sin in myself and others, appeared as that abominable thing which a holy God hates—and I earnestly strove to avoid sinning, not merely because I was afraid of hell, but because I feared to displease God, and grieve His Holy Spirit. I attended my studies in school, with far different feeling and different motives, from what I had ever done before.*

This dramatic change in Ann Hasseltine's life occurred in July 1806, and on September 14, 1806, the day of her first Communion service as a member of Bradford Congregational Church, she wrote in her journal, *"I have this day, publickly* [sic] *professed myself a disciple of Christ."*

Not only had Ann changed; others of her family had as well. Shortly following Ann's private commitment of her heart and life to Christ, her dear Papa had his own experience of salvation. One evening as John was returning from the fields, he glanced up at the house and in the twilight candle glow of Ann's room, he could see his cherished daughter kneeling beside her bed in quiet prayer. It pierced his heart—his beautiful young daughter, so glowing with life and vitality, humbling herself in prayer. Convicted, Hasseltine walked to a quiet nearby copse and, kneeling under a tree, gave his own heart to Christ, begging for forgiveness and redemption.

That summer Rebecca professed her faith as well, as did son John. In August 1806 Ann, her parents, and her brother were baptized into the fellowship of the Bradford Congregational Church. None welcomed them more warmly than Parson Allen, who saw in this family something special indeed. And within just a matter of months, the other Hasseltine children professed faith as well.

Just a month later, John, the beloved older son, lost his life at sea. The family was stunned when the news of John's death reached them by courier from Salem. In the midst of their grief, however, they cherished the knowledge of John's recent experience of salvation, and it gave solace to their broken hearts. They had the blessed assurance that they would experience a heavenly reunion with their treasured son and brother.

John's death profoundly affected Ann's future steps, as her life, already on an entirely new trajectory, suddenly took on new understanding and urgency. Her big brother was gone forever, and it struck her that she herself had no guarantee of another day. Ann found an entirely new understanding of the words of Psalm 90:12: "Teach us to number our days, that we may apply our hearts unto wisdom."

At the shocking news of the death of their son, John and Rebecca had to regroup and come to grips with such a loss. The frolic room was subdued now and often used for gatherings of young people who sought strength and comfort from one another. As they discussed vital life issues and how their faith could grow, their minds were newly focused on the eternal—a focus that had previously seemed so unimportant.

A similar wave of spiritual transformation was sweeping the nation, part of what became known as the Second Great Awakening. In Bradford, the amazing transformation of their community had begun with the coming of a quiet and humble teacher, Abraham Burnham.

Never in her life was Ann Hasseltine known to do anything half-heartedly. During recess at the academy, Ann still loved to ramble, and now it was frequently with her friends who had experienced a similar conversion, including Harriet Atwood. Their discussions were full of the wonder of experiencing Christ's redemptive grace and the joy it brought to their hearts. Ann's change from life-of-the-party to committed-to-serve-Christ was deep and permanent.

Ann immersed herself in learning more about God with the same enthusiasm she had previously devoted to good times with friends. One of her friends commented to another that Ann still loved social pleasures, but their complexion was completely changed. She now longed for her friends to know the joy of personal commitment she had discovered, and it showed in all she did. Ann wrote in her journal, *"My chief happiness now consists of contemplating the moral perfections of the glorious God. I long to have all intelligent creatures love him."* She also recognized a new purpose in her training at the academy and poured herself into it with renewed zeal.

Ann began taking notes on the books she was reading; commentaries by the Englishmen Job Orton and Thomas Scott were among many theologians whose writings spoke to her heart. The works of Jonathan Edwards on redemption fascinated her; she found that the ideas of the eminent theologian frequently clarified biblical truths for her questing mind. If any passage gave her great difficulty, Ann marked it, and as soon as some clergyman visited the home or she was able to talk with some pastor at a meeting, she begged for clarity and an explanation. Her bedtime reading was so deep as would now appear daunting to the average young person, but she was determined to learn more every day and to make up for lost time.

Ann often came up with a new question, and she would ask Parson Allen to loan her a work by Samuel Hopkins or Joseph Bellamy, or perhaps a book of theology written by Phillip Doddridge. The parson was astounded at her spiritual thirst. He had never encountered a young person quite so teachable, certainly never one so interested in Scripture.

Ann set the pace for the whole family in spiritual authenticity. The Hasseltines' newfound faith and involvement in the ministry of the parish helped ease the pain of their loss of young John. In later years, Ann frequently looked back to her childhood and recalled her loneliness after Bille died and the painful time when her wonderful big brother, John, was no more. She was left with one brother, Joseph, and she intentionally developed a new closeness with him.

As Providence would have it, while the community of Bradford was experiencing revival, an event was taking place in the far western corner of Massachusetts that would have direct bearing on Ann Hasseltine and the future God had in mind for her. In the same month that Ann had accepted Christ's saving grace, a group of five young men at Williams College got together to pray for the millions of people in the Orient who had never heard of God. As they gathered that August afternoon, a sudden rainstorm came up and they sought shelter under a nearby haystack. From that haystack prayer meeting, there was born a movement used by God to impact the world with the gospel.

This small gathering rapidly evolved into a larger group who called themselves "The Brethren." Most of them became students of theology at the newly organized Andover Seminary (only nine miles from Bradford) and frequently met to pray about missions. A dynamic young seminarian named Adoniram Judson soon joined the group, and before long the romance between Adoniram and Ann began—a marriage of minds, hearts, and spirits that would bless and change a people far away, as well as impact their own nation to an extraordinary degree.

CHAPTER 5

Meantime in Malden
1788–1809

THE PARSONAGE
THE FIRST HOUSE BUILT IN 1651
BURNED IN 1724
PRESENT HOUSE BUILT IN 1724
ALSO BIRTHPLACE OF
REV. ADONIRAM JUDSON
THE MISSIONARY TO BURMA

Adoniram's birthplace in Malden, MA is the
oldest extant house in the city.

ON AUGUST 9, 1788, IN NEARBY MALDEN, MASSACHUSETTS—
slightly more than a year before Ann Hasseltine's own birth—a boy
was born to Rev. Adoniram Judson and his wife, Abigail. Rev. Judson
was a graduate of Yale University and pastor of the thriving Malden
Congregational Church. The stately minister immediately determined that their son would also be named Adoniram and was surely destined for greatness. Years later a biographer noted that Rev.
Judson seemed to desire no fame for himself but coveted eminence
for his child. Time proved the validity of that ambition, but never in
the way that the proud new father could have visualized.

Adoniram Junior showed early and pronounced signs of being all
that his father could wish for. He was exceptionally quick at learning

new skills, and his adoring mother carefully guided and nurtured his early steps. Along with many other things, little Adoniram learned at the knee of his mother how to decipher the marks lined up in the books that frequently engaged the attention of his parents. One week when her husband was out of town on church business, Abigail taught their three-year-old son what those little marks meant. When her husband returned from his trip, Abigail had a surprise for him.

Pastor Judson gave a contented sigh that evening as he settled into his favorite chair beside the fireplace to relax and catch up on Malden's recent news. With a smile, Abigail motioned for their son to climb into Father's lap, whereupon she handed him the large family Bible. Little Adoniram proceeded to read for his father an entire chapter from the Old Testament, barely stumbling over the long and unfamiliar names sprinkled throughout.

Amazed, the proud father exclaimed, "Son, my son, some day you will be a *great* man!" The young boy, gazing with big hazel eyes into the face of the father whom he felt surely knew everything, would never forget this declaration. Adoniram's father took no pains to hide his great expectations for this treasured namesake of a son. A quarter of a century later, lying in the filth of a notorious death prison, the missionary Adoniram would recall those expectations and ambitions and wonder what his father would think of his son's greatness now if he could only see his horrendous predicament.

Just across Main Street from their home was Bell Rock Park, and the energetic Adoniram loved to play "big church" with his friends, who were always the parishioners while he was their pastor. When he was still three years old, his sister, Abigail, was born, and she was his adoring fan for the rest of her long life. She loved to recall that her brother's favorite hymn when playing church was "Go Preach My Gospel, Saith the Lord."

Those were uneasy times in many churches in the new nation, with controversies over doctrine often disturbing the even tenor of the Judson household. The family moved several times during Adoniram's boyhood, including to a pastorate in Wenham when he was four. There were fewer problems with church polity there, and the Judson family became an important part of the community. The family put down roots in Wenham and remained for eight years. When Adoniram was six, Elnathan was born, and his mother was in her element.

Always nurturing and involved in her children's lives, Abigail had a particular aversion for dirt. Adoniram quickly learned that his loving mother had strong opinions about what was good and what was undesirable. Dirt was bad and cleanliness was highly desired. The little fellow grew up to be especially fastidious. Decades later this loathing for dirt would make life almost unendurable when he found himself surrounded by inescapable filth and stench in a foreign prison.

Nevertheless, those early years in the neat, bustling town of Wenham held happy recollections of friends and school. The one sad memory that marred the even tenure of Adoniram's childhood was the loss of his baby sister. Mary Ellice was born when he was eight, and he adored her. An unexplained fever took her life when she was six months old, and printed indelibly on Adoniram's heart was the stricken look on his Mama's face for many months after their loss. (Nearly one hundred years later, Adoniram's youngest son, Edward, would write about that traumatic experience in his father's life, saying, "The keen ploughshare of sorrow tears up the fresh turf of a child's heart." Edward undoubtedly spoke from personal experience as well, having lost his beloved father when Edward himself was just five years old.)

Adoniram immersed himself in the challenge of classes at school, excelling in every subject. Math and languages were among his favorites, and he read voraciously. The primary schoolboy quickly gained a reputation for solving puzzles and enigmas, and he readily accepted any new challenge to his problem-solving skills. As much as young Adoniram was known for his energy and enthusiastic approach to any endeavor, he was fonder of books than of play. He read all the books he could get his hands on, some of which, had his dignified father known of them, would surely have shocked him to no end. In all his reading in the Bible, Adoniram was most fascinated by the Book of Revelation because it presented the biggest enigmas and challenges.

When Adoniram was ten, his father sent him to Salem to study navigation with the well-known Captain Morton. The captain would have delighted in keeping this brilliant young boy to continue to tutor and train, but Adoniram had too many interests to stop with just one. His fertile mind conjured up wonderful dreams as he learned about the sea and strolled along the fascinating wharves of Salem. Those massive, mighty ships coming from exotic and faraway shores were exciting to behold, and he could often catch the scents of sandalwood and spice as one of the traders from the East unloaded at the dock.

In grammar school Judson was at the top of his class in every subject, notably ahead of all the other children in both Latin and Greek. His studious habits and obvious skills soon earned him the nickname "Old Virgil dug up," to which he answered with pleasure. (The name was an allusion to Virgil was a well-known poet of ancient Rome.) His friends found him remarkably good natured and always ready to help. His spirit of determination remained an essential part of his personality and helped him to endure unspeakable hardships in years to come—horrors that most people cannot even envisage.

When Adoniram was eleven, his father's health became precarious, and he resigned the Wenham church, although the parishioners pleaded with him to stay. The family moved yet again, this time to Braintree, just south of Boston. Adoniram now found himself in a strange neighborhood and thrown on his own resources, academically as well as socially. Yet again, this difficulty worked to his advantage, as it fostered in him special skills in self-reliance.

As Adoniram Senior got a little stronger, he began to do some itinerant work with the Home Missionary Society in Vermont. Realizing the circumstances at work in his own life as a conservative cleric, often fraught with church controversy, made him even more determined that his son succeed and become a man of note. Very close to the Judson's house was the modest home where President John Adams had grown up. Adams was in Washington serving as president at that time, but each time they passed Adams's boyhood home, Adoniram's father would comment on the amazing possibilities before his son, for surely he had as much native ability and talent as the president of the country himself.

In 1802, when Adoniram Junior was eleven years old, Rev. Judson's health was robust enough to accept a pastorate in historic Plymouth with the newly formed Third Congregational Church. The church was founded by the conservative element that had recently split from the first church founded by the 1620 Pilgrims. The congregation called Adoniram Judson Sr. as their first pastor. The Judsons purchased land on the street where the new church stood and built a brown-shingle, two-story house on what was known as Watson's Hill—the place on which Chief Massasoit of the Wampanoag tribe had camped the fateful spring of 1621. Chief Massasoit had sent Squanto and Samoset as emissaries to the desperate Pilgrims and thereby helped save the struggling young colony. Young Adoniram enjoyed the thought of living on a piece of American history, little realizing that one day he himself would be making missions history.

The Judsons had just settled in Plymouth when Adoniram Junior grew dangerously ill, often in critical condition and close to dying, and had to convalesce for more than a year. Until this juncture in his life, he had not spent much time in thought and reflection; however, now leisure time to reflect was about all he had. As he slowly recovered, he gained enough strength to read and study on his own, while still having ample hours to think and daydream. Among his readings were numerous books about great men who had made their marks on history. Maybe he himself would make his mark by becoming a famous poet or a statesman, or perhaps, he considered, a great orator.

However grandiose those dreams, Adoniram's early training frequently intruded on these solitary thoughts. All his life he had been taught that real fame must come from goodness and holiness. Often he would muse about pulpit possibilities; maybe he would lead a large and wealthy congregation. He could visualize the sea of faces looking up expectantly, drinking in his every word. And then he would think about the humble country pastor who worked faithfully year after year and never sought anything for himself. His heart assured him that this was the pastor with true greatness. In later years, Adoniram clearly recalled that convalescent day when the words of Psalm 115:1 rang out so clearly that he felt he had heard them spoken aloud: "Not unto us, not unto us, O LORD, but unto thy name give the glory." The shock of that moment was so real that he sat almost bolt upright in bed at the words.

Adoniram began to agonize over the stark contradiction between personal ambition and what he knew was true greatness. The easiest thing to do was simply to train his mind not to think on these disquieting reflections. And still the shocking insight of that singular moment was so clear that he would remember it the rest of his life. As he recovered, Adoniram not only rebuilt his health but applied himself to serious study and, on his own, made up the missed year of school and beyond.

By 1804 fifteen-year-old Adoniram was ready to enter college. Father felt Yale was too far away and Harvard was far too liberal in its theology. Brown University was nominally Baptist, but Pastor Judson found its theology much closer to his own than that of liberals in the Congregationalist denomination. Brown it would be, and in August 1804, one week after his sixteenth birthday, Adoniram Judson Jr. matriculated at Brown.

So advanced was Adoniram in his private studies that Brown admitted him to the second-year class. Judson was of medium height and slender in build, with clear-cut features, striking hazel eyes, and curly, dark chestnut hair. There was a warm radiance in his frequent smile. He was not easily forgotten, and when he spoke, his powerful bass voice belied his slender size.

In later years, various classmates recalled his consistent brilliance and commented that never had Judson failed or even hesitated in

34

recitation. Many of those classmates would become prominent citizens, including government and industry leaders, a United States senator, and a Supreme Court justice, yet in the classroom Judson exceeded them all, graduating in 1807 as Brown's valedictorian at the age of nineteen. Had Father realized the liberal ideas his beloved son picked up during those years, he would have been appalled. His son's special friend was the erudite Jacob Eames, slightly older, nearly as brilliant, and a self-proclaimed deist. The two spent endless hours discussing philosophy and how they were going to become great men through their own efforts. In their estimation, no higher power was needed.

After graduation, where should he begin to make his mark in history? Adoniram Judson Jr. excelled in so many fields and had so many interests that it was hard for him to know just where to start. When he was asked to begin an academy in Plymouth, he decided that would be a good place to start while he decided what area of achievement interested him most. During that year he not only acquired valuable teaching experience but also managed to write two textbooks, one for mathematics and another for English grammar.

The following August, in 1808, Adoniram decided that teaching school was far too dull and ordinary. He was seeking fame and fortune and announced to his staid and puzzled parents that he was closing the school in order to travel. Mother and Father were so very conservative; he was strangely reluctant to reveal to these he loved so dearly that he found their thinking far too narrow and irrelevant. After all, he had no wish to hurt them. Initially Adoniram explained to his perplexed parents that he would first go visit Uncle Ephraim, a minister in Sheffield, about a hundred fifty miles away, and then he wanted to see something of the broad world beyond, especially New York.

To the traditional elder Judsons, this revelation couldn't have been more shocking than if he had announced he wanted to visit Sodom and Gomorrah. As they talked and pleaded with him, eventually the truth came out. Adoniram no longer believed in a personal God and the need for a Savior. His mother burst into tears, and his father tried every argument at his command. The staid logic of Pastor Judson was no match for the clever skills of Brown's top debater, however. Adoniram could handle each of his father's assertions with consummate ease, but his mother's wrenching tears haunted his thoughts and dreams for months to come.

On August 9, 1808, his twentieth birthday, a defiant Adoniram Judson set out to "find himself" and sow a few wild oats along the way. What he actually found would forever change the trajectory of his life, to say nothing of the life of a beautiful young woman known as the Belle of Bradford. The two would together make their mark in history—and on countless hearts.

Missionary woods, where Adoniram made his commitment to missions, is commemorated by a memorial stone.

From Plymouth to Andover 1809–1810

ON HIS OWN. FREE OF CONSTRAINTS. FOOTLOOSE AND FANCY-FREE. Adoniram was excited to be completely in charge of what he did and where he went. It was exhilarating, and he could scarcely keep a grin off his face as his horse tripped along on the road to Uncle Ephraim's home in Sheffield. Uncle, like Father, was a conservative Congregationalist minister, and Adoniram took care not to talk about controversial topics during the visit. Uncle Ephraim and Aunt Chloe had lost their only son just last year; he had been only in his early thirties. Judson's tender sensibilities made him keenly aware of their sorrow for his late cousin, and he took pains to comfort and encourage their aching hearts.

Uncle Ephraim gladly offered to stable Adoniram's horse while he continued on his trip, making his way to Albany, New York. Judson was excited to travel back on Robert Fulton's newly launched steamboat, the *Clermont*. It had just made its famous maiden voyage from New York to Albany when a jubilant

Adoniram boarded the boat in Albany for its return trip to the great city.

Adoniram's heart pounded with excitement as he stepped off the steamer and found himself in New York at last, where he aspired to a career in the theatre, either as an actor or a writer of great drama. However, this tenacious new aspirant to the stage had not considered the fact that summertime in New York was the slowest time of year for the theater. Nonetheless, diligent inquiries led him to a little band of actors who were trying to hit it big in the city's theaters. He joined the rather seedy group, and it was a wild and reckless time for the twenty-year-old minister's son from a staid and proper home. To the average traditional mind in that early decade of the 1800s, anything associated with the theater was risqué indeed. Judson realized his parents would be appalled at the very idea, but in his present state of mind, that did nothing to deter his pursuit of fame and fortune.

The band of strolling players were living a vagabond life, and Adoniram, with headstrong willfulness, went right along with their questionable behavior. They had developed a system of checking into a cheap boarding house, staying a few days, and then surreptitiously disappearing into the night, leaving unpaid bills behind. When Judson was once mistakenly addressed as "Mr. Johnson," he decided not to correct the error. Somehow it made him feel less guilty than using his honorable family name. "Mr. Johnson" left a trail of mischief behind, behavior that would hound his conscience and bring him to the point of retracing his steps a few years later and making good on every debt he had left behind.

It took only about six weeks for Adoniram to become thoroughly disgusted with the way he was living and to determine that greatness was not found down this particular path. Nor was honor. Growing up, he had been taught integrity, courtesy, and self-discipline by word and example. Surely he had been spending his time with people who mocked such verities.

Early one morning, he quietly left. He made his way back to Uncle Ephraim's to reclaim his horse and to pursue success along a more principled and reputable pathway to fame and fortune. To his surprise, his aunt and uncle were away on a trip to a neighboring community when he arrived, and an earnest young cleric was filling the local pulpit for several weeks.

Judson was intrigued to discover that the young minister, about his own age, seemed to have no great ambition but was content to watch over the flock in his care. He spoke of his faith with a solemn but gentle earnestness that made an impression on Adoniram's unsettled mind. This minister was not pompous or judgmental, but sincere and settled in his convictions. He was also eager to be an encouragement to this brilliant young man who asked such searching questions.

Judson left the next morning, impressed by what he had heard. He had a lot to think about as his horse ambled its way toward western Massachusetts. Maybe he would travel out west and find some exciting way to make his mark in new and unexplored territory. As his horse ambled along, Adoniram considered the parts of his own mind that surely needed exploring as well. Haunted by vague thoughts of *what now?* Judson failed to enjoy the beauty of the New England countryside in autumn.

Late that evening, Judson reached a small village with just one inn. As the landlord lighted the way to the only room available, he apologized, saying that Judson would be obliged to stay in the room next to someone who was very sick. "This young man is seriously ill, sir, maybe even dying," the innkeeper explained. Weary as he was, and wrapped up in his own uneasy thoughts, Judson assured the landlord that a few noises would certainly not disturb him.

Adoniram was generally a sound sleeper. But that night sleep wouldn't come. And in the stillness of the night, noises from the adjoining room became very distinct, increasing as the night progressed. They were most disturbing in their intensity—groans, a gasp, a moan. Then the sick man began calling out; over and over he groaned, "Oh God, lost—lost. God—lost." Judson assured himself that neither the noise itself nor the thought of someone dying bothered him. Death happened with frequency in early nineteenth-century

New England. The truly disturbing thing was the thought of his own death. Adoniram knew that in his present state of confusion, he was certainly not prepared to die. Surely Father's ideas of God's judgment and the ever-looming possibility of eternal damnation could not be fact. But what if they *were* true? How could he face death? What if he were the one who was dying?

In the night reaches, everything looms larger than life. Most certainly the grave did. Since he had been a toddler, Adoniram had been drilled in the importance of meticulous cleanliness. His flesh crawled at the thought of an earthen grave, of himself lying in that cold, solitary, dark, dank place. Was that really the end of humanity? Surely it could not be. Haunting thoughts overwhelmed him as he lay on his solitary bed, and sleep came only in snatches and starts.

After what seemed forever, the sun rose, and Adoniram's distressing anxieties and fears vanished with the light streaming in through the window. What a coward he had been! It crossed his mind that his agnostic friend Jacob Eames would surely laugh at his nighttime fears; he would certainly not tell Jacob he had spent a night with such haunting thoughts.

Tired but quite cheerful on such a bright morning, Adoniram headed down the stairs, prepared to pay for his night's lodging. Asking for his bill, he casually inquired about the sick man: "It seems quiet now. Is he better?" The sober-faced innkeeper responded, "He is dead." "Dead?" Judson was shocked. And then he asked the obvious question, "Do you know who he was?" "Oh yes," the innkeeper replied, "a young man from that college in Providence. Name of Eames. Jacob Eames."

The reality of his friend's death hit Adoniram with stunning force. Eames dead? His friend was gone, gone beyond all reasoning and logic and philosophies. And he had been in the very next room. Something told him that such an occurrence could not have been simple coincidence. A higher power had to be involved. If that were the case, it shattered Judson's confidence in his ability to reason and to control his own destiny. Hours passed before he was even coherent enough to leave the inn. Not far down the road, heading further west, he suddenly reined in his horse, paused a long moment, and turned in the opposite direction, toward home.

The young man who had always loved a puzzle, who had never found one he could not solve, now had one that required soul-searching thought. Always impulsive and never one to procrastinate, Adoniram considered what he knew of his parents' God and his own ideas of an impersonal Creator. In a state of bewilderment, Adoniram rode to his family's Plymouth home. It was September 22, 1808. Adoniram had been away not quite six weeks, but it seemed more like a lifetime. His parents were overjoyed to see him, but they realized at once that something was wrong. For one thing, he was quieter than usual, certainly not eager to talk about where he had been or what he had done. Furthermore, he seemed restless and preoccupied. Then once again, Providence intervened in Judson's life.

Two eminent leaders of the conservative element of Congregationalists came to confer with Adoniram's father. Edward Griffin and Moses Stuart wanted to discuss the new divinity school where they were preparing to teach. Andover Seminary was north of Boston and not far from Plymouth. Adoniram Junior not only listened with deep interest to the discussions but also made an immediate impression on the two professors. He exhibited great keenness of mind yet quietly admitted that he was not a believer. Both men were drawn to Adoniram Judson and agreed that the seminary would be glad to accept him as a special student should he wish to matriculate. He was clearly interested, yet hesitant, deferring for the moment. Sensing superior potential in Pastor Judson's son, they left their invitation open.

Deciding to embrace a faith he had been firmly rejecting for some period of time was no easy matter for one who thought as deeply as Adonriam. He was in a sad quandary. Two days later, he decided to accept an offer to teach at a private academy in Boston. He began the new job but took to it his doubts and apprehensions about the condition of his soul. Could he bear to remain lost—eternally lost? Who would have thought Eames could suddenly die in the prime of life?

What made Adoniram think he himself would escape such a fate? Each night was endless, each hour of darkness an eternity before dawn would finally break. Over and over his mind echoed those haunting cries: *"Oh God, God, lost."* Scarcely had he begun to teach when he came across the book *Human Nature in Its Fourfold State* by Thomas Boston. It was an old book about human sin and God's redemption through Christ, but he read it with new eyes of understanding. Ever quick to make decisions, Adoniram resigned the job he had just begun and headed for Andover Seminary.

The young seminarian who enrolled at Andover in October 1808 was marked by two shining qualities: an enthusiasm for life and a passion for excellence. Just as in college, he was admitted to the second year because of his excellent academic record. Ever a fascinating conversationalist, Judson was always comfortable in social situations, both quick-witted and full of vitality. He made friends easily. He was known for his kindness and a rather stately courtesy that commanded respect, clearly inherited from his distinguished father.

In no time, Judson was engrossed in the somewhat spartan and academic atmosphere, immersed in study and lectures. He spent much time thinking on his own, working through just who God really was and how he himself related to God. November arrived and with it colder weather, but Adoniram walked alone each day in the wooded grove behind the seminary, pondering the greatest of all life's puzzles. He saw no blinding light; he heard no audible voice from heaven; but little by little, his uncertainties dissipated. December 2, 1808, was a day he never forgot, recording in his journal, *"This day I made a solemn dedication of my life to God."* The one who had been so full of doubts and questions never again doubted the miracle of Christ's saving grace. Adoniram Judson, twenty-one-year-old seminary student, was a new person. The one who had in the past been so driven by the desire for greatness now directed his ambitions toward honoring God.

Two months after his personal commitment, he asked himself, "How can I so order my future being as best to please God?" As always, he reveled in his studies, but now he also pondered on what purpose God might have for him. Could it be that God was preparing him for a pulpit? As he weighed this question, a vision came to mind of that long-ago afternoon at home in Plymouth when he was a sick fourteen-year-old, bedridden and daydreaming of future greatness. Would not the pastor of an obscure country church be greater in God's sight than the pastor of some prestigious city church? His heart told him the answer.

Judson began looking for a sign as to just what God had in mind for him. In September 1809, as he began what would be his final year in seminary, a sign did appear in the form of a printed sermon by a chaplain with the powerful British East India Company. Titled "The Star of the East," it targeted the crying needs of that part of the world for the gospel. That simple sermon by Dr. Claudius Buchanan fell like a spark into the tinder of Adoniram Judson's heart; the simple reading of a small pamphlet became the means of transforming his plans for the future. Not only did it affect him; it also impacted the course of Christian missions history.

The Great Commission struck Adoniram Judson with force. There was a world out there lost without the message of Christ, and the entire United States had not sent out one foreign missionary to tell the story. On a small hillside across the pond from the old seminary building at Andover stands a massive stone with a tablet marking the place in "Missionary Woods" where Judson made his signal commitment. One cold February morning in 1810, the Great Commission of Matthew 28:19, "Go ye therefore, and teach all nations," came into his mind with power and never left in all the years that followed. Judson made his decision. How it would happen, and when it would happen, he had no idea, but he never doubted it would become a reality.

It was time for winter vacation, and Adoniram went home to Plymouth. He was hesitant yet again to tell his parents what was in his heart, but not for the same reason this time. He knew his loving parents still treasured fond hopes for his future, and he doubted they would want to hear what God was impressing on his heart. These were not plans for a great pulpit somewhere but impressions of a place far away.

And sure enough—Adoniram arrived home to find Mother and Father eager to share exciting news of their own for him. They had just learned that the eminent pastor of the prestigious Park Street Church in the heart of Boston wanted Adoniram Jr. to come be his assistant. They could scarcely wait to disclose these good tidings, but his heart sank as they disclosed their portentous news. Adoniram hardly knew how to respond. His parents would be appalled at his willingness to give up an opportunity of such eminence and instead bury himself a world away in the midst of unknown dangers and perils.

Quietly he said to them, "I shall never live in Boston; I have much farther to go." His parents were stunned. Surely not! His mother's shock and his sister's grief were wrenching to see as they wept in disbelief. There was nothing his father could say. He would not doubt the work of the Holy Spirit in his son's life. But Rev. Judson was full of questions. How could this ever come to pass? No one had ever gone from America's shores to share the Good News. Who would support him? Would he have to go alone? He would be going into obscurity. And to where? Adoniram himself had no immediate answers, only the quiet assurance in his heart that the Lord who had spoken to him and called him would make that way clear. And indeed, in a matter of months, the path would begin to emerge and the hand of God would be seen at work in lives both at Andover and nine miles up the road in Bradford.

CHAPTER 7

Phillips Hall circa 1808 (now known as Foxcroft) was the original residence and classroom building for Andover Seminary.

Destinies Meet 1807–1810

AT THE SAME TIME DIVINE PROVIDENCE WAS DEALING WITH Adoniram's heart, God was just as clearly working in a life in Bradford, a life whose path was about to intersect with Judson's. Ann Hasseltine had graduated from Bradford Academy in 1807 and decided to teach while seeking God's purpose for her life. Like many young women of her generation, she wanted to find a soul mate and experience the joy of motherhood. But she was not content with simply getting married, having children, and settling into matronly pursuits; Ann did not feel that this was the sole extent of God's plan for her. Just what the Lord's call might be, she did not know. In fact, Ann was at a loss to think of whom she might talk to who would even understand the questions and uncertainties in her heart.

In her spare moments, as she rambled from the solitude of the woods to the peaceful Merrimac, Ann contemplated her destiny. The more Ann studied the great theologians, the more she felt God had a divine purpose for each human being. Surely she was born to resemble the One who was her Savior. More and more, Ann sought to understand just how she could reflect Christ's character in her life. Many a night she sat at her desk, her journal open before her. She frequently paused and brushed the feathered quill back and forth across her lips as she considered her soul's yearnings, trying to articulate just what was in her heart. *Surely there is a Divine purpose that shapes our ends,* her heart told her, and she longed to place herself totally in God's hands. One day in 1807 she wrote, *"I desire to give myself entirely to Christ . . . to be entirely devoted to Him."*

As a budding young teacher, Ann exhibited some special skills while she taught at nearby Byfield, such that she was asked to take charge of a small school in Haverhill. She went on to expand her skills and experience by teaching in Newbury and Salem. After a long day of teaching, Ann often mused about her experiences in her journal, one night writing, *"I was enabled to open the school with prayer. . . . The little creatures seemed astonished at such a beginning. Probably some of them had never heard a prayer before. May I have grace to be faithful, in instructing these little immortals, in such a way as shall be pleasing to my heavenly Father."*

The more time Ann spent in private devotions and in the study of Scripture, the more convinced she became that God had a distinct purpose for her. Sometimes her journal became a place where she could invoke her prayers as she pondered weighty thoughts. More and more, Ann's mind began encompassing the needs of souls far from America's shore. Her journal in March 1809 detailed what she had learned of David Brainerd, the first to work among American Indians. Brainerd's writing inspired her to record, *"It excites a desire in me to live as near to God as that holy man did. . . . I felt my heart enlarged to pray for spiritual blessings for the heathen world and the African slaves. I feel a willingness to give myself away to Christ, to be disposed of as He pleases."* In the crucible to come in the years ahead, Ann would look back on those words she recorded in her journal and note the rugged and dangerous path on which the Lord had directed her steps.

As Providence provided, about this time the Hasseltines took in a fascinating young boarder who was attending Bradford Academy, just two doors away. Henry Obookiah was no ordinary student; he had come from thousands of miles away in Hawaii and was a new believer who absorbed both encouragement and inspiration from the effervescent Hasseltines. Ann was intrigued with the young man who was the first from his land to come to know the Savior. Surely it was no accident that God had led him here to their home.

By 1809 nineteen-year-old Ann was growing restless. Her mother knew the signs well. The more unsettled she grew, the more she rambled. Still Ann had not confided in anyone. Her thought pattern was quite circuitous but always came back to the burning question: Is this God's divine purpose for me? A bright young woman could teach and, maybe with a bit of good fortune, marry a clergyman. Indeed, her twenty-eight-year-old sister, Becky, would soon marry Rev. Joseph Emerson, the well-known Beverly pastor. Her January wedding was an unforgettable time for the Hasseltines. Becky was the first daughter to marry; Joseph was a widower with a charming three-year-old daughter named Nancy. The mother of the bride, Rebecca, had about despaired of ever having a grandchild, so she was already doting on the child, who was excited to be part of the upcoming wedding ceremony.

Ann, like the rest of the family, was caught up in the excitement of a wedding in the Hasseltine home. But after the festivities were over and life began to return to normal, Ann increasingly thought about her own future. In her quiet times of intense Bible study, she liked to take a passage and glean from it all that her broad-ranging intellect could contemplate. During these early months of 1810, Ann had been spending hours considering Romans 12:1-3 and thinking just how her own life could be a "living sacrifice." Surely she wanted to commit herself wholly to the Savior she loved. But how? Ann prayed earnestly to understand in what way she could present herself as such an offering to Christ.

Spring arrived and a restless Ann still rambled. She missed her old-est sister and thought even more than usual about her own future. Never as calm and collected as Becky, she certainly did not feel will-ing to wait seven or eight more years to see what God had in mind for her. A beautiful New England spring passed into summer, and still Ann searched for an answer. Unbeknownst to the seeking young teacher, her divine destiny would become clearer quite soon.

Meanwhile, Adoniram had returned to Andover early that spring, fiercely determined to find God's way to follow through with his newfound calling. He quickly discovered that the Spirit working in his life was dealing at the same time with a group of his fellow stu-dents. Adoniram learned from his classmate Samuel Mills about the haystack prayer meeting that had taken place back in 1806 at Williams College. Four of the six young men present that historic August afternoon were now Andover students and had just formed a group known as the Brethren. Coincidentally, three of the four were named Samuel—Samuel Nott, Samuel Newell, and Samuel Mills. Their friend James Richards made up the quartet.

When Mills pulled Adoniram aside one morning to tell him about the Brethren and their concern for the lost of the world, Adoniram grasped Mills's arm in excitement to explain about his own sense of call to foreign missions. Mills, an organizer and a politician, immedi-ately pointed out to Adoniram an obvious difficulty: "All right, Judson," Mills confronted him, "You want to be a missionary to the Orient, but who is going to send you?" Mills well knew there were no foreign missionary organizations anywhere in the still new United States of America. Adoniram, his usual impetuous self, quickly replied that he would somehow find a way to go. Exactly how he would get there, where he might go, or who would send him, he had not really thought through; it was enough that foreign missions was God's call for his life.

Adoniram promptly joined the Brethren, as did another student, Edward Warren. Later that spring Luther Rice came to Andover and also signed the Brethren's constitution. For several weeks, the eager young students discussed mechanics, ways, and means. How could they implement their calling? Since so much was unknown territory, they decided to meet with sympathetic professors and seek their advice. Always swift to act, Adoniram wrote to the London Missionary Society in April, inquiring about the possibility of being sent out by the British. While formerly ridiculed for his enthusiasm, he now had eight friends with a commitment like his own. Ever the optimist, Adoniram felt confident that an opportunity would open up.

And open it did. Even for Adoniram, events began happening at a remarkable speed. The Congregational ministers of Massachusetts were planning to meet in June, just nine miles up the road at the Bradford Church. Among the organizing church fathers was Samuel Spring, one of the denomination's most influential leaders and himself a true believer in missions. Spring contacted several other men who were planning the upcoming conference, and the seminarians met with the group of leaders to discuss possibilities. The elder ministers could not help but sense the sincerity and enthusiasm of the seminarians who met with them. One of the leaders summed up their impressions of the students' ideas by saying, "We had better not attempt to stop God."

Surely God's time was perfect. It was late June, and the General Association meeting in Bradford was scheduled to occur in a matter of days. Adoniram was chosen by the Brethren to write and present their proposal before the association, for none of them doubted the power of his compelling voice and persuasive skills. With this landmark moment would come another remarkable event in Judson's life, one which he could never have imagined, but one which would forever change and bless him.

As news of this meeting quickly spread around Bradford, its residents anticipated an influx of visitors. By horse, by stagecoach, on foot came the church leaders and other participants, hosted by Parson Allen and church elders. Ann's papa came home beaming that Wednesday evening, announcing that several of the church elders, and a few of the young seminarians from Andover, would be their guests at lunch tomorrow. This meant a lot of work for Rebecca and her daughters, but also much excitement, for word had been spreading that a group of divinity students would present a "bold project" to the church leaders. John Hasseltine heard that the seminary's top student, Adoniram Judson, would present this unprecedented request. John told his wife and daughters that several of the town's leaders intended to go to tomorrow's sessions to hear more, himself included. Rebecca assured John that she and the girls would have lunch ready when he brought the guests home.

Ann was looking forward to Thursday with much more excitement than she dared to admit, for had her siblings known, they would have teased her unmercifully, especially Polly, to say nothing of Joseph, her teenaged brother. Ann heard from several sources that Adoniram Judson was not any ordinary seminarian; he had already turned down the associate ministry at the prestigious Park Street Church. The gossip around Bradford was that he had some high-minded idea of becoming, of all things, a foreign missionary.

A thrill shot through Ann when she first heard this rumor. This was the first she had heard of someone who was thinking thoughts similar to her own. Now here was Papa saying this same Mr. Judson would be their guest tomorrow!

Thursday morning, June 28, dawned bright and crisp. After Rebecca, an excellent cook, and her well-trained daughters had prepared the meal, Ann eagerly helped her mother set the long table in the pleasant west room with the dishes her brother, John, had brought home for Mama from his first sea voyage. Rebecca used them only on special occasions, and surely this one qualified, for the church fathers were highly respected. The oak floor sparkled as mother and daughter bustled around preparing for their guests. Ann managed to find time to gather June flowers from the back garden to arrange in a delicate vase and place on the gleaming white mantel next to grandmother's silver candlesticks. A row of pies stood waiting to be enjoyed after the women served platters of fried chicken and a selection of fresh vegetables from the garden.

Ann was standing in a shaft of sunlight in front of the white mantel in the west parlor when Parson Allen ushered Adoniram Judson through the parlor door. Adoniram had already heard a number of intriguing comments about the "Belle of Bradford" from several ministers in the area, but this was his first opportunity to meet the vibrant young woman Parson Allen had described to him. Ann was not shy when introduced to him, but if she expected him to immediately impress her with his wit and charm, she was disappointed. He stood speechless, his hazel eyes wide, as he came face-to-face with Ann Hasseltine for the first time.

Ann served their guests and kept their glasses filled with water, all the while keeping her eye on Mr. Judson. She had heard so much about his powerful voice, his erudition, his keen intellect, but she saw none of that. He merely toyed with the food on his plate, only occasionally glancing up, and if he caught her eyes on him, he immediately looked away. Ann was puzzled; maybe he was concentrating on the presentation he would make to the church fathers that afternoon.

It was something far different, however, that had Adoniram sitting in uncharacteristic silence: he was immediately smitten by Ann Hasseltine. She was so beautiful, and the stories he had been told about her personality and charm were sadly understated. Months later he told Ann that he had sat there trying to compose a poem that was worthy of her loveliness, finding it terribly difficult to either eat or speak. For her part, Ann had to admit to feeling let down. Here was the widely esteemed young minister, sitting like a statue, taking no part in the friendly conversations flowing around him.

Parson Allen sat at Judson's side, a tiny smile on his face and a gleam in his eyes, quietly enjoying the silent drama taking place in the room as he noted Ann's many surreptitious glances and Adoniram's apparent paralysis. Ann just wished that there were not so many guests, for she longed for some opportunity to talk with Mr. Judson about this call to foreign missions. How had he come to this point?

How could she herself be sure about what she had been experiencing? She had a hundred questions and no real chance to voice them. Ann could only nibble at her lip in frustration.

The ministers and students finally departed for the afternoon session, where Judson made a powerful presentation. Ann later learned that he had boldly acknowledged that the men knew countless dangers would lie ahead, but asserted, "We consider ourselves as devoted to this work for life." John Hasseltine, unaware of the byplay that had occurred in the west parlor earlier that day, came home that evening happily recounting the charged atmosphere at the meeting when Judson made the presentation. Those young men had been in earnest; they were willing to give up home and friends and make the perilous journey to the heathen world. All those present had felt the electricity in the air as Mr. Judson passionately appealed for support for the divine call he and his fellow seminarians were experiencing.

The following day, news quickly spread around Bradford. The council selected by the church fathers had convened in special session the previous night, and on June 29, 1810, announced their response to the plea of the seminary students. In a first for the Congregational denomination, and a first for the new nation, those church fathers had voted into being the American Board of Commissioners for Foreign Missions. The church in the United States was finally responding to the call of the Great Commission, and as history would tell, this response would begin with Adoniram Judson and Ann Hasseltine.

CHAPTER 8

Dr. Stanley Hanna, great-grandson of Adoniram Judson, and the author examine the priceless Judson miniatures housed in the archives of the American Baptist Historical Society.

The Courtship 1810–1811

THE EXCITEMENT ENGENDERED BY THE BIG CONFERENCE FINALLY subsided, and Bradford settled back to being a quiet New England town—for everyone except Ann Hasseltine. Her mother, Rebecca, shook her head in puzzlement and wondered why her daughter was more jittery than usual. Ann would often be gone for hours at a time, and even when home, she was frequently distracted and absent-minded. She confided in no one, but her perceptive mother realized something still plagued her mind.

The paths alongside the Merrimac were a burst of color, with daisies and buttercups vying with each other for beauty, and honeysuckle begging for someone to breathe in its subtle fragrance. But Ann was oblivious to the beauty as she mulled over the significant decision reached by the Congregational leaders and the commitment the seminarians had made. Ann had a hundred questions she wanted to ask Adoniram Judson, but she had to wait for him to initiate a conversation; a young lady of that time would never approach a gentleman. Her frustrations grew by the day. What chance did a woman have to fulfill God's purpose for her life? Ann's mind continually played back that luncheon in the west parlor, and she tried to imagine what it would have been like to talk with Mr. Judson, to learn what he might be thinking.

At the same time, just nine miles away, Adoniram sat in his classroom, struggling to keep his mind focused on what his professors were saying. His head was teeming with ideas and strategies for beginning his mission, but in the midst of all his planning, Ann Hasseltine's face kept intruding. Ann had entered his soul like sunlight. Her image had moved into his mind and heart and taken up residence already. He simply could not stop thinking about her. Judson, always determined to be in control, was now having trouble managing his own heart. He was going to have to do something about his topsy-turvy thoughts.

Exactly one month to the day after meeting Ann, Adoniram entered in his journal: *"1810, July 28, commenced an acquaintance with Ann Hasseltine."* In Judson's mind, "commencing an acquaintance" was tantamount to proposing. That July 28 morning, he sat down at the desk in his room at Phillips Hall and wrote his first letter to Ann, a letter asking that she consider becoming his wife.

Two days later, the afternoon mail coach arrived at Kimball Tavern and left an envelope addressed to Miss Ann Hasseltine. When John brought the mail home and handed the letter to Ann, everyone in the family was curious. It was not often that any of them received personal correspondence. Ann quickly headed up the stairs to her room to read the letter in private. Heart pounding, she broke the wax seal and stared at its contents. Adoniram Judson, who had met her just once and never had a conversation with her, was asking that she marry him. Marry! And this was not just any proposal. Judson was also asking her to leave her family, her friends, her town, all that she knew, perhaps never to see them again, and go with him to the other side of the world. Her knees went weak, and she sank into a chair. How could Mr. Judson possibly have known how God had been speaking to her heart these many months? Ann was astounded. This could not be coincidence. The hand of God *was* evident in her life. But how on earth could she possibly answer? She knew too little. She knew so little about *him.*

The Hasseltine family was most curious to know who the letter was from and what it said, but it took Ann several days to bring herself to the point of confiding in her mother. Finding Mama in her favorite spot by the bay window in the parlor, Ann silently handed her the letter. Upon reading Adoniram's startling words, Rebecca's loving heart was struck with the thought: *Our Ann, our rambling Honey, might indeed be traveling to places unknown, places not even to be imagined.* Such a thing was unheard of. How could her own heart bear it?

At first Rebecca could only sit in her rocker and stare at the letter, her hands shaking. Ann knelt at her knee and said with pleading eyes: "Mama, what do I do?" Rebecca had no answer; she could only take Ann's cold hand in her own warm one and respond: "Honey, I don't have an answer. Just take your time. Ask our heavenly Father what he wishes." And giving a little sigh, Rebecca continued, "Surely God must have an answer even though we do not." Although Rebecca spoke with calm tenderness, all the while her heart was sinking at the thought of never seeing her beloved daughter again.

Ann's next move was to tell Papa what was disrupting her peace of mind. As John Hasseltine absorbed the contents of the letter, he somehow managed to control his tongue. He and Rebecca had already lost their oldest son to the sea. How could they bear releasing this precious daughter, never to see her again? Was she seriously considering such a move?

Ann continued to pour out the misgivings of her heart in her journal. Several days passed, and at last she hesitantly asked Abigail to come to her room and talk with her about an important matter. Abby had been her confidant since childhood and was the most attuned of all the sisters to Ann's own spirit. Sitting beside Ann on the bed, the loving, practical Abigail first had to recover from the initial shock of such an unheard-of idea. Never as impetuous as her dear sister, Abigail tried to absorb what Ann was telling her. Marriage? Go around the world—ten thousand miles away? Who had ever heard of a woman doing such a thing?

Abby quietly took Ann's hand. "Ann," she began, groping for words, "what can I possibly tell you to do?" Abby shook her head in perplexity, sounding hesitant. "Sister, you must seek what God wants for you. No one else can know. But ask yourself, Ann"— Abby paused again, "do I really know this man well enough to trust my future to him?" Then Abby waited long moments before adding, "But, sister, I guess it comes to trusting God with your future, does not it? The Holy Spirit must surely guide you." Abby reached up to gently touch her sister's cheek and say, "Only your own heart can give you the right direction."

For twenty years, Ann had been known as the most impulsive of the Hasseltine household. Not this time. This was a life-changing decision, an awesome proposition. Only heaven knew what perils were out there, wide oceans away. And that was the crux of it—only heaven knew. Ann spent countless hours in prayer and in examining her own heart. She wrote in her journal during that time, "*I never felt more engaged in prayer for special grace, to prepare me for my great undertaking, than this evening.*"

Waiting like this was not typical for Ann; she had always been noted for her decisiveness of character. Several more weeks went by with no action on her part. Still she had not replied to Mr. Judson's audacious letter from Andover. Meanwhile, in Andover, Adoniram had no choice but to pray and be patient. Each day he eagerly scanned the pile of letters that reached Phillips Hall, and each day he was disappointed when nothing came from Bradford. Concentrating on Advanced Hebrew and systematic theology had become a huge challenge.

At long last, a letter addressed in a clearly feminine hand arrived. His heart beating rapidly, Adoniram tore open the envelope. It was not a rejection. Relief made him lightheaded for a moment. But then, her words were not exactly encouraging either. Ann hedged a bit, writing that her parents would have to consent before she could even consider such a monumental step. No doubt she was borrowing some time in which to reflect on just what she should do. Maybe this was all too sudden for her.

Judson's own response was typical for him. He immediately sat down and wrote John and Rebecca Hasseltine. Forcing himself to be honest, he explained just what he was asking of their daughter. This was no simple, "May I have your daughter's hand in marriage, to protect and cherish her all her days?" His request of them was instead a remarkable document in its candor:

> *I have now to ask, whether you can consent to part with your daughter early next spring, to see her no more in this world; whether you can consent to her departure for a heathen land, and her subjection to the hardships and sufferings of a missionary life . . . to every kind of want and distress: to degradation, insult, persecution and perhaps a violent death.*

Judson wrote more in the same vein, never glossing over the dangers and troubles that likely lay ahead, concluding with, *"Can you consent to all this, in hope of soon meeting your daughter in the world of glory, with a crown of righteousness?"* Surely no loving New England father had ever received such an austere and bleak request for a daughter's hand. He and Rebecca were being asked to allow Ann to cross that same ocean in which John had perished. It is a tribute to two remarkable parents that they did not sink into total despair or react in denial, but rather allowed their cherished Ann the freedom to make her own choice and to know they stood behind whatever she decided. Although Rebecca Hasseltine always felt like Ann, her "Honey," was destined to ramble, such wanderings as this had never even crossed her mind. Thus did two extraordinary parents affirm to their cherished child, "Whatever it is that God prompts you to do, you will have our blessing."

Ann was struggling with a question no woman in America had yet been called on to consider: Should she marry Mr. Judson, leave her loving father and mother, and probably never be able to see them again? Some mornings she would think, *How can I even contemplate such a preposterous thing?*

After some weeks, Ann followed up Adoniram's letter to her parents with a response to him. Her answer was yes, but even as she accepted his proposal, Ann made it clear she had many considerations that needed working through. Forthwith, the jubilant Adoniram became a regular visitor to the Hasseltine house.

When word of the remarkable proposal began making the rounds in Bradford parlors, all sorts of opinions were proffered. "Crazy, wild, and romantic," one matron would tell another over tea. "Utterly impossible," another would retort. "How can her parents even consider such an absurd idea?" One of John Hasseltine's friends even went as far as to say he would tie his own daughter to the bedpost rather than allow her to do such a foolhardy thing. Not John Hasseltine. He respected his daughter enough to allow the decision to be hers.

So it was that the courtship actually came after the engagement was secured. Ann wondered how many young women might have had a similar situation of getting to know a suitor *after* the proposal. Her leather-bound journal throughout the autumn months was full of Ann's questions and her earnest desire to know just what God wanted for her and for them as a couple as she contemplated the life-changing decision she had made. Early in their engagement, she wrote, *"Endeavored to commit myself entirely to God, to be disposed of, according to His pleasure. . . . I do feel His service is my delight."* A few weeks later she added, *"For several weeks past, my mind has been greatly agitated. An opportunity has been presented to me, of spending my days among the heathen. . . . A consideration of this subject has occasioned much self-examination . . . but I now feel willing to leave it entirely with God. . . . O Jesus, direct me."*

After receiving Ann's reply, Judson spent necessary time in classes, but used every possible moment to go up the road to Bradford to woo the beautiful young woman who had captivated not only his heart but his imagination as well.

On a free day, Adoniram would come to the Hasseltine home and the couple would stroll under the low covered bridge over the Merrimac River. Sometimes they would gallop their horses through the fields surrounding the Hasseltine home; both were excellent in the saddle and loved exploring the beautiful countryside. Other afternoons they would ramble on foot, often wandering down to the banks of the Merrimac and dreaming about the days to come. One afternoon, as they gazed out over the river's glistening waters, Adoniram waxed eloquent as he took Ann's hands in his. "My beautiful girl," he began as he gazed into her glowing eyes, "in all my life I never met a girl other than you who could brighten my life merely by walking into a room." He paused a moment, and then went on. "When we are together, you see, I feel I have come home. And I am convinced," he concluded, "that where you are will always be 'home' to me."

Rebecca would often look out the bay window beside her rocking chair and see the couple in deep conversation, their faces alight with excitement and glowing health. She would concentrate her mind on such moments, treasuring them as points in time to which she could come back on those lonely days when Ann would be so far away, far from her loving mother's sight. Then she could dwell on those clear memories. And as the weeks passed, there was no mistaking the radiance on Ann's face as she looked into Adoniram's eyes. For his part, Adoniram could scarcely take in the wonder of such a keen mind and incisive intellect wrapped up in such a lovely form. And to think, she was going to marry him!

Adoniram was such a man of action, full of ideas and never lacking in confidence. Both of them noticed that their ideas did not always march neatly side by side, but in the first flush of tenderness and love, each made allowances for the other. One Sunday during this golden autumn of their courtship, Adoniram wrote his fellow mission volunteer Samuel Nott, *"I have done nothing scarcely since I saw you, beside making a compilation of extracts for the Collection of Letters attending to this missionary business and riding about the country with Ann. Pretty preparation this last article, for a mission-ary life—isn't it?"*

Even as she and Adoniram were getting to know each other and talking of their possible future, Ann continued to record in her jour-nal the questions and perplexities about the future. This was no whimsy. This was real. In September she wrote her dear friend and cousin, Lydia, in Salem, telling her of this life-changing commitment, explaining, *"I feel willing, and expect, if nothing in providence pre-vent, to spend my days in the world in heathen lands. Yes, Lydia, I have about come to the determination to give up all my comforts here . . . and go where God shall see fit to place me. My determinations are not hasty, or formed without viewing the dangers, trials, and hardships attendant on a missionary life."*

Ann had reached a firm determination as to what God wanted of her. As such she poured out her heart in her journal on October 28: *"I have at length come to the conclusion, that if nothing in provi-dence appears to present, I must spend my days in a heathen land. I am a creature of God, and He has an undoubted right to do with me, as seemeth good in His sight. I rejoice, that I am in His hands. . . . He has my heart in His hands."*

With the matter settled in her heart, Ann was as eager as Adoniram to move ahead with God's plan for them—this bold plan to make a path where none had ever gone. What might be the direc-tion of that path? One Sunday afternoon in December, Adoniram brought Ann a copy of a book that had just come to his hands and excited his imagination. It was *An Account of an Embassy to the Kingdom of Ava* by Michael Symes. The intriguing tales of the emperor of the Burman Empire on his golden throne in Ava captured Adoniram's attention. Could this be the place where God might direct them?

Another intrigue had also arisen. The recently formed missionary committee of the denomination was not yet doing anything about appointing these new missionaries. They met but feared that not enough money could be raised anytime soon. This was not what Judson wanted to hear. At last the committee decided to consult the London Missionary Society and agreed that Judson was the one to send as emissary to England, as he was already in contact with that society. This opportunity suited Adoniram's adventurous spirit right to the core, and he told Ann he was to make the trip in January. She was not excited about his leaving her in a few weeks, but she agreed that something needed to be done to get them on their way.

Boyhood home of Adoniram Judson, Plymouth, MA. The original banisters remain in the house, which is structurally much as it was 200 years ago.

A Journey and an Appointment 1811

JANUARY 1, 1811. COULD THIS BE THE YEAR ANN HASSELTINE would change both her name and her country? So many new challenges appeared in the offing for Ann, leaving her excited and apprehensive at the same time. After all, where was there a model to follow for this combination? Nowhere. Hers was an untrod path with no footprints to follow.

That New Year's morning, Adoniram wrote his fiancée what could only be termed a very unromantic love letter. Ann opened the envelope addressed in the now-familiar handwriting to read:

It is with the utmost sincerity, and with my whole heart, that I wish you, my love, a happy new year. May it be a year in which your walk will be close with God. . . . May this be the year in which you will change your name; in which you will take a final leave of your relatives and native land; in which you will cross the wide ocean, and dwell on the other side of the world, among a heathen people. . . . If our lives are preserved and our attempt prospered, we shall next new year's day be in India, and perhaps wish each other a happy new year in the uncouth dialect of Hindostan or Burmah. We shall no more see our kind friends around us . . . or enjoy the conveniences of civilized life.

Adoniram continued in the same vein, enough to chill the blood of any except the most valiant of hearts, and ended with a mournful little poem he wrote picturing what might be her end, or his: *"By foreign hands thy dying eyes are closed; By foreign hands thy decent limbs composed; By foreign hands thy humble grave adorned . . . at least either of us will be certain of* one *mourner."* Judson was no doubt on a flight of fancy; he could not have known the unerringly prophetic accuracy of what he was picturing.

Ann was not deterred by Judson's meanderings. She wasn't delighted, however, at the thought of her fiancé leaving for England soon, just when there was so much to plan and do. But with the Board of Commissioners dragging their feet about sending them to foreign lands, what choice was there? Ann could not share Judson's excitement about his trip to England; he had already become integral to her happiness. Because Adoniram had contacted the London Missionary Society the previous year, the Congregational leaders determined that he could best represent them to seek support for the American volunteers without them being wholly under LMS's direction. Convincing the American Board of Commissioners to work jointly with the London Society was not going to be easy. Since war between the United States and England seemed frighteningly eminent, there was some reluctance on the part of the American Board to work hand in hand with the London Society, due to communication difficulties. Likewise, the LMS would probably have the same concerns.

Accordingly, on January 11, Judson kissed his fiancée a fond good-bye, promising her he would be back almost before she could realize his absence—"Quick as a fly can wash his little hands!" he joked. Ann recognized hyperbole when she heard it. She knew this was no easy voyage and would likely take two months each way, even if the weather was favorable.

Adoniram left Boston harbor aboard the *Packet* destined for Liverpool. His first overseas voyage would be good preparation for the longer journey lying ahead in coming months. It wasn't long, however, before this trip took on the aspects of a nightmare. The seas proved dangerous, for only three weeks out crewmen of the *L'Invincible Napoleon*, a French privateer, boarded the *Packet* and captured the American vessel. Since Judson spoke no French, he was thrown in the hold as a prisoner along with the American crewmen.

For the first time in his life, Adoniram was staring a true hardship in the face, and it stunned him. Fastidiously clean almost to the point of obsession, he was overwhelmed by the filth in the hold. To make matters worse, it was February on the high seas and the weather was miserable. Sailor after sailor was terribly seasick, and the filth and odor were overpowering. Judson could only think of Ann and home and the big church he had turned down. For the first time in his life, he felt misgivings. This negative reasoning was soon pushed away by the thought that God had permitted this capture as a trial of his faith, and he immediately resolved in the strength of God to bear it. Maybe this experience was preparing him for greater trials in years to come.

After fumbling about in the dim prison light for his Hebrew Bible, he managed to keep his mind busy by mentally translating from the Hebrew into Latin. A short time later the ship's doctor passed near-by, and out of the shadows he heard a voice using refined Latin. He immediately responded in Latin, inquiring who on earth was using such scholarly language in that filthy hold. In no time, Adoniram was released and allowed the luxury of a thorough scrubbing before joining the officers on deck.

Trouble was far from over, however. The French took their prisoners to Bayonne, France, and a highly indignant Adoniram was marched with the *Packet*'s crew through the streets to the local jail. Judson knew a few words of French by this time and began loudly exclaiming about the indignities taking place, hoping that someone along the way would step in to help. Then it occurred to him that there might be someone along the route who understood English, so he began loudly protesting his treatment in his own language. Miraculously, a voice out of the crowd of onlookers responded in English, asking him what on earth was going on. Judson quickly explained his plight, whereupon the stranger assured him, "Go on, now. Calm down and quit yelling. I'll see what I can do." Judson took him at his word and thanked God for such a speedy answer to prayer.

Providence had provided for his rescue by a Philadelphia businessman who indeed returned to the jail that night. After greasing the palms of the guards, he looked over the prisoners, spotted Adoniram, threw his own voluminous cloak around them both, and herded him to freedom. His kind rescuer also found him a place to board with an American family living in Bayonne until Judson could find a ship to take him on to England. He could never have conceived of his trip to London being interrupted by six weeks in France. Finally, an American vessel was located, and he was on his way across the English Channel, arriving in London on May 6, nearly four months after leaving Boston.

While Adoniram's wild adventures at sea had been taking place, Ann was learning all she could about the Burman Empire and seeking to prepare her heart spiritually for the monumental task of missions service that lay ahead. Adoniram had loaned her Symes' book about the embassy to Ava. Ann carefully studied its pages to learn more of that mysterious land. However, there was no one with whom to consult, no wise and experienced older missionary to guide her thinking. This was solely an act of faith, blind trust in the One who was calling them.

Ann had eager listening ears in the quiet Harriet Atwood. A classmate for years, Harriet had always adored Ann and looked up to her older, more vibrant friend. By this time, Harriet's father had died and Harriet lived with her widowed mother close by in Haverhill. Like Ann, she had been teaching school and loving the experience. Ann told Harriet stories she had read about the fabled land of Burma, and Harriet was immediately fascinated. Little did Ann realize that summer afternoon that she had done far more than entertain her friend. In less than a month, Harriet herself became a mission volunteer and, about the same time, met missionary candidate Samuel Newell, Adoniram's classmate at Andover.

Meanwhile, one of the first things Judson did upon reaching his destination in England was write a long letter to his beloved, including with it a beautiful little watch brooch that he had purchased to remind her of his love and devotion. Adoniram longed to share every new experience with her, for she had become as important to him as breathing. He was anxious to get back to her side and begin preparing for their future together.

For the next six weeks, he remained in England, however, staying at the Missionary Seminary at Gosport and meeting frequently with leaders of the London Missionary Society. The encounters proved successful, as all those spending time with the passionate young American were impressed with his plans and listened intently to the proposal coming from the American Board. The society was indeed willing to employ Judson and the other volunteers. However, there was a condition: the work would need to remain in British hands. Adoniram knew this stipulation would likely prove a stumbling point for the American Board. His trip was to be a fact-gathering trip, however, and that is exactly what Judson did. He learned all he could about the society's involvement in missions in India, just what they did and how they did it. This information would prove immensely helpful to the fledgling American mission board.

During the time he waited for a passage home, Adoniram was frequently asked to speak. His deep, powerful voice was always a surprise to listeners, coming as it did from such a slender young man of medium height. In one service, when Adoniram finished his presentation, the English minister explained that this American gentleman was a prospective missionary, adding, "If his faith is proportioned to his voice, he will drive the devil from all India!"

At long last Adoniram ventured to Gravesend, boarded the ship *Augustus*, and by June 18 was on his way to New York and his beloved Ann. After the ordeals of the trip to England, this return voyage seemed calm and uneventful. Arriving in New York harbor on August 7, Judson could scarcely wait to get to Bradford and his sweetheart; it would be wonderful to share the past months with the one so closely attuned to his own heart and thoughts.

A radiant Ann could only drink in the joy of seeing his beloved face and hearing over and over again the staggering adventures that he had encountered. And one of the first things she did was call his attention to the watch brooch he had sent her from England. The gleaming gold case adorned her sprig muslin gown, and with shining eyes, Ann grasped Adoniram's hand and proclaimed, "I'll cherish this all the days of my life; I've been wearing it each day and counting the hours until you came back to me."

Along with the joy of being together again, the excited couple began to consider all that must be done. There was a wedding to plan as well as numerous preparations to make before departing for the mission field. September was a busy month, for on Thursday, September 5, Adoniram officially received his master of arts degree from Brown University and then on Tuesday, September 24—not three weeks later—completed his studies at Andover Seminary. Events were beginning to take shape, for it appeared that Judson's return from England was the signal for the Board of Commissioners to finally meet and take action.

Consequently, the commissioners met in Worcester on September 18, 1811, and two of the aspiring mission appointees, Adoniram

Judson and Samuel Nott, represented the group of four, all of whom were Andover students. The board carefully studied the report Adoniram had brought from the Society in England. Clearly the English society was willing to send the young Americans, but strictly under their own control. Each young man indicated his willingness to go however he could be supported. Wise heads among the conservative church leaders realized that if they wanted to follow through with the young missionaries being supported and directed by their own board, they would have to take action right away, with no more time for foot-dragging. The commissioners decided to take a leap of faith into the unknown to appoint the four and somehow raise the needed funds. September 18 marked the day a Christian body in the United States first appointed missionaries to serve overseas.

Luther Rice was among those young men seeking mission support from the American Board, but the church fathers felt that they would not be able to muster enough funds for five. From that moment on, Rice determined to raise that support on his own and join the others in the beginning of their American foreign mission service. Luther was also wooing a young woman, Rebecca Eaton, and hoping she would go with him, so multiple challenges lay ahead of him in the upcoming months.

Two things occurred almost simultaneously that encouraged the American Board to swift action. It appeared that the United States could go to war with England at any moment, making the likelihood of working closely with the English missionary society extremely difficult. Should American vessels set up a blockade, it would be impossible for the young missionaries to set sail. And miraculously, at this same time, Mrs. John Norris, a wealthy Salem widow, made a munificent bequest of $30,000 to the board for foreign missions. It transpired that this most generous gift would be tied up in court for years, but just the knowledge of that much money backing them gave the American Board the courage to get out and solicit other funds in a hurry. After a great deal of deliberation, the board decided that a single man would receive $444.45 a year and a married one, $666.66.

Meanwhile, Samuel Newell had met Harriet Atwood and was hopeful that she would accept his marriage proposal in time to sail. Newell was doing a nine-month stint in Philadelphia, learning basic medical techniques and skills to use while overseas. This made the courtship slow in progressing, as did Harriet's concern over her physical strength. Never a strong girl, she often wondered if she was fated to suffer the same consumption that had taken away her father so early in life. Frail as she was, there was nothing frail about Harriet's determination to serve Christ, and she seemed to gain strength from Ann's buoyant faith and confidence.

Nobody had to look far for naysayers—they were thick on the ground. One well-known minister dismissed the news of the appointment by disparaging the young appointees with the statement, "We learn nothing favorable of their talents or experiences." Plenty of people around Bradford had opinions, and most didn't mind expressing them, whether sought or not. One upstanding matron offered her unsolicited judgment held by many others as well: "It is altogether preposterous for a woman to consider such a rash undertaking!"

Despite this flurry of uninvited criticisms, Ann continued preparing to take a step no woman in America had taken before: marry the man she loved and travel far from her family's home to a distant land, probably never to return, all in response to God's call. Many people dismissively labeled the young couple's decision foolhardy. Yet regardless of the negative sentiment, the bone-deep determination bred in Ann's heart and soul was not deterred. People were not calling her; God was. She and Adoniram were headed for shores unknown and experiences beyond belief.

The original mantel in the west parlor, in front of which Ann and Adoniram exchanged their wedding vows, still remains.

The Wedding 1811–1812

ANN AND ADONIRAM LOVED WALKING IN THE WOODS AND ALONG the Merrimac, reveling in the riotous beauty of that New England autumn. It was somewhat bittersweet, however, because both realized they might never see such beautiful foliage again in their lifetimes. The tropical clime for which they were bound had no such seasons. There would be no changing leaves or gently falling snow, but instead only large cities and deep jungles of green. The couple drank in the autumn colors, knowing that they would soon be memories tucked away in their hearts to treasure in the years ahead. Both had a flair for the dramatic, and their current circumstances surely encouraged drama, for theirs was a one-way path with no turning back.

The usual order in a courtship had been reversed, for Ann and Adoniram had in essence committed to their marriage before getting to know each other. The fall of 1811 was their opportunity to get to know one another in depth, and both were surprised at how many character traits they shared. Ann occasionally smiled to herself to recognize in her beloved some new attribute closely akin to one of her own. One obvious similarity was the marked tendency of both to always feel that they were right; furthermore, neither Ann nor Adoniram suffered fools gladly, a tendency that would sometimes make it difficult for them to deal with people less gifted. Both were likewise adept at devising plans to obtain his or her own way. These commonalities would make for some interesting family dynamics in the months and years to come.

The young couple certainly shared a strong will; however, this tendency would prove invaluable in light of the massive challenges that would soon confront them. There was no question that both exhibited a decisiveness of character and a depth of compassion that never ran dry. Each likewise shared a vivid conception of what duty meant. Once determined, there was no subsequent hesitancy or faltering. Sometimes late at night John and Rebecca Hasseltine would lie in bed and reflect on what might be confronting their Honey in the days ahead. "I think she's met her match in finding someone who knows how to consistently devise a plan to achieve his own aims," John would chuckle. Rebecca would smile in response and add, "Indeed, and our soon-to-be son-in-law will discover that she can match him plan for plan."

In October 1811 Ann poured out her heart in a letter to a friend in another city who was contemplating a similar calling:

> *Our undertaking is great, arduous, and highly important. . . . To enter a path untrod before by any American female requires much previous consideration. . . . A life of self-denial is before us; and we must begin by cutting the most tender ties. . . . We may soon be called to part with our dearest earthly friends and be left alone in a land of strangers—thus we may end our days in a heathen land. . . . [but] He will strengthen and support us in every trying hour—although*

He may appoint for us a path full of dangers, yet He will provide a way for escape. . . . We have every thing to engage us, for all heaven is engaged in the same glorious cause for which we leave our native land.

Had Ann been able to look back at these words some fifteen years later, she would have realized the staggering accuracy of each conjecture she had recorded. What *was* clear was that Ann had soberly counted the cost of what might lie ahead.

Soon autumn's foliage started dropping, the first rains of winter began, and the trees were quickly stripped of their beauty. When the first snow fell, the engaged couple was still waiting for news of a ship they could sail on. While they were waiting, the entire Hasseltine family was caught up in the urgency of packing and, at the same time, preparing for the wedding. Ann's mother and siblings quickly prepared a trousseau, with a lot of fine stitching done by candlelight each evening around the rocking chair in Mama's room. Rebecca Hasseltine was not a woman to do things halfway. Never mind that her beloved child was going to a tropical climate, where one hot, steamy day would follow another. She was also determined that her Honey would have a sufficient supply of sturdy leather half-boots, which meant nothing less than a dozen. Ann would eventually adapt to Burmese-style clothing, but those New England half-boots would forever remain a staple of her wardrobe. And each time she put on a pair, they would remind her of a loving mama and home.

Meanwhile, Adoniram was busy planning what to take and how to get there. Impending war with England was complicating a process never easy at best. Finally, in December 1811, his trip to Salem revealed a possible passage. A certain ship owner, Mr. Pickering Dodge, had received assurance that his brig, the *Caravan,* could be cleared for sailing by mid-February. In addition to her cargo, Adoniram discovered that the *Caravan* could take on four passengers. That would mean space for Ann and Adoniram, plus Samuel

Newell and his soon-to-be-bride, Harriet. As Judson and the other appointees feverishly planned, Gordon Hall, Luther Rice, and Samuel Nott and his bride, Roxanna, were able to obtain passage on the *Harmony* out of Philadelphia, which was expected to leave at about the same time as the *Caravan*.

Ann was not much concerned about her wedding wardrobe, for Mama had that well in hand. Rebecca ordered the newest in bridal wear, finding in Boston a white satin scoop bonnet to go with the cream-colored wedding gown with hand-embroidered trim all around the hem. It would certainly be striking with Ann's black curls. The bride-to-be had a major disappointment, however, when Adoniram explained to her that his parents weren't going to be able to come to the wedding. Rev. Judson was growing older and was not well that winter. Ann was forced to swallow her regret that she could not meet the parents of the one who had become so dear to her.

By now it was already early in the new year, and 1812 promised to be crowded with change. Adoniram, who had always felt a terrible aversion to saying good-byes, traveled to Plymouth to take leave of his parents. Never had farewells proved more difficult for him than on this occasion. This would prove to be a permanent leave-taking. Adoniram realized with anguish that his mother, Abigail, was almost certainly seeing her firstborn son for the last time. His mother's tears were nearly his undoing. His father was always dignified, whether in the pulpit or with his family. On this occasion, however, he departed from custom and clasped his son to his heart for a heartbreaking length of time. Both he and Adoniram choked back tears.

That fact that brother Elnathan and sister Abigail were planning to come to the ordination in Salem was balm to Adoniram's heart. Ann would at least be able to meet them, and as for himself, he would be able to postpone for just a bit longer two more farewells that would be wrenchingly difficult. Adoniram could not bring himself to say a final good-bye, so rising in the early hours of the following morning, he slipped away without a word. The hollow feeling in his heart, however, remained as he and his faithful horse steadily made their way through the wintry day. Judson was a bundle of mixed emotions. Although heavy of heart over his last time with his parents, at the same time he was excited about what lay ahead, anticipating both marrying his beloved and then sailing for lands unknown, all within just a matter of days.

Tuesday morning, February 4, the Hasseltine house was already a beehive of activity. The wedding was the next day, and there was so much to do. Mama was in charge of the kitchen, with Polly and Abigail her willing assistants, while Ann would come in occasionally with a question for Mama about whether to take this dress or that cloak. As Ann passed through Mama's sitting room each time, she could not help pausing to trail her fingers over the delicate cream and pink flowers in the wallpaper. She would never see those familiar flowers again; it seemed an insignificant trifle but it was home and family, and such thoughts brought a lump to her throat.

Ann was busy most of the day as she packed her trunk as carefully as possible, tucking bits and pieces of memories of home into the corners, knowing that these would be increasingly precious to her in months and years to come. Home and dear ones would be so far away, and her small family portraits might make them seem a bit nearer. Among the portraits was a miniature of her older brother John, gone now for seven years. She and Adoniram, for their part, were leaving behind beautiful ivory miniatures of the two of them. Papa had insisted that they sit for the portraits so the family would have these reminders of their dear ones who would be so far away. Ann would have been astounded to learn that those tiny images would one day be replicated and seen around the world.

Adoniram would be coming in time for the wedding tomorrow morning, and Ann's heart was a welter of emotions. Sometimes the excitement was nearly overwhelming as she knelt by the chest, packing for the years to come. Occasionally she would have to stop, sit back on her heels, take a deep breath, and ponder: *However can I manage these good-byes in the midst of so much excitement and coming change? O God, am I doing just what you want me to do?* The questions did not have definitive answers apart from her faith, and over and over she would pause in her busyness and seek heavenly direction.

During the night a heavy snow fell, and Ann woke early the next morning to that soft silence that a blanket of snow brings. It was early enough that no one in the house was yet stirring. Immediately the thought came: *My wedding day. By the end of this day I will no longer be simply Ann Hasseltine. I will be Ann Hasseltine Judson, Mrs. Adoniram Judson.* The very thought brought a smile to her lips, and her heart skipped a beat. So much change, dramatic change. As her eyes adjusted to the dimness of the early morning, she could make out the outline of the mahogany chest that had always stood at the foot of her bed, the tallboy near the door, and her beloved little desk, where she had sat for so many hours pouring out her heart in her journal, studying Scripture, and reading books of theology and poetry.

She dressed quietly so as not to disturb the household and slipped downstairs. At the landing where she turned to the right for the final flight of steps, she ran her hands lovingly over the smooth dark railing, reminiscing about the many times she had inelegantly slid down this banister when just a little girl. That had stopped the day she decided she was too old and dignified for such childishness, but those fond memories lingered on.

Quietly descending the remaining steps, Ann turned to the left and walked over to the mantel where, in just a matter of hours, she and Adoniram would stand together to exchange their vows. She bent down to stoke the fire that had been laid in the hearth, and both light and warmth leapt up to give a glow to the room. Ann stood there for a long moment, turning to the door and recalling her first sight of Adoniram as he had entered this very parlor that June morning. The words leapt to her mind: "'Til death do us part." This would be part of their vows that very day, and what it might mean in the days ahead she had no way of knowing. It had to be enough that they would go together into this unknown and that the presence of almighty God would surely go with them.

The snow did nothing to deter the wedding guests, who began arriving for the momentous occasion. Relatives and friends from Salem, Beverly, Haverhill, and other nearby towns made it in time. Parson Allen was beaming as he came in wearing his usual tailored black suit and shiny shoes with their large silver buckles. Parson was feeling particularly pleased today, picturing himself as the middle-aged cupid who had first introduced this unique couple to each other, and now here he was, about to officiate at their exchange of vows. Harriet Atwood slipped in, smiling with joy at being able to attend the wedding with her fiancée, Samuel. In just a matter of days, she too would be marrying and had been spending her days feverishly preparing for the monumental journey ahead.

As usual, Rebecca had everything in order for the wedding, while husband John appeared his usual jovial, hospitable self. He was try-ing not to let his emotions show at the thought of not just giving his daughter away in marriage, but actually giving her to travel a world away, to see her no more.

The groom arrived in plenty of time. But the usually urbane, con-fident Adoniram Judson who was always in control exhibited a few signs of wedding day nerves as he frequently brushed back the wavy chestnut hair from his brow. In a few minutes, Adoniram joined Parson Allen at the mantel, smiling to himself as he recalled his first glimpse of Ann in this very room. So much had happened since then. And now family and guests crowded into the two parlors, joining minister and groom as they awaited the arrival of the bride.

A hush fell over family and friends as they caught sight of the bride descending the staircase. Ann seemed to float down in a cloud of ivory as she gracefully entered the parlor and turned to join Adoniram by Parson Allen. Her sole adornment was the beautiful gold watch brooch Judson had sent her from England. Taking his daughter on his arm, John Hasseltine led her to stand beside the groom. Judson's eyes lighted with tenderness as he looked into the radiant face of the young woman who was joining him to travel to the ends of the earth.

If Ann was nervous, she gave no such indication as she stepped up to his side. As Parson Allen began the solemn and beautiful words of the age-old litany that would unite them in holy matrimony— "Dearly beloved, we are gathered together today in the sight of God and of this company"—Ann's heart swelled with the magnitude of the moment. As she spoke her vows, Ann felt as if a moment of destiny was enveloping them. For this, God had been preparing her heart and spirit. She would not fail.

As each was asked to repeat their vows, both spoke in clear, strong voices, responding to the minister's questions with a firm, "I do." When Parson Allen asked who gave this woman in marriage, John Hasseltine had his most difficult moment but did not hesitate to affirm, "Her mother and I do." It was like a holy vow to the man whose beloved child he was indeed giving away.

As Parson Allen concluded with "I now pronounce you husband and wife," family and friends broke into spontaneous applause. The celebration then began, with the food and festivities spilling over into the frolic room, with many a round of song and cheer and wedding guests enjoying the sumptuous wedding breakfast, crowned with a massive plum wedding cake.

The conclusion of the wedding day was not typical for a New England wedding, however, for the Bradford Parish Church was having a solemn meeting that afternoon to serve as a farewell for the two young couples who would in a matter of days or weeks be leaving for parts unknown. With the church just a few doors away from the Hasseltine home, the guests easily made their way through the snow to the church sanctuary, attending what would be a first in America—a farewell to young missionaries for a lifetime. The church would be packed with family and friends, along with much of the population of Bradford, all coming to be part of what would be a historic moment in the history of missions in America.

The deacon's bench, on which the five young men ordained for missions service in 1812 sat, remains on display in historic Tabernacle Church in Salem, MA.

The Good-byes
1812

WHO EVER HEARD OF A WEDDING CELEBRATION FOLLOWED IMMEdiately by a long and mournful religious service? That is the perfectly accurate description of the wedding day of Ann Hasseltine and Adoniram Judson. Similarities between the nuptials of Ann and Adoniram and that of most New England couples ended following the ceremony and the wedding breakfast, for next in the day's activities was a solemn service held at the parish church where the Hasseltines were members.

This was a different kind of event, for pastor and church were saying farewell to both Ann Hasseltine (now Judson) and Harriet Atwood, two beloved young people who would no longer be sitting in their pews on Sunday mornings but would instead be thousands of miles away, learning a new language and living among a very different people. The common core was the need of the human heart, no matter the country or language, for the love of God through Jesus the Savior.

The parish church was crowded that snowy February afternoon, and each one present was moved with the gravity of the moment and the seriousness of the mission that lay ahead. Parson Allen presided with mixed emotions. He had known the Hasseltines since Ann had been a toddler, and he had watched her grow up. During the years, Harriet Atwood had frequently attended the Bradford church, and Parson had many memories of the two girls laughing and dancing with their friends in the frolic room at the Hasseltine home. Parson Allen addressed much of his message directly to Ann and Harriet, noting that they, as missionary wives, would have a special duty to the women of the land to which they went:

> *It will be your business, my dear children, to convert these women to whom your husbands can have little or no access. Go then, and do all in your power to bring them to the knowledge of the truth. . . . Teach them to realize that they are not an inferior race of creatures but stand upon a par with men. . . .Teach them that they have immortal souls.*

The solemn truth of the task ahead hit the new bride afresh, and her mother as well. For the sake of her cherished daughter, Rebecca Hasseltine struggled throughout the service to maintain her own self-control. Parson's emotional farewell concluded with: *"To the care of the great head of the church, I now commit you. To His grave I also resign you . . . and may you all return and come to Zion with a song and with shouts of everlasting glory."* There were few dry eyes in the sanctuary as each thought of the reality of what lay ahead for their two Bradford girls.

Ann, sitting beside her new husband, frequently bowed her head in order to maintain her composure, thankful for the new white scoop bonnet that she could use to shelter her face from loving but curious eyes. Parson Allen's words were nearly her undoing, but even as he spoke them, Adoniram reached out and grasped her hand in his warm grip. Her heart swelled in gratitude at the tangible reminder that not only was God going with her as the vanguard, but her husband would be at her side as well.

The newlywed Judsons left immediately after the service to go to Beverly and spend the night in the Emerson manse. Beverly was about three miles from Salem, where the commissioning service for the new missionaries would take place the next day, so the new couple left with Ann's sister Becky and her spouse, Rev. Emerson. The painful good-byes with Mama and Papa would come only too soon. The elder Hasseltines were unable to attend the commissioning, but at least the newlyweds would have one last time in Bradford before leaving for Salem to await the sailing of the *Caravan*.

Rebecca Hasseltine looked and sounded much braver and more matter-of-fact than she felt as she embraced her child, took Ann's face between the palms of her hands, and spoke softly, "My dear child, God sustain you by the moment." As Ann relished her mother's embrace, the thought raced through her mind that, no matter how difficult this was, the next parting would be the final one and much, much harder. Mother and daughter, so very much alike, looked deeply into each other's eyes, and Rebecca murmured, "Honey, this is going to be rambling indeed!"

The piercing winds of a New England winter had swept through the valley of the Merrimac, and Thursday morning all roads leading to Salem were covered with a deep layer of snow. The sun, however, was shining on the glistening white surface as hundreds made their way toward Tabernacle Church. This historic spot would once again be marked by a moment in church history as America's first missionaries were to be ordained this winter's morning. Tabernacle had been the first church established in Salem back in 1629, and the legendary Roger Williams had once been its pastor. Dr. Samuel Worcester, the present minister, was a leading figure in the denomination and in the forefront of this missions thrust. Dr. Worcester would serve as secretary for the missionary board for many years and was the main advocate for funds to support the new missionaries. Less than a mile away from Tabernacle Church was the wharf from which Ann and Adoniram would be embarking in just days or weeks, along with soon-to-be-newlywed couple, Samuel Newell and Harriet Atwood.

Scores of students walked the sixteen miles from Andover to Salem, evidence of their determination to be part of this moment in their seminary's role in the beginning of missions. Others came from miles around, eager to be witness to the beginning of a daring new venture. The radiant newlyweds were both touched and gratified that each would have some family present for this momentous occasion. Adoniram's siblings, Abigail and Elnathan, were both at Tabernacle Church this morning, and they met their new sister-in-law for the first time. And Ann's sister Becky and her husband, Joseph Emerson of the Beverly parish, were there as well. It was a momentary comfort for the couple who would so soon be far away from kith and kin.

The sanctuary was so crowded that people were standing along the walls. Close to two thousand had come for this moment in history. Sitting on a narrow bench at the front of the auditorium, the five young men were questioned for several hours. Ann sat in the nearest box pew just behind the ordination bench. The consecration of ministers and deacons was quite a common practice. The setting apart of missionaries, on the other hand, was not. The very air was alive with emotion, as one presiding minister after another spoke of the dangers ahead and potential peril likely to come.

And then the five appointees knelt for the presiding ministers to begin the ceremonious laying on of hands. A presiding minister stood before each candidate, placing a hand on his head and offering a prayer of consecration. Years later, many who had been present that February morning recalled the moment: *"An irresistible sighing and weeping broke out. The entire congregation seemed moved as the trees of the wood are moved by a mighty wind. Pent-up emotion could no longer be restrained."*

After the ordination service, Adoniram had the opportunity to meet briefly with Dr. Lucius Bolles, pastor of Salem's First Baptist Church, located just across the road from Tabernacle Church. During those years of the new century, Congregationalists and Baptists were sometimes rather antagonistic over the question of infant or believers' baptism, but Dr. Bolles was excited about the new missions endeavor, and Adoniram urged him to rally the Baptists around the idea of foreign missions. That afternoon, the two formed a special bond in spirit that would last a lifetime.

Ann and Adoniram made one last visit to Bradford for Ann to say her good-byes. They could not linger long, for the *Caravan* was hoping to set sail in just a few days. Those last two days for Ann in her childhood home were full of precious memories for a lifetime. The final evening was consumed with last-minute advice and recalling of favorite family stories. Each one in the close-knit family was reluctant to let the evening end, but morning would come all too quickly.

The new bridegroom was determined to continue his practice of avoiding farewells and insisted, very early the next morning, even before daylight, that the two of them depart. Ann was unhappy at the thought—so much so that the young couple came close to having their first "domestic encounter" as they quietly prepared to slip out the door. Ann's heart was a reservoir of unshed tears as she tiptoed down the stairs and ran her hands lovingly along the dark banister for what would surely be the last time.

This February morning, however, young Mr. Judson had met his match in Deacon Hasseltine. As the horses pulled the carriage through the fresh snow that had fallen the night before, it was slow going. Ann and Adoniram had scarcely reached the covered bridge over the Merrimac River when a single rider pulled up beside them. It was Papa. He had stopped only long enough to throw a heavy cloak over his nightshirt. With a will that could match his new son-in-law's, he demanded, "You will come home and say good-bye properly." And for the second time in his life, and both times due to a Hasseltine, Adoniram Judson was speechless.

They returned to the house and took a proper leave; those precious final moments eased the pain in Ann's heart just a bit. Right before they walked out the front door, Rebecca tucked into Ann's little portmanteau a well-wrapped package of her famous gingerbread. "It will keep well, Honey, and be a bit of home." It was nearly the undoing of Ann's tender heart, and she wept over each crumb of gingerbread for those first several weeks at sea.

For the first days of their wait for the *Caravan* to sail, Ann and Adoniram stayed with Becky and Joseph in Beverly. The church brethren were working feverishly to accumulate enough money to support the missionaries for at least their first year. Such an amount was deemed necessary because it looked like the United States would soon go to war with England, and the board might not be able to get money through. It also looked like the *Caravan* would be the last ship allowed to leave Salem Harbor before an embargo began. On the day of the ordination, there was only $1,200 in the treasury. At the meeting congregants contributed $220, a bountiful sum for that day, but still far from enough. Dr. Worcester, minister of the Tabernacle Church, led the fund-raising, with the bare minimum needed determined to be $5,000. With the bequest of the wealthy widow Mrs. John Norris held up in court, more than $3,000 had to be raised in just days—a daunting sum for 1812.

People all around Massachusetts began rallying to the call. Andover students worked especially hard, sending letters to many possible donors. In two weeks, the committee had $6,000 in hand. Much of it came anonymously, some even mysteriously. While the Judsons were still with the Emersons in Beverly, someone opened the door one snowy morning and said not a word but tossed in a purse holding $50 and a note: "For Mr. Judson's personal use."

Luther Rice, joining in the project late, was left to seek his own support. His reluctant fiancée, Rebecca Eaton, never gave him a final *yes,* so the intrepid Luther, large of body and just as substantial in courage, got on his horse and set out to raise his support. With talent and personal appeal aplenty, he had the funds in hand within six days. His bold resolution was a foreshadowing of how he would soon galvanize an entire denomination to respond to the Great Commission.

Time was of the essence now. The ship might sail as soon as weather conditions were favorable, so Ann and Adoniram went to Salem to stay with Ann's cousins, the Kimballs. Valentine's Day came and went, and the *Caravan* could not set sail on a still-stormy sea. She boasted just two masts and square-rigged sails and was only ninety feet from stem to stern. Nonetheless, the two young missionary couples were fortunate to sail on this small ship. Not only had the owner, Pickering Dodge, employed a particularly fine and capable captain, twenty-seven-year-old Captain Heard, but Dodge had given Heard specific instructions as to how to care for the missionaries while they waited to set sail. He suggested the captain serve them a fresh dish once a week or more often, along with puddings and rice. Ann and Adoniram and the Newells, who had just married the week before, were able to put their trunks in their cabins and have all in readiness for when the weather might smile on them.

As Ann later wrote in her journal, *"The* Caravan *was a regular Noah's Ark."* The deck was a small farmyard inhabited by a motley collection of pig pens and chicken coops, with all of the creatures quite vocal. At least there would be some fresh food for the voyage, and it would be most welcome, for it would take months to reach India, their first destination.

A terrific storm hit on February 17, so still the couples waited onshore. But the next day word came to board the ship. They headed to Derby Wharf to take the little skiff out into the harbor where the *Caravan* was anchored. Boarding the ship, they were again compelled to wait for favorable weather conditions to sail. Thus it was that although a number of people had gathered in Salem in previous days hoping to witness the missionaries' historic embarkation, only a few remained to watch on the morning of February 19 when the *Caravan* finally lifted her sails and set out for the Far East. It was the last vessel to leave Salem before the War of 1812.

Meanwhile, snug in their parlor in a comfortable Salem home, it is said that two silk-clad dowagers sat sipping their tea and enjoying a cozy midmorning gossip. One queried the other, "I heard that Miss Hasseltine is going to India! Why does she go?" The woman's companion retorted, "Why, she thinks it her duty. Wouldn't *you* go if you thought it was your duty?" Indignant, the companion responded, "I would not think it my duty!"

Gazing at the shore for as long as they could see it, the two couples stood at the ship's railing with hearts pounding. *This is a one-way trip.* The finality of that thought assaulted Ann's mind once again. In a matter of minutes, the spray and mist of the February day closed them off from the sight of shore, and their great adventure—and the birth of American missions—began.

A Sea Change 1812

Stained glass window hanging in Salem's First Baptist Church, commemorating the historic February 19, 1812, sailing of Ann and Adoniram Judson. Courtesy of First Baptist Church, Salem.

ANN'S EMOTIONS WERE IN AS MUCH TURMOIL AS the wintry waters over which she gazed. Her thoughts tossed and whirled, going from elation at the thought of actually beginning this journey to fulfill their call, to wrenching pain at the thought of never seeing Mama or Papa or her beloved home and dear ones ever again. As she and Adoniram stood at the *Caravan's* rail, Adoniram caught a glimpse of Ann's taut face and took her hand in his comforting warm grasp. Ann swallowed the lump in her throat; excitement, trepidation, apprehension, joy, grief, and resolve were all fighting for space in her jumbled thoughts. Harriet and Samuel stood nearby, and Ann gave thanks again for the comforting thoughts of having a dear friend and bit of home on the high seas with them.

When land was no longer in sight and the bitter-cold wind blowing off the water brought stinging tears to their eyes, the ladies retreated below while the men walked the decks. Ann went into the relative warmth of the cabin, thinking it would ease the pain of parting just a little to be able to sit at the tiny desk bolted to the wall and write in her journal. That slim volume was a reminder of the many hours spent at her desk at home, and she once again poured out her heart: *O America, my native land, must I leave thee? Must I leave my parents, my sisters and brother, my friends beloved? Farewell—but never, no, never to be forgotten.*

Writing proved to be a challenge, however, as the little ship pitched and tossed with the waves. Ann was eager to get her "sea legs" as her husband already had, but the queasy protestations of her stomach soon took her to the bunk for some hoped-for relief. Much later she recorded in her little book: *Sea-sick all day, and unable to do anything.* Within just a few days, however, she noted: *Somewhat relieved from sickness, and able to read a little.* Ann soon became more philosophical about being on the high seas, commenting in a letter to her friend and cousin Lydia Kimball: *I feel no worse on the whole, than if I had taken a gentle emetic [laxative].* Ann was able to walk on deck in just a couple of days, but poor Harriet continued to feel deathly ill for more than a week.

Sickness wasn't their only problem, either, for on their fifth day at sea, the *Caravan* sprang a leak and all hands were called to the pumps, including the passengers. The little brig nearly sank, but fortunately the hole was found in time and plugged. By this time, all four passengers had begun to enjoy the voyage. After all, these days were their honeymoons, albeit not the usual wedding trip, to be sure. Ann was irrepressible, and her usual buoyant spirits returned and were a light aboard the ship. Harriet and their husbands warmed in her glow.

Eating was a challenge, despite the presence of "fresh" creatures on the deck, oinking and clucking around them. *"Everything tastes differently from what it does on land, and those things I was most fond of at home, I loathe the most here,"* Ann wrote to Lydia. They soon determined that the main reason for their sluggishness must be due to lack of exercise. *"Jumping the rope was finally invented and this we found to be of great use,"* she continued. When they tired of skipping rope, the four newlyweds decided to exercise by dancing, which brought back delightful memories to the two young women of happy evenings in the Hasseltine frolic room.

The weather slowly turned warmer, and the two men and Ann had increasingly normal appetites. Harriet was still a little off-color, and it was plain by now to see that she had been experiencing morning sickness as well as seasickness. Her baby's birth was estimated to be in November, either in India or Burma. The seventeen-year-old bride was more excited than frightened by the thought of having her first child in a foreign land and was thankful to have her dear friend nearby. Nonetheless, Harriet couldn't face the thought of coffee or tea without milk and was always craving some food that simply was not available on board ship. Oh, for a piece of soft white bread!

Each Sunday, the two honeymooning couples conducted worship services, and Captain Heard and several of his crew joined in. Years before, Ann's brother John had talked about the salty language of sailors at sea, and Ann wrote home about her surprise that she had not heard any profane language since setting sail. She had a strong suspicion that their noble captain had given his sailors stringent warnings about guarding their language around these missionary passengers.

With the days getting more pleasant as they sailed farther south, they spent much of their time alternately exercising and reading. Ann wrote copious letters home to family and friends, telling mostly of her reading experiences, occasionally tossing in a tidbit about her wonderful spouse who was "the kindest of husbands." In truth, in such constricted space and with limited activities available, Ann and Adoniram were continuing to get to know each other and test out their similarities and differences. Ann would sometimes be taken aback by some statement of Adoniram's that was completely opposite of what she had always thought, and then soon realize in another conversation that they thought so much alike in countless important ways. She was ever astounded at the breadth of knowledge and keenness of mind Adoniram displayed. On occasion she even wondered if he could read her mind, so quickly did he comprehend her meaning. She loved to call him "Mr. J," which was about as close as she could come to a special, endearing nickname.

Sometimes Adoniram would surprise her with a little poem he had jotted down to express his love for her, or with some little treat he would bring to the cabin to indulge his bride. When Ann felt those piercing hazel eyes capture her gaze and heard that deep, resonant voice, she felt like her blood turned to clotted cream. *Was ever a bride so fortunate as I?* would flash through her mind as she fastened her eyes on his and thanked him for the treat or words of praise.

Ann and Adoniram decided individually to reread the New Testament in Greek, determining that this would be a valuable mental exercise to keep their minds sharp. Adoniram had begun his own translation of the New Testament into Greek while at Andover and happily continued that project. It didn't take long until one particular word began trouble him: the Greek word most often translated as "baptism." Having grown up in the Congregational church, he had been baptized as a baby by sprinkling, as were all infants of that denomination. Search as he would, however, nowhere in the New Testament could he find reference to such a form of baptism. Clearly, John the Baptist had used total immersion to baptize believers, and Christ himself was baptized this way as an example.

The more Adoniram studied the Greek word for baptism, the more troubled he became. He confided his thoughts to Ann, shaking his head in rueful dismay and stating, "It appears we Congregationalists have been wrong about baptism and the Baptists right." Ann was shocked. However, this new bride was nobody's fool, and God had not given her an astute brain in order to waste it. She already knew better than to argue with Brown University's top debater. Ann simply dug in her heels (in her trim half-boots) and asserted, "Well, *you* may become a Baptist, but I won't!"

Ann did attempt to quietly reason with him, reminding him that he had been the leader in speaking out to the Congregational fathers, pleading with them to begin a mission-sending society, and "now you would tell them you want to become a Baptist? Mr. J," she implored with those earnest brown eyes, "just think about this. We are supported by the Congregational denomination. The Baptists are not even organized. All our missionary friends are Congregationalists, and we would be alone and adrift in a strange land with no companions and no support."

Judson was not deterred. He agreed on every point but, grasping her hands in his, implored her in turn, "My Dear Love, just promise me you will do the same study of the word and text that I have. Your Greek is excellent. You examine this issue for yourself, and we will pray mightily for God to grant us wisdom. We don't have to do any-thing rashly or suddenly," he continued, "but please assure me you will study this perplexing problem along with me, and we will ask the Lord to guide our thinking." Ann already had a good understanding of her husband's way of thinking and making decisions; she knew he usually made them very quickly, never doubting that what he did was right. This must really be a mammoth conundrum to his way of think-ing for him to delay a decision. She pledged herself to examine the issue in earnest along with him and to pray for wisdom. The Judsons were perplexed, but they were young and in love and on their honey-moon, headed to an adventure and a challenge such as neither had ever imagined. This baptism question could wait a bit longer, surely.

The farther they sailed from all that was known and familiar and loved, the more Ann Judson sensed her utter dependence on God. Frequently, as the ship was tossed by particularly violent waves or a thunderstorm rose nearby, Ann would think of the hymns that told of hearing the thunder, seeing the lightning, and feeling the waves threaten to swallow the soul. Here it was in reality. She came to real-ize in a totally new way that although they could not know what might lie ahead, God certainly did. Ann Judson's implicit faith in God's control over all things grew apace during those months at sea. Surely God who was sovereign over the waves of the sea would be in control as well of the hearts of heathen rulers.

In May, after three months at sea, Ann wrote Lydia again to update her on life on board their brig in the middle of the vast ocean:

> We found it exceedingly hot the first time that we crossed the equator. When going round the Cape of Good Hope, we had rough rainy weather for twenty days. I never knew till then "the dangers of the deep." I never felt before, my entire dependence on God for preservation. Some nights I never slept on account of the rocking of the vessel and the roaring of the winds. Yet God preserved us—enabled us to trust in Him and feel safe.

By May all the livestock on deck was only the memory of a meal, and the two couples, now seasoned young sailors after three months at sea, were growing anxious to see land again. The days changed from warm to hot and humid, a sure indication that they must be drawing near to exotic India and the tropics. Each of them speculated on where their fellow missionaries sailing from Philadelphia might be by now and which ship would reach Calcutta first. Harriet was over her morning sickness and looking forward to becoming a mother in her new land, even if it caused her heart a pang to think of her own mother so far away and unable to share in the experience of her first grandchild.

May came and went, until on Sunday morning, June 14, Ann called the others to come quickly to the rail and look with her. Yes, there—very faintly in the distance—was land! It was the coast of the state of Orissa in India. Ann wrote to sister Abby, *We came in sight of land after being out only one hundred and twelve days!* On Tuesday she added to her letter: *The scene is truly delightful. We are sailing up the river [Hooghly], a branch of the Ganges, and so near the land, we can distinctly discover objects.* Ann thrilled at the sight of a delicate butterfly and two strange tropical birds. And on Wednesday she bubbled to Abby:

> *I have never, my dear sister, witnessed or read anything so delightful as the present scene. On each side of the Hoogly [sic], where we are now sailing, are Hindoo [sic] cottages as thick together as the houses in our sea-ports. They are very small, and in the form of hay-stacks, without either chimneys or windows. The grass and fields of rice are perfectly green, and herds of cattle are everywhere feeding on the banks of the rivers. The pagodas we have passed are much handsomer than the houses—yet it is truly melancholy when we reflect, that these creatures, so numerous, so harmless, have immortal souls—and yet have none to tell them of Christ.*

Captain Heard gave orders for the ship to be anchored in the Bay of Bengal until he could obtain the services of a reputable pilot to steer her through the shallow waters. Often this process took days, but the very next day a ship arrived with an English pilot and the first Hindu the young missionaries had ever seen. Ann described him to sister Abby: *A little man with a dark copper color skin, he was wearing calico trousers and a white cotton short gown.*

By the next morning, June 17, the experienced river pilot had guided the *Caravan* out of the bay, and slowly they moved up the Hooghly River toward the massive city of Calcutta. Ann was entranced with all her eyes could take in, as were Adoniram and the Newells. They would run across the deck, sniffing the spice-laden breezes that came from the shore and pointing out new and exciting wonders to each other. Ann laughed happily, feeling like a child again in those moments of discovery.

At last Calcutta itself came into view, one of India's largest cities and commonly called "The City of Palaces." Solid brick buildings were painted a dazzling white; large domes and tall, picturesque palm trees stretched out as far as the eye could see. The harbor was full of tall-masted sailing ships, and the noise was stunning. Crowds milled all through the waterfront streets, chattering away in the strange-sounding Bengali language. Harriet's first thought was of sitting down to real milk and the fresh bread she had been dreaming about for months. Ann was intrigued by the new fruits the English river pilot brought aboard. Gingerly she tried her first bite of pineapple and found it sweet and delicious. Then she discovered a long yellow fruit, which she described as tasting a bit like a rich pear. She liked bananas!

Everything was new—sights, smells, sounds—and the great adventure in the Orient was about to begin. The exotic and mysterious East was now reality, and the elated American missionaries mentally stood on tiptoe to experience what might lie ahead once on shore.

A plaque stands near the harbor at Salem's wharf, commemorating the sailing of the Judsons in 1812. A replica of a ship similar to the *Caravan* stands in the harbor.

On February 19, 1812, the brig *Caravan*, with Adoniram and Ann Judson aboard, departed from Salem Harbor, launching the first American missionary expedition to a foreign land.

Settling in Burma in 1813, Judson started his Baptist missionary work and began translating the Bible into Burmese, a task he completed in 1834. After years of hardship, including the death of his first wife in 1826, he returned to America in 1845 to much adulation. He went back to Burma in 1846 and completed an English-Burmese dictionary in 1849, a year before his death.

Exotic India
1812

THE MYSTERIOUS EAST. IT WAS NOW REALITY, AND AS EXOTIC AND mystical as the land that had appeared in Ann's dreams these many months. *Red tape* was a new term to Ann Judson, but red tape was clearly part of the process of even being able to disembark. Consequently, she and Harriet were forced to exercise patience, at least outwardly, until Adoniram and Samuel could go to the police station and report their arrival in the country. That Wednesday morning, June 17, two excited young men followed directions to the port police headquarters, discussing as they went just how to explain they were in India only temporarily, merely awaiting passage to their final destination of Burma.

The four of them had spent many a long evening aboard the *Caravan* talking over what their challenges might be in the unknown land where the Burmese emperor reigned with an "off-with-their-heads" mentality. In talking with Captain Heard about Burma, they had become suspicious of the glowing reports Michael Symes had given in his book about Burma and the city of Ava, stories that had captured their imaginations. Their brig's captain reported much the opposite from all the information Judson had learned, firmly stating that foreigners were not welcome in Burma, nor were they respected.

Upon the arrival of the two young missionaries at the Calcutta police station, they were indeed met with no welcome and little respect. The British East India Company controlled India, and they had no liking for missionaries. Furthermore, rumor had it that America and England were soon going to war again. Judson and Newell were each given a certificate merely stating the two had complied with policy by reporting their presence—scant reassurance for their chance to receive permission to stay or even to proceed to another destination.

Nevertheless, certificates in hand, Adoniram and Samuel wanted to pay their respects to the renowned Dr. William Carey, the British dean of Baptist missionaries in India and famous in Christian circles. His reputation as a brilliant linguist had reached around the globe. At their first meeting, Judson was surprised to discover this man of such stature in the Christian world to be very unprepossessing in appearance, quite small and unpretentious, older and with just a fringe of white hair framing his kindly face. But there was about William Carey a presence, and his spirit and intellect quickly became apparent as he greeted the young Americans with glowing eyes, rejoicing in the thought of reinforcements to the tiny band of missionaries that was slowly forming.

Judson and Newell felt honored to stand in his presence and receive his counsel. About one thing Carey was quickly emphatic—don't consider Burma. Coming from this great man, such advice was unnerving. Carey explained that it would be next to impossible to establish a ministry there, no matter how desperately Burmans needed the Bible in their heart language. However, Carey immediately assured the startled young men that he and the Indian Baptist Mission would stand their friends and would help them in any way possible. Carey was

hopeful that they would be able to stay in India as long as they needed to. Times, he explained, were precarious just now.

And, as if to prove his point, the very next day, June 18, 1812,
America declared war on England. Now, not only did the British East
India Company disdain missionaries; the American missionaries were
suddenly the enemy. Whatever the political situation, however, the
two young couples determined to proceed apace with their plans to
go ashore in Calcutta and see what the next step might be, with God
as their guide. Thus, on June 19, Ann Judson first set foot in the Far
East, that part of the world that became her home for the remainder
of her life.

Dr. Carey had graciously invited the young Americans to stay with
him, at least until their fellow missionaries, Rice and Nott, arrived on
the *Harmony*. The plan was for Adoniram and Samuel to walk ahead
to Dr. Carey's and for Ann and Harriet to follow them, conveyed in
palanquins (covered chairs supported on two poles resting on the
shoulders of four bearers). Ann's ears were assailed with a cacoph-
ony of noise in the crowded streets, everywhere clamor and masses,
dirt and confusion. She lost sight of Adoniram or anyone familiar and
had a chilling sense of isolation. No wonder she had heard that foreign ladies did not go strolling through the streets of India! Ann was
soon put down in front of a large white house that impressed her as
more like a palace than a private residence. In a few minutes, Harriet
arrived and, with great relief, saw Ann's familiar face. Their husbands
came hurrying breathlessly up the drive about ten minutes later.

Ann felt honored to be meeting the great William Carey, of whom
she had heard so much since she was just a young girl. Dr. Carey's
reputation as a brilliant linguist had reached around the globe. His
translation of the gospel into Bengali had been a major achievement,
and his contributions in diverse areas influenced the entire nation of
his native England. Carey graciously welcomed them into his
Calcutta home, with its high ceilings built to ease the discomfort of
sweltering tropical days, room after whitewashed room appearing
clean and airy. Ann's New England eyes quickly registered the

strangeness of no fireplace and no glass in the windows. Added to the unfamiliar sights were the servants, each with his or her own appointed task.

For days Ann had been fretting to get on with things, to explore Calcutta and find their next step. The reality of Calcutta proved to be strange and loud, confusing and a bit frightening. The unusual was now the usual to her eyes, and Ann was grateful for the mission compound, especially Dr. Carey's garden. As a farmer's daughter, she was in awe of Carey's accomplishments in horticulture. She was quite knowledgeable about American gardens and wished that Papa could just see this man's brilliant accomplishments in horticultural experimentation. She wrote home, reporting that it was *"far superior to any in America, as the best garden in America is to a common farmer's."*

Even though surrounded by many strange sights, Ann welcomed not having a rolling floor under her feet. Perhaps the most gratifying moment occurred that same evening when they were able to attend a worship service and hear the beloved hymns she had learned in childhood. It already seemed like forever since she had heard the familiar sounds of home.

The next morning, Dr. Carey took them some fifteen miles away to Serampore in West Bengal to stay at the Baptist mission house while awaiting the other American missionaries. In Serampore, Ann saw idol worship for the first time and learned of child marriages and other odd and sundry customs so foreign to American understanding and experience. Her first exposure to Eastern religion was shocking, and each day brought a new sense of need to depend on almighty God for guidance.

The reception the young Americans received from the Serampore missionaries was balm to their unsettled hearts. They were welcomed with genuine warmth, which went far in calming their bewildered spirits. Having left their own country with such high hopes, they found themselves in a land where those controlling the government wanted them gone, and gone quickly, yet they had no clear answer as to where they might go. The time of respite in Serampore was a welcome change, surrounded by people with the same goals they personally held dear. They had long heard stories about the eminent men of faith known as the Serampore Three: William Carey, Joshua Marshman, and William Ward. And here they were in the flesh, welcoming and nurturing the new missionaries from the United States.

Nonetheless, the respite could only be short, for Ann and Adoniram were facing two serious dilemmas. The first and most pressing was where to go. They couldn't stay in India. Burma likewise seemed out of the question. True, Carey's son, Felix, was living in Burma but was tolerated by the despotic emperor only because he had some medical skills. China appeared inimical to missionaries, and Muslim control in places from Arabia to Persia to Turkey made those destinations seem unfeasible. Both couples thought of ministering to the slaves on the Isle of France (now known as Mauritius), but it seemed no ships were sailing there anytime soon. The deep desire of Adoniram's heart for many months had been to translate God's Word into the language of a people who had never before been able to read it, but many of these countries they were now considering already had the Bible in their own languages.

In late July, a summons came for the Americans to present themselves immediately at the police office in Calcutta. Captain Heard was refused clearance from port unless the American passengers sailed with him. Not only was it disappointing; it was humiliating. Nonetheless, Ann and Adoniram believed overwhelmingly that God had not brought them safe thus far just to reverse the divine call now. There *must* be some other needy country where they could go.

Joshua Marshman, one of the Serampore Three, actively sought to find the two couples a way to embark for some remote place that needed the gospel, and find one he did. The *Colonel Gillispie* was headed for the Isle of France. However, they could take only two passengers. Timing was nearing the point of desperation for the Newells. Harriet's baby would be born in November, now only a few months away, and it was critical that she get settled before her due date. The expectant seventeen-year-old Harriet was in anguish telling Ann good-bye that first morning of August before boarding the *Colonel Gillispie*. They each comforted the other with the knowledge that surely the Judsons could soon follow. Harriet wept as her lifelong friend put a gentle hand on her cheek and tenderly wiped the tears away. "Oh my sweet Harriet, take heart! This is just a short separation—we will surely be together again very soon."

Even as she attempted to comfort her friend, Ann was aware that this was one of her own recurrent fears—that she and Adoniram might end up all alone in some alien land. She held the trembling Harriet close to her heart for a long and agonizing moment and then turned away so Harriet would not see the tears streaming down her own face. In that wrenching moment, Ann had yet again to exercise her own wavering faith. Surely God had not brought them thus far just to let them down.

The Newell's departure finally allowed Captain Heard to leave port on the *Caravan*. However, an order came from the police informing the Judsons that they were forbidden from doing any form of mission work in India. Now what? Soon there were others in the same predicament with them, for on August 8, just four days after the Newells sailed out of the harbor, the *Harmony* arrived with Luther Rice and the Notts aboard. These, too, must find a place to go.

In the meantime, an English businessman in Calcutta, Mr. Rolt, graciously invited the Judsons to stay with them until such time as their dilemma was solved. Mrs. Rolt had been widowed when her first husband, also a missionary, had died. The comfortable Rolt home boasted a large and well-stocked library that included a multitude of books on theology from Mrs. Rolt's missionary days, much to the enjoyment and pleasure of the Judsons. Among this treasury of books were several that dealt with the subject of baptism, and as was his lifelong habit, Adoniram Judson was like a dog gnawing on a delicious bone when he encountered the subject that still teased his mind. He could not rest until the puzzle of baptism was solved. Months before, while on board the ship, Judson had thought to peruse the topic because they would be meeting Baptists in India, and he wished to be firm in his stance on pedobaptism (infant baptism). Of course, he had acknowledged by now both to himself and to Ann that his search was leading him to the conclusion that he was wrong and the Baptists were right.

Ann's journal was her faithful friend during these trying months in Calcutta, and she poured out her feelings about waiting: waiting to find passage to the Isle of France or to another country where they could go and serve, and waiting to find the answer God surely had for them concerning baptism. This question loomed large in their minds. John Hasseltine's daughter had learned well from that practical man: sometimes you had to make a decision that might not be popular but was necessary for peace of mind as well as for practicality. Here was the issue: baptism. Which was right: what she had always been taught about the correctness of pedobaptism, or immersion as practiced by the Baptists?

Ann disciplined herself to look at the issue from every viewpoint, and often when Adoniram took the Baptist view, she would deliberately play devil's advocate and support the Congregational stance concerning this command of the Lord. Ann was also by nature the more pragmatic of the two, and she understood all too well that to become Baptist meant that all relationships with their supporting denomination must be severed. That would mean being thousands of miles from family and all that was familiar *and* with no means of financial support. Baptists in America had not even organized into a denomination yet.

Adoniram recognized this troubling problem, but it did not stop him from being completely honest about what he was discovering. Christ himself had been immersed, and Judson determined that, in all honesty to both himself and his denomination, he must stand by what he now understood to be scriptural. Ann was distraught; this would leave them adrift and entirely on their own. But then faith and courage in the inner soul asserted itself, and she, weeping and stirred, came reluctantly to that same decision as her husband. They must be immersed and immediately tell the Congregational fathers what they now believed.

Ann's fears regarding the possible consequences are reflected in her letters home. She wrote to her friend Nancy, *"My dear Nancy, we are confirmed Baptists, not because we wished to be, but because truth compelled us to be. . . . [T]he most trying circumstance attending this change . . . is the separation which must take place between us and our dear missionary associates. . . . We feel that we are alone in the world, with no real friend but each other, no one on whom we can depend but God."* Ann was brutally honest about her struggle and dragged her feet far longer than did her husband, not because she wasn't clear in her convictions but rather because of the inevitable separations and loss of support that would result.

For his part, Adoniram wrote the American board and, with candor and resolve, apologized for their decision that no doubt would look ill-conceived and rash, but one nonetheless that they must make. He next wrote his Baptist friend in Salem, Dr. Lucius Bolles, explaining what had occurred and concluding, *"Under these circumstances, I look to you. Alone, in this foreign heathen land, I make my appeal to those whom, with their permission, I will call my Baptist brethren in the United States."* Judson also wrote Thomas Baldwin, pastor of Boston's Second Baptist Church, saying, *"Should there be formed a Baptist Society for the support of missionary in these parts, I shall be ready to consider myself their missionary."*

Thus it was that Ann and Adoniram met with Dr. Carey and the rest of the Serampore Three and declared themselves Baptists by conviction, respectfully requesting baptism. The English missionaries were amazed. Without hesitation, however, after speaking frankly with the two Americans about all that this must entail for them, the seasoned English missionaries stood by them in every way. Hence, on September 6, 1812, William Ward led Ann and Adoniram Judson into the baptismal waters at Lal Bazaar Church in Calcutta. Two Sundays later, Adoniram was invited to preach at the church, and his sermon was an incisive look at the meaning and purpose of a subject much on his mind—baptism. The eminent William Carey himself proclaimed it the best sermon on baptism he had ever heard.

Carey then assured the Judsons that his own English mission station would loan them the necessary funds to continue with their mission until such time as Baptists in America would take up their support. Not only did Carey make this bold move; he also wrote personally to leading Baptists in the United States to tell them that they now had a Baptist missionary couple headed to a field of service who needed their support. Dr. Carey did not mince words: "After God has given you a man of your own nation, faith and order without the help or knowledge of man, let me entreat you . . . humbly to accept the gift."

The die was cast. The Judsons were now Baptists, thousands of miles from home and with no supporting board, no missionary coworkers, and no place to go. Faith alone was their companion.

No Place to Call Their Own 1812–1813

Copy of an ancient Old Testament manuscript page used by Judson in translating the Scripture.
Two sections of old manuscript remnants were found in the Judson family trunk (now housed in the archives at Judson University, Elgin, IL).

DEAR LORD! WHERE ARE WE TO go? What can we do? The half-formed prayers ran endlessly in Ann's mind throughout each day. Although she was grateful that English Baptists would be loaning them sufficient funds to continue to a field of service, that field itself was the constant question that loomed in her thoughts, sometimes even waking her up in the steamy stillness of a Calcutta night.

Ann and Adoniram's friends had arrived on the *Harmony* in August, but that reunion was bittersweet, for the two of them had to sit down with Samuel and Roxanna Nott, Gordon Hall, and Luther Rice and explain their current position on baptism. The new arrivals were shocked. Did this mean that they would not be continuing in the same mission, working together? Yes, a somber-faced Adoniram Judson affirmed; the thought of parting with their coworkers was wrenching, but conscience allowed no other recourse. Ann realized that her husband was handling this entire issue much better than she. He had that gift of temperament that allowed him to make a decision and never look back. Her feelings were much more complex and clearly evident, as though written across her face. Roxanna Nott reached out a comforting hand, understanding the pain Ann must be feeling.

Then something unexpected occurred that brightened the hearts of both Judsons. Here they were, constantly under stress because of pressure from an inimical government trying to hound them out of India as well as facing grief over their inevitable separation from their Congregational friends because of doctrinal concerns. Yet to their joy and relief, they learned that Luther Rice, always considered the most obstinate friend of pedobaptism of any of the young missionaries, had, in the interminably long voyage from Philadelphia, reached the same conclusion as had the Judsons. Rice determined that he needed baptism by immersion, which meant that he would no longer be able to serve with the Congregational mission board either. On November 1, Luther Rice was baptized at Lal Bazaar Church. Now, without a supporting missionary board but encouraged by one another, he, along with Ann and Adoniram, daily searched for a way to leave the country before being physically forced out.

The Notts and Gordon Hall managed to leave Calcutta unobtrusively and go to Bombay, where they planned to begin a mission station in some quiet manner that would escape the notice of the powerful East India Company. Ann looked at her own situation and realized afresh each morning that only God could solve their dilemma. Then, mid-November arrived and with it came a terse order from the East India Company: the Judsons and Rice were to be deported to England and not permitted to leave their current place of residence; furthermore, their names were placed in the newspaper as passengers on a company ship. *What now?* Ann fretted.

Notwithstanding the edict, Adoniram and Luther slipped out of the house that night, still desperately searching for a ship that would accept them as passengers. Finally, they had a measure of success. They learned that *La Belle Creole* was sailing in two days for the Isle of France, where Samuel and Harriet were now living. Judson and Rice immediately took their story to the ship's captain, pleading with him to take them as passengers, even though they had no official pass.

La Belle Creole's captain, who apparently had no love for the over-bearing East India Company, agreed, remarking, "There is my ship. Do as you like."

Now the three Americans faced a problem of logistics. Somehow they had to get their luggage on board without the authorities discovering them. They had been ordered not to leave their place of residence, yet here they were, out on the streets, looking for a way to escape. Then another moment of divine intervention occurred. Their kind host, Mr. Rolt, came to their aid. About midnight, when all was quiet and still, Rice and the Judsons, assisted by a band of strong coolies hired by Mr. Rolt, made their way through the dark streets of Calcutta, through winding lanes leading to the wharf, paving the way for their surreptitious nighttime transfer of their belongings. With a little judicious bribe, dockyard gates mysteriously opened, and the three weary missionaries quietly went aboard. Promptly at dawn, *La Belle Creole* slowly eased its way through the harbor and out to open sea, and the three Americans breathed a collective sigh of relief.

The feeling of relief did not last, however, for someone had betrayed them. Toward evening of the second day at sea, a government dispatch boat pulled up beside their ship. A government document stated that the passengers on board must leave the vessel at once, even in the dark of night, because they had been ordered to be conveyed to England. Ann was distraught, and her eyes locked with Adoniram's as worry was plain to read on both of their countenances. The French captain, chivalrous in the presence of a lovely lady in distress, was moved to pity and forthwith suggested that Ann remain aboard with the luggage while the two men went ashore to the village of Budge Budge to see what measures they could take that would allow them to continue their journey.

Through a long night that felt to Ann like an eternity, and all the next day, the *Creole* lay at anchor awaiting orders. That evening a message came from headquarters, from the ship's owner, saying the captain must write a certificate that the passengers were not on board. The gallant captain suggested that Mrs. Judson go ashore and join her husband temporarily but leave the luggage on board. He would wait for word that they had gotten permission, and then the three could return to the vessel and sail for the Isle of France as originally planned. Ann quickly clambered down the side of the ship to sit precariously in the tiny skiff that would take her ashore. The ghostly darkness around her was frightening, and she prayed mightily during those interminable minutes. "*Cutcha pho, anna sahib; cutcha pho, anna,*" ("never fear, madam, never fear") the sailors of the little boat reassured the distressed foreign lady.

An anxious Ann finally reached the tavern where Judson and Rice were trying to come up with a plan. Escape seemed hopelessly blocked without a passport. In the meantime, Adoniram had learned of a friendly tavern some sixteen miles downriver at Fultah. Maybe they could safely wait there while searching for another ship. Ann would return to the vessel to get their luggage since it was too risky for Adoniram to be seen. When Ann returned to the *Creole,* she explained their plan to the captain, whereupon he kindly suggested that Ann remain on board until Fultah, as the British likely would not arrest a woman. Ann saw the logic of his idea and immediately returned to Budge Budge to share the latest arrangement with the men.

Alas, even as the three in the tavern were making plans, the *Creole's* captain felt compelled to take advantage of a favorable wind, and off the ship sailed—with the Judsons' luggage but without them. Again the question they had been asking themselves repeatedly in recent weeks arose: *Now what?* Ann left a worried Adoniram ashore and found a tiny skiff to chase after the luggage, finally catching up with the *Creole* the next morning. Recovering their baggage, she then had the boatman take her to the tavern in Fultah where Adoniram had asked her to wait for them. Meanwhile, Rice had once again gone to try to get a government pass, even knowing how slim the odds were for success.

An exhausted Ann finally landed in Fultah, alone and with very few rupees in her pocket. She entered the tavern and waited at a table by herself, perilously close to tears, wondering every minute where her husband might be and if he was in danger. Here she was, hunted like a criminal, knowing very few words of Bengali, and alone in a little tavern on a desolate coast in India. Despair was fighting with courage to see which would take control of her anxious heart. Ann alternately prayed and looked out the dingy tavern window, hoping against hope that the next time she looked up, her dearest love would appear.

Anxious hours later, a breathless Judson came through the tavern door. His eyes lighted on Ann, and she could read the relief on his face. But then she saw despair flickering in his eyes and understood without words that his search for permission had been unsuccessful. In short order, Rice came in as well. No success; all attempts to obtain a pass had failed. Three pairs of worried eyes looked at one another, and that nagging question hung heavy in the stale air: *What now?*

Scarcely had they begun to discuss their options when the door of the tavern was flung open and in walked a young Indian man. He approached their table and thrust a letter into Judson's hands. Hurriedly, Adoniram tore it open—a pass. A miracle. Where could it have come from? Who could have approved such a pass? They could scarcely believe their eyes. Long nights later a most thankful bride wrote in her journal, *"We knew not who wrote it, but our hearts were rejoiced. We blessed God and took courage."*

Of course, nothing was easily or readily solved in such a perilous situation. They were still in dire straits, for the *Creole* was already three days on its way. Again the trio hired a little skiff and chased after their ship. Ann was unable to sleep aboard the fragile vessel and was frustrated that Adoniram managed to slumber through the entire night. She also ruefully thought how *little* it was of her to want to rouse Mr. J and ask him to worry along with her.

Dawn finally broke, and during those long hours aboard the rocking skiff, the three had ample time to contemplate the same nagging question: *Where on earth would they settle?* They examined each option, even when it seemed impossible. Ever recurring was the thought of Burma, the first country to capture Adoniram's heart. Despite all the frightening accounts they had heard, Ann later recorded in her journal, *"We had almost concluded to go to the Burman Empire when we heard there were fresh difficulties existing between the English and Burman governments. If these difficulties are settled, I think it probable we shall go there."* Ann then recorded one of the most important of all reasons for choosing Burma: its people did not have the Bible in their heart language. Therein lay a powerful inducement to her husband to seriously consider living in such a menacing land. Translation had a strong pull on his heart.

Near sunset of the second day, they drew near Saugur, India, at the mouth of the great river Ganges, and sighted some vessels, among them the *Creole*, appearing reddish pink in the glow of sunset. Three exhausted exiles wearily climbed aboard and again blessed God and took courage. At least they could sail *somewhere*. As the sturdy ship made its way toward the Isle of France, the pioneers had ample time to contemplate their next step, although each was thinking more and more about Burma, despite its obvious drawbacks.

Constantly on Ann's mind and heart was her friend Harriet. It was already January, and her baby should be two months old by now. Ann's heart gladdened at the thought of seeing Harriet again and having an opportunity to talk of all that had transpired in both of their lives in these recent months. Ann could scarcely wait to see Harriet's child and to share her own news with Harriet. Ann was certain by now that she would become a mother in June or July and was excited at the very idea. Adoniram was the one doing the worrying just now, wondering where they would be in six months and how Ann and the baby would be cared for. Ann kept assuring him that she was stronger than he realized, and with morning sickness finally behind her, she was happily anticipating all that lay ahead.

The morning of January 17, 1813, dawned, and Ann could see the green outline of the shore of Port Louis, the largest city on the Isle of France. It was one of the most beautiful islands in the Indian Ocean, with blue skies reflecting in the waters of the reef-bound harbor. The

Judsons were exhilarated at the thought of seeing their friends again and comparing adventures of recent months. Maybe they could look together at possibilities for the future. As the captain dropped anchor, Ann and Adoniram waited impatiently for the Newells to come out to the *Creole*. The imminent arrival of the ship from Calcutta would have been news all over the town. As they stood at the deck's railing, they could see a skiff drawing alongside and the familiar face of Samuel Newell. But it was a Samuel they could scarcely recognize.

One look at Newell as he boarded the *Creole,* and Ann's heart nearly failed within her. What could have happened? Samuel could only speak in broken snatches, so overcome that he was finally going to be able to share his tragic tale. The Newell's ship last August from Calcutta had been battered unmercifully by winds and waves, and the voyage had stretched to three months. While still out in the Indian Ocean, Harriet had given birth to a tiny baby girl in their flimsy little cabin on the ship's deck. They named her Harriet Atwood, and the tiny child seemed happy and healthy, much to the their delight.

Just five days later, the ship was buffeted by a massive storm, and rain poured into the cabin. The newborn took cold from the sudden exposure and two days later died in her mother's arms. Even worse, Harriet began to fail as the consumption that had taken her father's life was now invading her own body. Samuel struggled to tell the agonizing story. He wept as he explained to his shocked friends that Harriet had not been frightened in any way. Their crippled ship finally reached Port Louis in November, and two doctors attended to Harriet daily, but their efforts were in vain. When one of the doctors told her she could not live much longer, Samuel recalled, Harriet immediately thought of heaven and exclaimed, "Oh glorious intelligence!" Ann was openly sobbing by this point, but although prostrate with grief herself, she tried to comfort Samuel Newell. He was a broken man.

The grieving Ann remembered how just a year ago Harriet had been so intrigued by the tales from the Burmese narrative. That night she wrote in her journal, *"Have at last arrived in port; but O what news, what distressing news! Harriet is dead. Harriet, my dear friend, my earliest associate in the Mission, is no more."*

The Judsons spent countless hours comforting Samuel and discussing with him what possibilities might now lie ahead of them. Samuel decided to travel alone to Ceylon and attempt to open a mission there. Prospects for any mission work on the Isle of France were frankly disheartening. The British would not allow them to evangelize among the slave population; they could preach only to the British soldiers stationed in this lonely outpost. This was not their calling.

Even while they spent endless hours weighing every possibility regarding their place of service, another problem reared its head. Luther Rice had developed a serious liver ailment while in India, one that nearly took his life. It now flared up again, as violent as before, and it appeared his only chance of recovery was to return to the United States. Nonetheless, there was surely a glimmer of hope in this adversity, for Baptists in the States needed to be rallied to the cause of missions. They had no central organization, and who better to rally them than the dynamic and persuasive Luther Rice? With this purpose firmly in mind, Rice found a ship leaving for America, and Ann recorded in her journal, *"March 12, 1813: Brother Rice has left us and taken passage for America. Mr. J and I are now entirely alone—not one remaining friend in this part of the world. The scenes through which we pass are calculated to remind us that the world is not our home."*

Of all the options the two now prayed over, neither considered returning to America. Nevertheless, they had to go somewhere. A ship in harbor was soon leaving for Penang, Malaysia, although it was stopping first in Madras. Of course, that raised the question of the dreaded East India Company again. Ann looked at Adoniram. He looked back into her worried eyes, took her hand in his warm clasp, and voiced their mutual determination: "God being our helper, we will chance it."

Adrift 1813

Map of Burma then and now, showing the ancient and modern names of important cities.

TIME WAS WASTING. ADONIRAM went to the Port Louis docks daily, talking to ship captains, checking with the port office, searching for a passage he and Ann could take. They were thinking about opening their mission work in Penang (in modern Malaysia), even though it did not seem the best place for translating Scripture. Ann tried not to let her dear love know how anxious she was to find a home on some shore before the baby was due. She curved her hands protectively around the little one growing in her. Never far from her consciousness was the thought of Harriet and what had happened to her and her baby just months before. God forbid! Here it was April already, and she had less than two months remaining before the little one came.

Suddenly Ann was struck with dysentery, a highly infectious and often fatal disease in those days. She became so sick that both she and Adoniram feared she wouldn't survive. A long two weeks later, Ann wrote in her journal, *"Have been confined to my bed for a fortnight past. God has mercifully carried me through a scene of great pain and weakness. . . . May I be grateful for divine mercies received and humbly devote to his service the life he has spared."*

One morning early in May, Adoniram, full of news, rushed through the door of their small room. He had found a ship! *The Countess of Harcourt* was embarking for Penang on May 7. However, a worrying stipulation accompanied this good news: the ship was first going to Madras, India. That meant the couple could encounter the dreaded East India Company again. As husband and wife looked into each other's eyes, Adoniram smiled, gave a little nod, and declared, "Nothing ventured, nothing gained." He booked their passage.

Shortly before sailing, Ann made a sad pilgrimage to the remote little cemetery where Harriet and the baby lie buried. She stood alone and looked at the small white gravestones in the midst of all the tropical profusion of green and bent nearly double with grief. Long minutes later, Ann walked slowly back to her conveyance, turning for one more glimpse of that hallowed spot. Sitting motionless at her little desk in her room that evening, Ann heaved a deep sigh before picking up her quill and recording, *"The visit revived many painful, solemn feelings. But a little while ago, Harriet was with us and joined us daily in prayer and praise. Now her body is crumbling to dust in a land of strangers. But her immortal spirit has doubtless joined the company of holy spirits around the throne."*

Excitement mixed with trepidation as the solitary young couple boarded the *Countess* the morning of May 7 with Judson carefully helping Ann up the rickety gangplank. Their baby was due soon, and they longed to get settled as quickly as possible. Ann's body felt as unwieldy as her anxious mind, but she reminded herself often to bless God and, yet again, to take courage.

For once, no unexpected crisis at sea occurred, and the Judsons were grateful for smooth waters and sunny days. Ann walked as much as possible on deck, trying to maintain her strength for the days to come. She remembered that Mama had always maintained that exercise was important just before labor. Those weeks aboard the *Countess* gave the couple ample time to consider remaining options for a field of service. In both of their minds was the ever-present thought of that earliest country to capture their hearts: Burma.

To view the burning question from all angles, Ann would intentionally bring up the known difficulties in that field, recalling what
Dr. Carey had told them and what they knew of the despotic and
erratic government. Yet somehow they could not let the idea drop.
Felix Carey (Dr. Carey's son) had been visiting in Calcutta part of
the time they were also there. He had been living in Burma for a
few years and trying to gain a foothold there in the face of great difficulties. Nonetheless, Felix alone, among all those who warned
against Burma, had urged them to consider it still, as the needs were
so great. There was no Scripture in the people's own language, and
Burmans were a people lost and without hope.

Felix himself had been trying to find time to translate the Gospels
into the difficult and intricate Burmese language—an endeavor that
captured Adoniram's imagination and enflamed his own dreams of
translating the Scriptures. But Felix had a bit of protection from the
hostile Burmese government. He had married a young woman whose
Portuguese father had married a Burman woman. Thus the government looked upon Carey as somewhat acceptable since his wife was
part Burman. She could speak no English and lived in the mission
house Felix had built right outside the wall surrounding Rangoon,
the capital city. Felix knew something about medicine, and that made
him acceptable to the Burmese government.

On June 4 the *Countess* docked in Madras on India's southern tip.
Word was sent that same day to the Bengal government: the renegade
American missionaries were once again on Indian soil. News of the
couple's arrival in the city reached the ears of an English missionary
almost as soon as the *Countess* had docked, and Rev. Loveless, with
the English mission, hurried to the wharf to invite the Judsons to the
comfortable home he shared with his wife, a gracious American
woman from New York. Ann bonded with Mrs. Loveless immediately, deeply grateful for the presence of a fellow American woman when
she might give birth any day. Mrs. Loveless took the young bride into
her heart as they discussed many topics. She reassured Ann that when
pregnancy caused her to feel awkward and clumsy, her natural grace

and godly character were in no way diminished. As they talked of what the Judsons might do next, Mrs. Loveless joined in the chorus of all who had protested. No, you must not consider Burma.

Yet neither Ann nor Adoniram could forsake their desire to serve in Burma, despite all the naysayers. Judson went each morning to the Madras docks trying to find a ship. A young Dutch businessman, Mr. Von Someron, was especially kind and helped Adoniram each day in his search for a passage. Mrs. Loveless also had a special friend in the city, Mrs. Stevens, a retired lady from America who was living quietly in Madras with her two daughters. They clearly came from wealth and were serious in their faith and their desire to bless others. Mrs. Stevens gravitated toward Ann and admired her spirit and courage. While Adoniram was looking for a ship, Mrs. Stevens was intent on gifting Ann with everything possible to help her when the baby came.

Ann wrote to her mother and sisters about this special lady and her bounty, describing to Rebecca the lovely linens, fabrics, sewing materials, clothing, and even *"a nice straw bonnet and ten pairs of superfine English stockings"* that Mrs. Stevens had showered on her. Mrs. Stevens was determined to tempt Ann's appetite as well, and she prepared all sorts of jars of preserved food and delicacies for the expectant mother.

It increasingly looked like there was now no ship headed to Penang, so that possibility seemed unlikely. The sense of urgency grew every day, for at any moment word might come from the Bengal government to arrest the Americans or deport them to England. All their newfound friends in Madras continued to say, "Not Burma! Anywhere but Burma!" Nonetheless, Adoniram returned to the Loveless home on Sunday afternoon, June 20, to announce, "There is a ship—and yes, its destination is Rangoon!"

The Judsons were determined to be on that ship to Rangoon, the capital city of Burma. Ann wrote a letter to Mama that night to tell her:

> *We have at last concluded, in our distress, to go to Rangoon, ere it will be too late to escape a second arrest. O, our heavenly*

113

Father, direct us aright! What wilt thou have us do? Our only hope is in thee, and to thee alone we look for protection. I sincerely hope we shall be able to remain at Rangoon, among a people who have never heard the sound of the Gospel or reading their own language, of the love of Christ.

All their new friends in Madras were most anxious about Ann, for her baby was due at any time. Mrs. Stevens helped the Lovelesses obtain the services of Mrs. Jarvis, a European nurse who was willing to accompany the Judsons in order to help Ann when the baby came. The nurse's presence brought a great sense of relief to the nervous couple, and Mr. J, Ann thought to herself, was especially delighted because he knew next to nothing about helping with the delivery of a baby. The *Georgiana,* that *"crazy old vessel,"* as the Judsons named the little brig, appeared on its last legs, and nothing about it inspired confidence in someone sailing on her. Mrs. Jarvis appeared sturdy enough, however, and that calmed Adoniram's worries a bit, along with the fact that the nurse and the captain could both speak English.

The day of departure arrived, and they boarded the *Georgiana.* As Mrs. Jarvis turned to help Ann walk to the tiny makeshift cabin that had been prepared on deck, she suddenly gasped, stumbled to the deck, and lay there in great distress. Ann knelt at her side, trying to raise Mrs. Jarvis's head, but the stricken nurse could only take two or three strangled gasps before she died on the spot. All efforts to revive her were in vain. The Judsons were in shock.

As help came from shore to take her body away, Ann looked at Adoniram with wide, questioning eyes: *What now?* He took a deep breath, grasped her hands, and asked, "Oh my dear love, shall we leave the vessel? There is no time to find more help. The ship is ready to sail." So affected was he that his voice cracked. Ann had never seen him in such distress. "Mr. J," she said, sounding like the strong one now, "we have set our eyes to Burma. Our heavenly Father is still with us." The die was cast. They would go to Rangoon.

The *Georgiana* was sailing under the Portuguese flag. Smelly, dirty, and rickety, all it could offer them for protection from the elements was a canvas shelter that had been erected on the cluttered open deck. That night, lying on their cot in the temporary cabin, Ann and Adoniram alternately prayed and talked about the days ahead and what they must do about the impending birth. Already it had been a long seventeen months since they had left Salem with their lofty hopes and dreams. Maybe they were finally nearing their field of endeavor. Pray God it was so, and only the Lord could prepare the way.

Those three weeks at sea were a time they would later recall with mingled horror and sadness, its dangers and sorrows forever etched on their memories. Following the trauma of losing Mrs. Jarvis without warning, Ann went into labor just days after boarding the ship. The winds were blustering in every direction and the waves choppy the entire day. As the boat tossed incessantly from side to side, its motion only exacerbated Ann's pain. There was no doctor, no medicine, and Ann's mind fixed with agonizing worry on memories of Harriet and what had happened to her. Yet even in her wretchedness, Ann thought of her husband and prayed over and over again—*O God, do not let this man be left alone. He must not be left to go on alone. Spare us, O Father.* Never had Mama and home and safety seemed so far away or so longed for.

Adoniram was completely beyond knowing what to do and frantic with worry, struggling to help in a situation completely outside of his skills. He knelt beside the little cot and tried in vain to ease Ann's pain, bathing her brow in cool water, squeezing her hand as she cried out. After a night that seemed endless, the sun rose over the Bay of Bengal, and Ann gave a final exhausted gasp. Their tiny son entered the world, but he never drew a breath. Grief now bowed their hearts in overwhelming sorrow. Adoniram gently wiped the tears from Ann's eyes and handed the tiny, perfectly formed baby, wrapped in one of Mrs. Stevens' soft linens, into her waiting arms. Together they gazed long minutes at the precious little face, and both wept and prayed for peace and mercy to endure such sorrow.

Later that same day, as an exhausted, grieving Ann finally slept, Adoniram took the tiny form and gently consigned their unnamed son to the Bay of Bengal. Tears streaked his face as he turned and slowly returned to the canvas shelter. But there was more fear and danger yet to come. Ann, alarmingly weak from loss of blood, was dangerously ill for days on end. Now Adoniram agonized over losing his wife as well as their firstborn child. To add to the alarm, the old vessel was not powerful enough to stay on course, and they were threatened with wrecking on a cannibal shore as the *Georgiana* drifted perilously between the Little and Greater Andaman Islands.

Yet in danger, hope struck a note. The islands lay between India and Burma, where the Bay of Bengal met the Andaman Sea, and the little vessel was blown off course into a spot where the waters were still as a millpond. At long last, while the ship was becalmed there, Ann was able to rest. Upon finally experiencing some relief, her tired mind remembered one of the last things Harriet had said before she and Samuel left Calcutta: "He who takes care of the ravens will not forsake his own children in the hour of their affliction." God had not forsaken her, and Ann Judson survived the greatest affliction that had come her way in all her twenty-four years. Yet again, she could but take courage.

When Adoniram realized that his wife was going to live, he sank beside their cot, clutching her hand and weeping tears of relief, even as she gently stroked his head, as if to assure him that all would be well. Sailing into the quiet waters of the Andaman Sea had spared her life. If they could have looked ahead through the years that followed, the bereft young parents would have realized the significance of the Andaman Sea in their lives, for it was on a cliff beside that same sea as it touched the shores of Burma that the earthly remains of Ann Judson would one day be laid to rest.

Nearly a week later, the *Georgiana* was at long last able to catch favorable winds, and they slowly drew nearer to Burma. Husband and wife were filled with conflicting emotions. Had they not been striving for this very moment for years? Now they wondered if their dream had evolved into a nightmare. It was Tuesday, July 13, 1813, when the shores of Rangoon, Burma, at last appeared on the horizon. The decrepit and creaking *Georgiana* reached the entrance to the Rangoon River, the mouth of the great Irrawaddy, and slowly entered the harbor.

In the hazy distance was a straggling, squalid shoreline. It was like a cruel parody of a dream for two exhausted and grieving wanderers. Their first views of Calcutta had been colorful and exhilarating. In stark contrast, Rangoon was a wretched-looking jumble of a place. The city had been recently flooded by monsoon rains. Ann was still too weak to stand, so as Adoniram stood by the rail and strained for his first view of the shoreline, he could only describe for Ann the depressing sights that met his weary eyes.

The grimy little city slowly emerged through the drifting mist. From their perspective on the deck of the *Georgiana*, Rangoon seemed scarcely better than a neglected swamp. Occasional tumbledown shacks with bamboo walls and thatched roofs stood on stilts. Slightly behind the harbor's edge appeared the outline of a timber stockade, some eighteen feet high and stretching a scant mile along the water's edge. Everywhere were scattered the tips of pagodas, some a dull gold, others whitewashed, and the air was heavy with the smell of swampland and decay.

Then a break in the clouds occurred, and in the first wavering rays of sunshine, one massive spire glinted in the sun, a spire reaching up over four hundred feet. It was Shwedagon Pagoda, laden with gold and one of the wonders of the world. The Judsons' hearts leapt. This was the "golden shore." This was the challenge they had accepted, that God's golden scepter of salvation would be lifted high above all else, even the soaring Shwedagon. They had arrived at this moment with the determination that this was literally a *"mission for life."* Ann later wrote in her journal, *"It was in our hearts to live and die with the Burmans, and we in this place induced to pitch our tent."*

117

The Golden Land 1813

Shwedagon Pagoda, Rangoon, Burma. The 2000-year-old pagoda was the first sight the Judsons saw upon reaching Burma.

"MR. J, IT IS PERFECTLY ALL right to leave me resting here while you see a bit onshore," Ann urged her husband. It was late afternoon on July 13, but the sun had not yet set, and Adoniram was eager to take a closer look. Taking her hand in his, he gently kissed it and told her, "Dear Love, I'll bring you a report forthwith," and she smiled in assent. Her impulsive Mr. J was likely never to change; if something needed doing—get to it.

Adoniram took a skiff to the dock for a brief look around while it was still daylight. That glimpse did nothing to uplift the heart. Huddled all around the base of the glittering spire of the pagoda was a miserable cluster of huts along narrow streets clogged by pungent filth. He could not help but contrast this unappealing sight with their own temperate, orderly New England, now a world away. He had come ashore with the half-formed idea of finding Felix Carey's mission house, which he correctly judged to be a rather large building standing just beyond the city stockade walls. Nonetheless, at the last minute his courage failed, and feeling increasingly disheartened as he looked around, he decided to return to Ann so they could commiserate together.

Ann took one look at his face as he came into the flimsy canvas shelter, and her heart sank. "My Dear Love," he began, giving her a rather wry smile, "I haven't much of cheer to report." He then launched into a rather jumbled account of the squalor and neglect that permeated the dock area. Ann listened with deepening dismay, for he was always the positive one, and there was nothing of hope or encouragement in his account of the brief reconnoiter ashore. Exhausted from the trauma of childbirth and losing their baby, Ann mirrored his depression, and tears slowly rolled down her wan cheeks. This should have been their happiest moment. After all, for a year and a half they had been rambling, trying to reach the place God had called them to serve. They were finally here, and now all they seemed able to do was weep and pray.

Adoniram later recorded his feelings about that memorable evening. He, as well as Ann, kept a journal, although not using it as frequently as she. About those first hours in Rangoon he wrote:

> *All seemed so dark and cheerless, and unpromising—that evening of the day . . . we have marked as the most gloomy and distressing that we ever passed. Instead of rejoicing as we ought to have done, in having found a heathen land from which we were not immediately driven away, such were our weaknesses that we felt we had no portion left here below and found consolation only in looking beyond our pilgrimage. But, if ever we commended ourselves sincerely and without reserve, to the disposal of our heavenly father, it was on that evening.*

Ann later noted in her own journal that it was indeed one of the unhappiest days of their lives. But the practical and irrepressible Ann soon recovered most of her strength and all of her courage and wrote, *"We felt very gloomy and dejected the first night we arrived, but we were enabled to lean on God, and to feel that he was able to support us under the most discouraging circumstances."*

After that first night, they took heart; tomorrow was another day. The following morning, America's pioneer missionaries set foot together in Burma for the first time. Ann was still too weak to walk, so to go ashore she sat in a palanquin carried by four Burmans. In this manner, the Judsons got their first close look at what was to become home, impossible as that seemed in those first hours of unfamiliar smells and confusing sights and sounds.

Their new reality was a noisy, scraggly, arguing mass of humanity, jostling for position in muddy lanes strewn with every imaginable kind of garbage, some of which the two could identify neither by ghastly odor nor rotting appearance. The son of fastidious New England housewife Abigail Judson was staggered by the filth and could only imagine the dismay of his dear mother. They had never heard so much tinkling of temple bells, even in India, and the streets of Rangoon were dotted with saffron-robed Buddhist priests with their shaven heads and begging bowls. Sad-faced lepers pleading for a morsel of food, thrusting out stumps of hands where the disease had eaten away fingers and joints, abounded in the crowded melee of people. And all around were naked children, if you didn't count the many necklaces they wore as clothing, and to Ann's amazement many of the little ones were smoking cigars. *What would Mama make of that?*

In front, behind, and all around the bewildered missionaries were throngs of people, men in their *lungyis*—colorful waistcloths drawn and knotted at the waist—and women with their silk petticoats and bright scarves in a rainbow of colors. Some of the women had gold earrings, but others had long cigars stuck through massive holes in their earlobes. A startled Ann could scarcely turn her wondering gaze away from the sight. As she peered out from under her bonnet in astonishment at the strange sights all about them, she soon discovered that she was also a curiosity to the women crowding around her palanquin. A foreign Englishman, or possibly a man from Spain or Portugal, was only occasionally seen on the streets of Rangoon, but never a foreign *woman*. Ann Judson was a wonder to the chattering women on Rangoon's streets.

About this time, the four palanquin bearers decided they needed a rest and a cigar, so they set down Ann's chair. The women all jostled around, one curious woman after another bending down and trying to peer under the strange-looking headgear on the foreign lady. A few bolder ones reached out tentative fingers and stroked shining curls, at which Ann lifted her head and showed her captivating smile. The delighted audience broke into joyous laughter at the sight of the pale but lovely lady with the amber eyes, so like yet unlike their own. The tale of Ann's radiant smile was surely told in many a little Rangoon house that night.

Of necessity, the first stop was the customs house. The law required that a tenth of every cargo be set aside for the emperor, and so the luggage of all travelers was thoroughly inspected, criticized, fingered, discussed, and sometimes laughed over. Adoniram was stripped and thoroughly searched. Many travelers tried to conceal precious booty on their persons, and the customs officials knew all the tricks. To their disgust, this foreigner had nothing hidden. Ann fared a bit better, but women in the customs house checked her over thoroughly, oohing and aahing over the strange and uncomfortable-looking clothing she wore.

Ann and Adoniram were themselves wide-eyed, gazing at all the extraordinary sights assailing their eyes in their new chosen home. Just beyond the customs house and inside the stockade was Sule Pagoda—many centuries old already, its shining cleanliness a vivid contrast to the squalid refuse scattered near its base. The Judsons stared up, marveling at the pristine white structure, gleaming and immaculate, and then down in dismay at the filth around their feet. Ann was doubly grateful for the sturdy half-boots on her feet and silently thanked Mama for their protection.

The Judsons' little procession slowly made its way through the muddy lanes and past collections of dilapidated bamboo and teak buildings. Soon they passed the place of execution with its nearby enclosure where dead bodies were burned. With a shudder, they left this sight behind and proceeded out the stockade gate and to the nearby mission house of Felix Carey. Ann described it in a letter to Mama:

We felt a great disappointment in not finding Mr. Carey at home. . . . He was ordered up to the capital by the king, to vaccinate some of the royal family. . . . Mrs. Carey is a native of the country, though of European descent. She speaks very little English, but is very kind, and does everything to make us comfortable. The house is large and convenient, made wholly of teak wood, but the inside is unfinished and the beams and joints all bare. It is however, the largest and hand-somest house in all Rangoon.

After the filth in the inner city of Rangoon, the mission house was a wonderful oasis. The area around the structure appeared to be a jungle, with thick groves of trees and bushes, primitive and some-how menacing, but the house itself was nestled in the midst of a two-acre garden filled with shade trees and all manner of mango and other fruit trees. What a relief after the sights that had just assaulted them! Although the house was not finished and had very little furniture, it was large and comfortable and comparatively cool, considering the searing heat they had felt all morning. Mrs. Carey knew only two or three words of English but spoke with her smiles and gestures, making the couple feel welcome. She seemed happy to have the company. The Careys had a little boy who had just turned three, named Felix for his father, and Mrs. Carey had recently delivered another son. Ann's heart cried each time she played with the little boy or cuddled the baby, thinking of what might have been.

There was no time for grieving, however. They had a language to learn and a mission to fulfill. The first order of business was for Ann to regain her strength after her close brush with death. She struggled not to dwell on the absence of her loving mother and the conven-iences of home. The savory food of a comfortable New England home was now just a fond memory, and the reality of Burmese food was becoming a daily trial; both Judsons found it increasingly diffi-cult to cope with eating only Burmese dishes.

In those early days, Ann often recalled Harriet's longing for some fresh bread and butter, and now she also had that craving. There were also no potatoes and no cheese. Rice was now the daily staple, and fowl their only meat, which was cooked with curry and cucumbers. Ann, the farmer's daughter, thought longingly of the steaming bowls of fresh vegetables served nearly every day in Bradford. Ah, for some creamy mashed potatoes and Mama's roast beef dinner!

In this Buddhist country, it was against the law to kill livestock for food. From time to time, however, an animal would "accidentally" die, and then there was a bit of beef or pork for a change.

In the first weeks in Rangoon, Ann wrote to her parents about the strange food but added, *"We are blessed with good health and good appetites, and feel that instead of murmuring that we have no more of the comforts of life, we have great reason to be thankful that we have so many."* But the gregarious Ann Judson, always loving people and enjoying being with them, wrote of a sore deprivation: *"There are no English families in Rangoon. There is not a female in all Burmah with whom I can converse."*

Ann described the poverty of the people and the oppressive rulers who made their lives more difficult in a letter to Mama:

> *Many of the poor natives live on leaves and vegetables that grow spontaneously, and some actually die with hunger. Everything is extremely high [i.e., expensive] and therefore many are induced to steal; there are constant robberies and murders committed. Scarcely a night but houses are broken open and things stolen. But, our trust and confidence are in our heavenly Father. . . . I think God has taught us to find comfort and peace in feeling that he is everywhere present. . . . O for more love to him and greater willingness to suffer in his cause!*

Despite these struggles, the Judsons were curious about the people and eager to learn more about the Burmans' Buddhist faith. They contemplated where to begin. No one in Burma spoke English, and there was no dictionary, no grammar book. The challenge was daunting. So, the first step would be to learn Burmese.

Finding a teacher was top on their agenda. Judson inquired throughout the city about a possible instructor. After much gesturing and attempting to explain, a frustrated Adoniram finally located an elderly Hindu scholar who was willing to ignore caste enough to sit with him, and eat with him as well. However, the scholar balked at the thought of teaching a mere woman. Women were considered inferior beings. He finally consented, though with great reluctance, and then was amazed at the speed and acuity of Ann's language acquisition. A normal day of study usually stretched from seven in the morning until ten at night, with infrequent breaks. Ann and Adoniram found themselves falling into bed at night, as tired as they had ever been in all their lives. Ann wrote Mama about the details of a typical study day:

> As Mrs. Carey has the whole care of the family, being familiar with the language, and having several servants at her command, I am free from every concern of this nature and can devote all my time to study. We rise at six, commence study at seven, breakfast at eight, and after breakfast have family worship. We then go to our study and attend to the language closely, till half past one, when we dine. We generally exercise for half an hour after dinner then attend to our study again till near sunset, when we take a walk, either out among the natives or in our verandah; take tea at dark, after which we have family worship, then study till ten, at which time we retire. I go to bed feeling as much fatigued as any farmer can after a hard day's work.

The two students became experts at pointing. They would point, and the teacher would name the object in Burmese. It became more difficult by the day, however, when they confronted the complications of adverbs, adjectives, and prepositions, only to discover that

Burmese grammar and syntax were completely different from any language they knew. Of all things, punctuation and paragraphing were also not used. (After more than a year, Adoniram maintained that if he had a choice of being examined on the contents of Burmese book or a French book that he had studied for two or three months, he would without question choose the French.)

Ann confided to the family at home: *"It is a most beautiful, easy language to write, but very difficult to read, or pronounce. Words all join together and there are no capital letters."* She described their teacher: *"Our teacher is a good natured, intelligent man. He sits in a chair by us or will eat with us, the same as an American. When he first came, he paid very little attention to me, appearing to feel that it was rather beneath him to instruct a female. But, when he saw I was determined to persevere, and that Mr. Judson was as desirous to have him instruct me as himself, he was more attentive."*

Studying such a complicated language was grinding work, and some days they wondered if they would *ever* be able to communicate the gospel in Burmese. However, their Hindu scholar was both astounded and gratified at what he considered their sterling progress. He even went so far as to tell Ann that he was going to *her* land when he died, which for a Burman was a great compliment.

With many an exhausting day and even more endless nights, Ann would weep inwardly from sheer loneliness and discouragement and sometimes whisper in her prayers a plea to God to "call her again." And, in a hundred small ways during those long, dark nights, God would reveal himself to her aching heart and she would give a sigh, bless God, and determine that tomorrow was another day. *What might God have in mind for them?* Ann would search for some small hope for the next day: maybe mail would arrive from America, or maybe in some way she could make a difference for someone. And at long last, a weary Ann would fall asleep. She was determined to persevere. She must.

CHAPTER 17

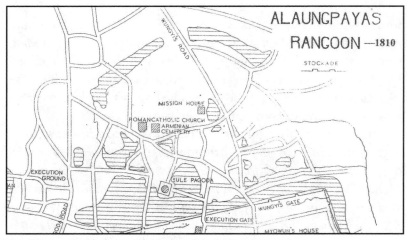

Map of Rangoon, showing the location of the first mission house.

Alone
1813–1814

IT WAS NO ACCIDENT THAT GOD HAD CALLED TWO BRILLIANT LIN-guists to the task of learning an extremely difficult language. The Judsons could never have imagined studying without a textbook, a grammar book, or even a dictionary, but that was exactly what they were forced to do. Study was nearly all-consuming, even to these two motivated minds. Before long, Ann's spoken Burmese became fluent; she had a keen ear for tone and sound and could accurately mimic what she heard. She also assumed some of the household duties, which strengthened her language skills, as she was forced to use Burmese to communicate with everyone except Adoniram. It soon became appar-ent that Ann's written skills were also exceptional, and she wrote and translated the first Burmese catechism with surprising speed.

In contrast, her dear husband struggled in spoken Burmese, although his brilliance in feeling his way into the structural heart of the language was remarkable. This ability was ultimately one of the main reasons he would, twenty years later, be able to complete his extraordinary translation of the Bible into Burmese, one that would still be in use two hundred years later.

Ann wrote to her family describing Adoniram's daily routine: *"Could you look into a large open room, which we call a verandah, you would see Mr. J bent over his table, covered with Burman books, with his teacher at his side, a venerable looking man with a cloth wrapped round his middle and a handkerchief round his head. They talk and chatter all day long, with hardly any cessation."* Adoniram immersed himself in Burmese literature and in Buddhist teachings, legends, and poetry, so that he could understand the way the people reasoned. Even their thought patterns were different, and how could he reach the *hearts* of the people if he could not see inside their minds?

Despite their commitment to language study, both Ann and Adoniram recognized the importance of becoming part of their larger world in Rangoon. Visiting religious sites, conversing with vendors in the market, and meeting people on the streets would make them much more useful in preparing for their ultimate goal of reaching the hearts of Burmans with the Good News. One of their first visits was to the towering Shwedagon, Burma's most massive religious shrine. Built soon after the death of the Buddha some four hundred years before Christ, it had been enlarged and beautified through the centuries, and its golden spire reached nearly four hundred feet into the air, nearly as high as the great pyramids of Egypt. Small wonder that those seeing it for the first time were in awe. The Judsons were shocked to be told that it contained more than sixty tons of gold. The vane at the top was studded with approximately fourteen hundred precious rubies and sapphires and crowned by five thousand diamonds weighing two thousand carats. They were also aghast at all these riches, when the masses worshipping here were living in wretched poverty.

At the same time, Ann loved her forays into the markets and stalls of Rangoon and quickly became a familiar sight to the shopkeepers. *"Nay kaung bar lar"* ("Good morning"), Ann would say, and the vendors in the market would laugh out loud with pleasure. Some vendor would invariably inquire, *"Be hmar lar de?"* ("Where are you from?"). That was nearly always followed with the question, *"Woon ma tit yauk lar?"* ("Are you the number one wife?"). Ann had to ask her venerable teacher how she could explain that in America men had only one wife. The market women would then commiserate with her because that must mean her husband was a poor man. As if to verify what they thought about the poor foreigners, Ann would usually say about the price that vendors were asking for their vegetables and fruit, *"Zay kyee de, Zay kyee de"* ("Price too high.") Small wonder Ann's language progressed so quickly and naturally; she used it every day.

Day-by-day annoyances also came to be routine. It was a fact that Rangoon's humidity encouraged the growth of little creatures. Neither of the New England transplants got along very well with the host of bedbugs, cockroaches, spiders, centipedes, mosquitoes, and beetles, not to mention the bats—all of which seemed to vie with one another for the most rapid reproduction. Also in the competition were the legions of rats; every time Adoniram saw one, his mind harked to what his fastidious mother would think if she found one of these creatures in her spotless house. The acorn had not fallen far from the tree, and her son found himself squeamish at these constant reminders of poor sanitation.

Nevertheless, the Judsons learned to cope and to quietly exterminate these little annoyances whenever possible. Of course, this took a good deal of planning, for no good Buddhist would kill any creature; it might be the reincarnation of some unfortunate person. No wonder such creatures proliferated! Ann's skin crawled the morning she encountered a cobra that had slithered its way into the cool mission house, and she quickly called for Mr. J's assistance in eradicating this deadly visitor. She judiciously decided she'd not write Mama about this particular uninvited guest.

128

Life was not all bugs and vermin, filth and hardship, however. Ann and Adoniram quickly learned to love and appreciate the people of Burma and their inquisitive minds. This sense of curiosity bode well for finding those who would want to learn the way of eternal life. The culture was so very different from their own that the Judsons had to look intently into Burmese history to understand the way the Burmans thought.

One philosophy by which nearly every Burman lived greatly disturbed the self-respecting New Englanders: "How can you not lie?" one Burman after another would ask the Americans in genuine sincerity. "Lying is essential." Another perplexing fact of life in Burma was bribery, which was the way to facilitate your path through life.

Both the Judsons, especially Ann, were intrigued by something else that seemed a great contradiction to them. Here was a culture where, on one hand, women were allowed much greater freedoms than in most Asian countries, yet they were at the same time repressed and regarded as mere chattel in other areas of daily life. The couple sought to figure out why the people thought and acted as they did; their determination in this area was surely the foundation of their later success in ministry. The two missionaries developed a genuine respect for the people of their adopted land, and this sense of admiration and understanding led to their becoming an accepted part of the community.

Nonetheless, loneliness was always a reality. Ann and Adoniram, back in those months when they were courting, had talked about the isolation they would likely feel one day when they would live far away from home. But talking about such a thing in theory and experiencing it in reality were far different. Loneliness hurt; sometimes in the still of the night, tears would trickle down Ann's cheeks, and then she would feel ashamed of herself, knowing that she and Andoniram were blessed in so many ways. And so she would pray for special grace and understanding and would slowly manage to fall asleep. That first August in Rangoon she wrote:

Have been writing letters this week to my dear friends in America. Found that a recollection of former enjoyments, in my own native country, made my situation here appear less tolerable. The thought that I had parents, sisters, and beloved friends still in existence, and at such a distance, that it was impossible to obtain a look, or exchange a word, was truly painful. While they are still in possession of the comforts I once enjoyed, I am an exile from my country and my father's house, deprived of all society, and every friend but one, and with scarcely the necessaries of life. These privations would not be endured with patience, in any other cause, but that in which we are engaged.

Ann concluded in a letter home, *"It is now a year and a half since we left America, and we have not received a single letter or heard anything from any of our friends. How would it rejoice our hearts to receive a large packet of letters from our native country!"* But when the sun would rise on another day, the Judsons would once again persevere in their studies and in building their relationships with people who had no inkling of a God who loved them and offered eternal life.

While the two were deeply involved in learning the language and the culture of their adopted country, they were simultaneously examining their own spiritual condition. There were no outside means of encouragement in their faith, no established church, no kindly pastor or Christian friend to offer comfort or guidance. Ann constantly examined her heart to see if she was thinking and living in a way that would honor God. Frequently running through her mind was the passage that she had examined so closely during the months when searching for God's direction for her life; the significance of presenting her body as a "living sacrifice" (Romans 12:1) was becoming clear. Repeatedly Ann would ask herself: *Do I really mean these words when I speak them?* One night she sat down with her journal and wrote, *"Nothing do I dread so much as becoming cold and worldly minded, and losing the life of religion in the soul. I find that the innate depravity of my heart is constantly showing itself. O for a more holy heart, more fervent love to God."*

In the absence of opportunities for worship with other believers and the encouragement that always gave, Ann would often meditate on the hymns that had touched her in earlier days, humming to herself the priceless words of assurance in the hymns of Watts, Newton, or Wesley. Watts's "Jesus Shall Reign" would often echo in her thoughts: "His Kingdom stretch from shore to shore, 'til moons shall wax and wane no more." Surely this was why they were here: to share the news of the Kingdom. Sometimes she would weep as she hummed Newton's "How Sweet the Name of Jesus Sounds" and came to the comforting words, "It soothes his sorrows, heals his wounds, and drives away his fear."

On September 13, Ann recorded what became a signal moment for the couple: the first Sunday morning they partook of the Lord's Supper in Burma. As Ann and Adoniram took the bread and juice, reading the precious words from First Corinthians and praying together, they felt a sense of communion and a bond that could not be broken on this earth. It was in that holy moment, in a strange land, when the two lonely young missionaries united in the sharing of Communion, that the Christian church of Burma was born.

About this time, Felix Carey returned briefly from the capital in Ava, and Mrs. Carey and little Felix were thrilled to see him. Mr. Carey noted the speed with which Ann and Adoniram were acquiring the language and wrote to his father, *"They are just cut out for this mission."* Felix had much of his father's talents in translation and had managed to translate six chapters of the Gospel of Matthew. He well knew the monumental task that lay ahead in making the Bible available in this challenging language and was relieved to find such capable missionaries carrying on the work he was about to leave, for he had been offered an enticing government post in Emperor Bodawpaya's court. He felt duty-bound to first visit his father in Calcutta, however, to explain his reasons for such a step, so Mrs. Carey and their two sons had him home only briefly.

By this time in 1814, Adoniram was feeling sufficiently comfortable with the language to pay a visit to the viceroy, the most powerful political figure in all of Rangoon and surrounding areas. Considering the viceroy's level of power and influence, Adoniram felt it might be wise to meet him. Much to his disappointment, the "audience" with the viceroy was not successful. Ann reported in a letter home that the viceroy *"scarcely deigned to look at him, as English MEN are no uncommon sight in his country."*

The Judsons talked about the disappointment that evening and decided to try their luck with having Ann seek a powerful audience. One never knew when they might need some powerful backing in this alien land, and clearly it behooved them to be on speaking terms with authority. Since a foreign man was no rare sight, they would attempt the sight of a foreign woman. Surely this was sufficiently rare. Ann had previously met the wife of a French businessman who lived in Rangoon, and she asked the woman to help her get an audience with the vicereine, the number one wife of the viceroy. This, the woman was happy to do.

Ann set forth one December morning, butterflies in her stomach and her favorite scoop bonnet covering her head and shielding her brown eyes. Later that evening she wrote home, pleased about her first foray into minor diplomacy: *"Dec. 11: Today, for the first time, I have visited the wife of the viceroy."* Ann described the vicereine's appearance when she entered the chamber, clad in rich Burmese attire and smoking a long, silver pipe. As she entered the room, the lesser wives who had been admitted that day retreated to a respectful distance and crouched on the floor, not daring to speak unless addressed. The vicereine looked with interest into the face of the beautiful stranger, the wife of the American teacher, took her by the hand, and led her to a seat on a mat where she herself sat. Ann wrote of this experience, *"One of the women brought her a bunch of flowers, of which she took several and ornamented my cap. She was very inquisitive whether I had a husband and children; whether I was my husband's first wife—meaning, by this, whether I was the highest* among them, supposing that Mr. Judson, like the Burmans, had many wives; and whether I intended tarrying long in the country." Ann then recounted the appearance of the viceroy himself:

> When the viceroy came in, I really trembled, for I never before beheld such a savage looking creature. His long robe and enormous spear not a little increased my dread. He spoke to me, however, very condescendingly, and asked if I would drink some rum or wine. When I arose to go, her highness again took my hand, told me she was happy to see me, that I must come to see her every day. My only object in visiting her was, if we should get into any difficulty with the Burmans, I could have access to her, when perhaps it would not be possible for Mr. Judson to have an audience with the viceroy.

About this time, reports of robberies in the area surrounding the city were growing in number, and the Judsons decided that they might be safer to move inside the stockade walls, which seemed to offer at least a bit of protection. In January they found a small house to rent, and shortly after the move they heard the chilling account of a band of about fifteen men, armed with knives and spears, who attacked a house in the neighborhood of the Carey's mission house, stabbing the owner and escaping with everything of value.

Two months later another alarming event occurred, one that reminded them of both the fragility of security and the uncertainty of life itself. One Sunday morning they decided to walk out to the mission house to visit Mrs. Carey and her children and to spend the day in quiet worship, a custom they had developed since their move into town. Just about the time they reached the house, one of the Carey's servants came running up to them with frightening news: a fire was raging inside the town. Ann and Adoniram immediately headed back to their little house to try to remove their belongings from harm's way.

As they ran in the direction of the stockade, they could see the flames spreading, but upon reaching the gates of Rangoon's stockade wall, they were horrified to find them locked. Naively, the people had thought that by locking the gates, the fire could be kept out. Ann and Adoniram frantically pleaded for the gate to be opened and, on finally gaining access, rushed to their house and rescued their possessions just in time. The house was a total loss, and Mrs. Carey graciously received them back at the mission house, and there they remained for the rest of their time in Rangoon.

The Judsons continued to immerse themselves in the language, with Adoniram spending long hours learning Pali and Sanskrit (the sacred languages of India) so as to more accurately understand the mind-set of the people and be able to translate God's Word into the language of the Burmans. It was exhausting work, but lack of determination had never been their shortcoming.

Felix Carey returned from Calcutta in April with mail, and the two Americans were thrilled to receive their first letters in more than two years, letters from friends in India. However, it also made them yearn even more for news from New England, for still no letters had reached them from home. It seemed a lifetime since they had sailed from Salem Harbor.

Meanwhile, Felix was making immediate preparations to take his family to the national capital, Ava, to begin a new life there. He was feeling a bit of guilt and regret about leaving mission service but at the same time was excited to think of the splendors of court in the capital. The morning of August 20 dawned bright and humid, and Felix and his family headed to the boat they had hired for their trip. Yet how quickly life can take a sudden, totally unexpected turn, and tragedy strike with no warning.

Judson's great-grandson, Dr. Stanley Hanna, with the author on a busy Rangoon street, next to the place where the first mission house stood.

Travels and Travails
1814–1815

THE MISSION HOUSE SEEMED EXTRAORDINARILY QUIET THE FIRST few days after Mrs. Carey and the children left with Felix for Ava. The Judsons had grown accustomed to the happy sounds of the children's voices and the patter of their busy little feet, especially during their unremitting daily language study. They missed those sounds, as well as the bright questions and observations of young Felix as he asked about what life in faraway America was like. "Do all Americans look like you do?" he would question them. "Are all their eyes round like yours?"

And then came some chilling news. About two weeks later, a messenger arrived at their door, holding out a note written in Felix Carey's distinctive handwriting. Not long before the Careys' small boat had reached Ava, a sudden storm arose on the Irrawaddy, and their vessel capsized. Frantically trying to reach his wife and two little ones, Felix saw them sink before his horrified eyes. All of his family was lost. Gone were the grand dreams of the Carey family together at the courts of Ava. Felix was still in shock and would remain in Ava, trying to sort through the tragedy. Adoniram read the dreadful news aloud to Ann, who sat in horrified silence, watching his hands tremble as he held the fateful letter. In their shock and grief, nothing seemed to help but pleading with God for mercy and comfort for the bereaved young father, himself only twenty-nine. Felix's first wife had died while still in her teens, and now he had lost both a second wife and two sons.

The Judsons returned to their intensive study of Burmese, and in their sorrow prayed anew for wisdom. It was painfully evident that life could be cut short at any moment, in the twinkling of an eye. "God give us grace to number our days aright" was their earnest petition. This loss reminded them all too painfully of the death of Harriet, cut down so early in life, and the stillbirth of their own son. The Judsons had been keeping up a correspondence with the widowed Samuel, even though mail was painfully slow both coming and going. Ann wrote to him about the loss of Mrs. Carey and the children and of their intense loneliness: *As respects our temporal privations, use has made them familiar and easy to be borne; they are of short duration and when brought in competition with the worth of immortal souls, sink into nothing. We have no society, no dear Christian friends, and with the exception of two or three sea captains, who now and then call on us, we never see a European face.*

But then she wrote of how it felt to look about them at the condition in which most of the people had to live, scratching out a bare existence and somehow imagining that they could purchase promotion to another state of existence by strictly worshipping their Buddhist idols and building pagodas. They often reflected, she told Samuel, that they could forget their native country and former enjoyments and feel contented with their lot, with just one wish remaining: to be instrumental in leading the Burmans to Christian faith.

In the house by themselves, Ann and Adoniram developed a daily routine in which they would pour vast amounts of time and energy into mastering the Burmese language. It was a major challenge, but they had no intention of backing down or giving up. Ann, perforce, also needed to spend a certain amount of time and energy directing the various servants who helped them maintain the house and thus afforded them time to study. Adoniram spent his mornings with his teacher, and Ann, attempting to keep the household running smoothly, discovered that housekeeping, specifically talking with the servants, had some side benefits. After a year, she was amazingly fluent in Burmese and sounded colloquial in her tones and terminology.

Mr. J was frustrated with the slowness of his spoken Burmese but consoled himself with the knowledge that his own studies would eventually bear fruit when he managed to translate the Bible into the heart language of the people. That was the burning goal that kept him motivated each day. Dr. Carey had loaned him some priceless portions of Scripture manuscripts in Hebrew, and he was determined that his translation work would be from Hebrew and Aramaic into Burmese—a massive challenge indeed. Ann would smile to herself as she went about her work, listening to the background hum of voices coming from the study on the verandah.

Mama would likely be proud of me, Ann occasionally reflected as she figured out ways to give a bit of variety to the limited items of food available to them. She developed quite a flair for preparing curry dishes and found new ways to dress up rice, plus countless ways to prepare chicken, their main source of protein. She used fruit from the garden to make preserves and managed to create a delicious mango pie that tasted a lot like Mama's peach desserts. Wheat flour was unavailable, but she developed a way to pound together banana-like plantains and ordinary rice to make flour. Ann thought of it as "missionary flour."

Adoniram was discovering that his wife was not only a brilliant scholar but also a dab hand at cooking. Rebecca Hasseltine had taught her well, and her daughter was following in those capable footsteps. Mama would have been especially pleased with the custard that her Honey had learned to concoct, and Ann soon learned that sugar and tea could be ordered from Bengal. Their sea-captain friends were a doubly welcome sight when they appeared periodically with supplies for the lonely couple. It almost felt like Christmas to open a canister of sugar and sit down to a cup of real English tea, hot and aromatic. She never drank a fragrant cup without remembering teatime with Mama and her sisters.

It was in the still reaches of the night, however, that Ann often suffered the most wrenching loneliness. Occasionally she would wake up before dawn and immediately think of home and the family gathered around the fireside. She would begin weaving dreams of telling Mama about all her eyes were seeing and her heart was experiencing. She would think of the soft touch of her mother's hand and the loving look in her eyes as she listened intently to all her Honey was telling her. A vagrant tear, and then another, would wend its way down her cheeks, and she would hold back a sob, concentrating instead on the hopelessness of the precious people about her. She would plead with God not just to comfort her own and Adoniram's heart in their loneliness, but to keep brightly burning in their hearts the message they so longed to share with these people who were living with no hope for eternity. Ann would brush the tears from her cheeks and bless God yet again for the privilege of representing the gospel to those who did not know.

On the other hand, Ann and Mr. J were steadily making new friends. Frequently, Burman acquaintances from the town would pay an evening call, often bringing little gifts. Building relationships, they knew, was the way to reach to the heart, and they never let a day pass without praying for a fresh portion of wisdom. The viceroy, Mya-day-men, had left Rangoon, and his successor was an elderly man with many wives and scores of children. This new viceroy actually came to visit the Judsons—which was a departure indeed! Ann was gratified to be able to establish a friendship with the viceroy's number one (most favored) wife, and this regal lady came to understand that these interesting foreigners were "holy people." Ann prayed daily for opportunities to share the Good News with this influential woman.

The Judsons had been in Burma for a year and a half now, and they were still completely alone in the mission, struggling to master the intricate language and fighting loneliness—that constant specter over their heads. Adoniram had been keeping watch on Ann for several weeks now. He was noticing that her skin seemed "shadowed," for want of a better description, and that her steps were slower, not her usual crisp moving from task to task. As he realized she was looking thinner, with her cheeks growing hollow and her skin unnaturally sallow, he grew steadily more concerned. "My love," he would ask her several times a day, "are you feeling well? Is something amiss?" Ann would sigh and raise her brows a bit in acknowledgment, offering, "I don't know, Mr. J. I just don't seem to have any energy." She would often bite the corner of her lip, a sure sign that she was puzzling over something. But then she would straighten her shoulders and let her eyes smile again and reassure him, "It's just the weather."

But Adoniram could not keep his anxiety at bay. Something was wrong. He was so closely tuned to his dear wife's every thought and action that he sensed trouble. There was not a doctor to be had in all of Rangoon, and although the Judsons had brought several medical books, these seemed to offer few clues. However, Ann's changed complexion made Adoniram wonder if it might be so-called bilious disease, which caused the liver to malfunction. They had to face the fact that the nearest European doctor was in Madras, a thousand miles away across the Bay of Bengal. *What should they do?*

As they sat on the verandah one January evening, Adoniram looked at Ann with resolution and declared, "We are going to Madras to get help for you." Immediately Ann protested, her voice shaking with emotion. "Oh no, we must not desert the mission! We cannot do that." They spent a serious hour talking through their dilemma. Adoniram was adamant on one point: she must have medical help. Ann, for her part, was just as determined that the mission could not be abandoned, even for a short span. He was getting deeper and deeper into the intricacies of the language and thought patterns of the culture; she was insistent that he must not stop such important

139

work now. Finally a reluctant Ann agreed to seek help, while Adoniram continued his studies.

Adoniram shivered at the thought of Ann, weak as she was by now, making the trip alone, but who could accompany her? As both well knew, the laws of Burma stated that a Burman woman was not allowed to leave her native land. Then Ann came up with a possibility. She suggested that they ask the viceroy, whose number-one wife was disposed in Ann's favor, to grant special permission. Taking a small gift, always an essential in the Burmese culture, the two Americans presented themselves at Government House with their request. The elderly viceroy not only immediately acquiesced to permitting a female Burman friend to accompany Ann but also insisted on covering the expense of the passage. Ann and Adoniram once again stood in awe of the mercies of their God.

On January 25, 1814, Ann and her Burman companion set sail for Madras, safely arriving after several weeks at sea—a trip that had been miraculously free of typhoons, pirates, or any other perils. What a balm to Ann, to see dear friends in Madras after an absence of close to two years! The Lovelesses treated her like a long-lost relative, as did the kind Dutch businessman, Mr. Von Someron. These friends were astonished at the accounts she gave of their many months in Rangoon and all that had occurred in such a short time. They were likewise amazed at the progress the Judsons had made in the difficult language and could only imagine the painful loneliness they were enduring.

Ann and her Burman friend were treated royally by all, although the English doctor's diagnosis confirmed what Adoniram had suspected. She had "bilious fever" (liver disease). The kind doctor would not allow her to pay anything for his services, and his generosity brought Ann's tender heart to tears again, as did the ministrations of friend after friend, showering her with treasures and treats to take back to Rangoon. The loneliness of the past months was eased by such loving attention, but each act of kindness made her ache to share it all with Mr. J, a thousand miles away and all alone.

Ann had not long been in Madras when it dawned on her that one of her medical conditions had little to do with liver disease or jaundice. She suspected that she was pregnant again. Her heart skipped a beat at the thought, excitement mixing with trepidation as to what could happen with this baby. The tragedy of their firstborn was ever an echo of pain in her heart. Ann consulted with the doctor, who confirmed her pregnancy and reassured her that her current illness would not endanger the baby. He made a number of helpful suggestions as to how to prepare for the baby's birth, which did much to allay her fears.

Ann enjoyed frequent fellowship in the Von Someron home. Mr. Von Someron was the guardian of three young cousins whose parents had tragically been killed, and Ann fell in love with seven-year-old Emily, who gravitated to her side every time Ann visited. One evening, Ann and Mr. Von Someron talked of the possibility of Emily returning to Rangoon with Ann and living with the Judsons. Ann's heart leapt at the thought, for she adored the child. A few days later, Emily was thrilled to learn that she would be traveling to Burma with her beloved Miss Ann.

Meanwhile, Adoniram fought worsening loneliness through each long day in Rangoon. Due no doubt to their isolation and circumstances, Ann and Adoniram were far closer in spirit than most married couples, and it was a perpetual ache for him to be apart from his dear love. He poured himself with dogged determination into learning every nuance of the language and its history, immersing himself in Burmese and seeking to understand the thought patterns behind Buddhism, the better to reach those who had no hope of heaven. The house felt hauntingly deserted, and nighttime was the hardest; he would reach out in the darkness of midnight, as was his wont, for a reassuring pat on Ann's shoulder, but there was no Ann next to him to respond. Nor was there anyone with whom he could pray, and that was the biggest ache of all. He and Ann were a devoted team, and he felt half a person without her loving presence. Judson eased his pain each night by imagining his joy when he saw her ship sailing into harbor.

Finally, that glad morning came. On April 13, nearly three months after Ann had sailed across the Bay of Bengal, a messenger came running with the news that the sails of the Madras ship had been seen coming into harbor. Adoniram felt the excitement of a schoolboy as he hurried to the docks to await the ship's arrival. Sure enough, as the vessel drew closer, there on deck he could make out the form of a "foreign" woman. *That must be Ann!* And yes, it was she, for as the ship grew closer, he could see the Ann he knew and loved, her face glowing with health and her eyes alight as she saw the form of her beloved Mr. J.

Then he noticed a young child who appeared to be standing by Ann's side. Puzzled, he watched the vessel draw nearer to the wharf and saw that yes indeed, a pale little girl was clinging to Ann's hand. And thus it was that Adoniram welcomed his cherished Ann home and had the pleasure of meeting a lively girl who would bring laughter and smiles into their busy, lonely lives.

In the privacy of their room that night, Ann and Adoniram clung to one another and could scarcely bear to let go—it had been so long since they had been together. In that moment of joy, Ann shared her news with Mr. J: they were going to become parents in about five months! Adoniram's heart leapt in elation, followed immediately by concern over her condition and what might be the implications for her health. His mind harked back to the tragic morning aboard the *Georgiana* when their son entered this world stillborn, to be buried at sea.

Ann could read his expression and at once took his face between her gentle hands. She looked into his worried hazel eyes and spoke softly, saying, "Mr. J, it will be different this time. I will be all right. It will not be the same this time." She gave him her beautiful smile, concluding, "Let's just thank God and let our hearts take courage."

Morning in Rangoon. Buddhist monks with their begging bowls, a custom dating back more than 2,000 years.

Little Roger
1815–1816

SEPTEMBER WAS A MONTH OVERFLOWING WITH JOY. NEITHER ANN nor Adoniram ever forgot the overwhelming exultation that flooded their hearts the morning of September 5, when a messenger arrived at the mission house with a large packet of letters. Ann went to the door and stared in disbelief at the package held out by the young man from the ship that had arrived from Calcutta that morning. Mail. Actual mail. Mail addressed to Rev. and Mrs. Adoniram Judson. Mail with a postmark from the United States. Ann's hands began trembling uncontrollably. It had been three and a half unbelievably long years with no mail from home.

"Adoniram!" she called out. "Come quickly!" Hearing the urgency in Ann's voice and thinking that she might be going into labor, Judson

143

hurried to the verandah door where she was standing. Ann turned at his footsteps, and he grew alarmed at the tears welling up in her deep brown eyes. "Dear love," he took her shoulders in his hands, his eyes full of concern. "Are you all right? Is the baby coming?"

Ann managed a smile through her tears and thrust the large packet toward him, exclaiming, "Oh Mr. J, look at what has come! You won't believe it—mail from home! Mail from home!" Tears of joy were now running down her face. He was nearly as overcome by the moment and stood there in disbelief for the longest time. Then they both came to their senses and with shaky hands began sorting through the precious letters.

Ann and Adoniram had imagined just such a moment for many months, but the reality of receiving mail nearly paralyzed them. "Where do we even start, dear love?" he asked. Ann glanced down at the priceless letters and laid them out on the little table beside them. There was the familiar handwriting of Mama, of sister Abby and sister Becky, and that of other treasured family and friends. Along with those whose script they recognized were several official-looking envelopes addressed to the Rev. Adoniram Judson Jr., and postmarked Boston, Philadelphia, Charleston, and other cities. The couple sat in uncharacteristic stillness, overcome by the importance of the moment. Then drawing a deep breath, Adoniram offered, "Let's open these official-looking envelopes first, and then we can get to the dessert." Grinning, he reached for one of the long, bulky envelopes.

In a shaky voice, Adoniram read aloud the momentous news: during the month of May 1814, "the General Missionary Convention of the Baptist Denomination in the United States of America for Foreign Missions" was formed, with headquarters to be in Philadelphia. Dr. Richard Furman of Charleston was its first president, and Rev. Thomas Baldwin of Boston was president of the newly elected Board of Managers. All of this was formed in order to appoint the Judsons as its missionaries. The two sat in stunned silence at the workings of Providence. All these many months they had been laboring alone, but not really alone. God had been at work in hearts in their native land.

Other bulky envelopes awaited their eyes, but they decided to next enjoy the thrill of reading letters from home. Ann chose first the letter from Mama and had to wait for her eyes to clear of their happy tears. It was the next best thing to a visit with Mama and a comforting hug. Meanwhile, Adoniram was reading news from his mother, from his sister Abigail, and even from his dignified father. Occasionally one or the other would interrupt to share a tidbit of news that just couldn't wait. Ann ended up reading and rereading her treasured letters until they looked tattered from wear.

In his elation, Adoniram wrote in his journal that day:

> *These accounts from our dear native land were so interesting, as to banish from my mind all thoughts of study. This general movement among the Baptist churches in America is particularly encouraging . . . in furnishing abundant reason to hope, that the dreadful darkness . . . is about to flee away before the rising sun. . . . None but one who has had the experience, can tell what feelings comfort the heart of a solitary missionary, when . . . [he] had proofs that there are spots on their wide earth, where Christian brethren feel that his cause is their own, and pray for his welfare and success.*

Ann read her letters from various pastors and friends, telling of Baptists around the nation who were organizing missionary societies, from a group of low-country women on remote Edisto Island in South Carolina to groups in Virginia, Georgia, Massachusetts, New York, and other states. Their sole purpose was supporting mission endeavors, beginning with the Judsons in Burma. The exciting news made it hard to sleep that night.

Both thanked God for Luther Rice. Providence had used Rice's liver trouble to return him to America, where he had rallied Baptists from Maine to Charleston to the cause of missions. Rice was commissioned by the newly organized Baptist convention in America to continue to set up local branches of missions support. He was a superb spokesman, uniquely used by God to bring scattered Baptists together. (Luther was never able to return to the Far East to join the Judsons in Burma. Instead, he was the catalyst who brought Baptists together to send forth the gospel to the world.)

One of the letters contained especially great news for their mission, news as good as an early Christmas present. A printer, George Hough, and his wife, Phebe, were being sent to Burma to support the Judsons by printing in Burmese anything they were able to produce.

And even more joy was on the way that month. Early on the morning of September 11, just six days after the blessings of news from home, Emily ran out onto the verandah and tapped Adoniram on the shoulder. "Mr. J," she spoke excitedly, "Miss Ann says please come quickly. She thinks Baby is coming!" All thoughts of study and translation left behind, he rushed to Ann's side. It was an agonizingly long day, but thankfully not under the horrific circumstances aboard the *Georgiana*. Shortly before ten that night, a healthy baby boy was born, and Ann laughed with joy through her tears of exhaustion. The Burmese woman who helped with the housework proved a competent assistant to Mr. J, who needed her moral support more than anything as his memories of the tragic birth on board ship still haunted his mind.

The new parents shared a supremely tender moment when Adoniram placed their son in Ann's waiting arms and they gazed in wonder at their beautiful baby. "We need a name, Mr. J," Ann smiled tiredly. "What are you thinking of?" Ann speculated that Mr. J would suggest his own father's name or maybe his brother's, but he surprised her. Clearing his throat, he responded, "Dear love, how about Roger Williams Judson as an auspicious name for our fine son?" Ann said with her radiant smile, "How appropriate! An historic Baptist name for our historic first mission child."

Little Roger, as they usually called him, was the focal point of the mission house from that day forward. He delighted not only his doting parents but all who saw him. Even the viceroy was excited at the sight of the chubby white baby with striking blue eyes—no other such child had even been seen in Burma. Ann and Adoniram continued their many hours of diligent study, with Roger by their side. When they went by his cradle without picking him up, Ann related in her journal:

> *[H]e would follow us with his eyes to the door, where they would fill with tears, and his countenance so expressive of grief, though perfectly silent, that it would force us back to him, which would cause his little heart to be as joyful as it had been before sorrowful. He would be for hours on a mat by his papa's study table or by the side of his chair on the floor, if only he could see his face. When we had finished studying . . . it was our exercise and amusement to carry him around the house and garden and though we were alone, we felt not our solitude when he was with us.*

The Judsons' feelings of loneliness and isolation became much more bearable with the arrival of baby Roger. And Emily felt like a proud big sister and talked endlessly to Roger about all the things they would learn and do together.

For seven glorious months, the baby thrived. Then early in May 1816, they began to notice that he had periods of fever and heavy perspiring during the night. Both were alarmed, but by morning Roger would seem fine. He was steadily gaining weight, and that was a good sign. Then the fever became a pattern, always higher at night. One morning the baby began coughing, and this time the fever did not abate. With absolutely no medical help, Ann and Adoniram were frantic with worry. For two endless days they stayed by his side, their hearts torn with anguish and helplessness. The second night, exhaustion overcame Ann, and Adoniram took over Roger's care. Ann wrote in her journal about the agonizing experience of that night: *"The little creature drank his milk with much eagerness (he was weaned), and Mr. J thought he was refreshed and would go to sleep. He laid him in his cradle—he slept with ease for half an hour when his breathing stopped without a struggle, and he was gone."*

Little Roger Williams Judson, aged seven months and twenty-three days, was no more. The grieving parents hardly knew how to cope with such a devastating loss. The joy of their lives was suddenly extinguished. Emily often placed her hand into Ann's for mutual comfort during the sorrowing days following their tragedy, for she was deeply grieving as well. On May 7, Adoniram wrote:

> *Our little comfort, our dear little Roger, has become insensible to our parental attentions and fond caresses. . . . His sweet face has become cold to our lips and his little mind, which to a parent's discernment at least, discovered peculiar sensibility and peculiar sweetness of disposition, has deserted its infantile tenement and fled. Had I lost a wife, I might not thus lament for a little child eight months old. . . . Nothing but experience can teach us what feelings agonize the soul of a parent when he puts his face to that of his dear, his only child, to ascertain whether there may not be one breath more. . . . Our little Roger died last Saturday morning. We looked at him through the day and on the approach of night we laid him in the grave.*

Every afternoon Ann slipped down to the garden to Roger's grave, located in a quiet and secluded enclosure of mango trees. Many days she stood at the grave and sobbed as she bowed to the force of her grief, calling out to God for mercy and comfort. In the still of that night, she relied on the comforting arms of the Holy Spirit's presence to lull her to sleep and assure her of divine consolation. Yet sometimes the bereft mother and father would turn to each other without words and cling to the comfort of their mutual sorrow, both of them weeping as they prayed for strength and mercy.

Ann finally summoned the courage to take pen in hand and write Mama and Papa:

My dear Parents, little did I think when I wrote you last, that my next letter would be filled with the melancholy subject on which I must now write. Death, regardless of our lonely situation, has entered our dwelling . . . our little Roger Williams our only little darling boy, was three days ago laid in the silent grave. Eight months we enjoyed the precious little gift, in which time he had so completely entwined himself around his parents' hearts, that his existence seemed necessary to their own. . . . Thus died our little Roger . . . we buried him in the afternoon of the same day, in a little enclosure the other side of the garden."

A week later Ann managed to finish the letter, saying: "*We feel the anguish a little abated, and we have returned to our study and employment; but when for a moment we realize what we once possessed, and our now bereaved state, the wound opens and bleeds afresh.*"

A few days after Roger's death, the wife of the viceroy heard the mournful news and came at once to proffer condolences, bringing along some two hundred officers and attendants in her train. Just a few days later, the sympathetic vicereine came again to take her foreign friends on a trip to the countryside to "cool their minds," as she expressed it. Within the hour, a magnificent elephant with a *howdah* (a seat with a canopy) on his back appeared at the gate of the mission house to take them for the outing. The vicereine herself was atop another elephant, and the Judsons and Emily rode in the place of honor behind her. Ever in Ann's mind that day was the fond wish that she might be able to return the kindness by leading her to accept the greatest of all gifts—salvation. From that moment forward, Ann continually prayed for such an opportunity.

Young Emily marveled at the extraordinary picnic outing with the elephants, and many years later she regaled her own grandchildren with tales of the splendor of the day. She was a real comfort to Ann and Adoniram during the intense grief of that hot summer in

Rangoon. She picked up Burmese words and sentences with ease and was learning English rapidly under Ann's expert instruction.

Despite their hardships and sorrows, the Judsons never lost sight of their consuming goal and calling: sharing the Good News of salvation with the people of their adopted country who had never heard. Ann commented in a letter to her parents:

> *You doubtless are expecting to hear by this time of the Burmans inquiring what they shall do to be saved, and rejoicing that we have come to tell them how they may escape eternal misery. Alas, you know not the difficulty of communicating the least truth to the dark mind of a heathen, particularly those heathen who have a conceited notion of their own wisdom and knowledge, and the superior excellence of their own religious system. Sometimes when I have been conversing with some of the women, they have replied, "Your religion is good for you, ours for us."*

She wrote of one of the biggest hindrances to their acceptance of the truth of God's gift of Christ Jesus: *"Mr. J will be telling them of the atonement by Christ and they will reply that their minds are stiff."* It was a favorite saying of the Burmans, and how graphic a picture of reality it painted. Their minds *were* stiff and basically closed to truth. *"But,"* concluded, *"these things do not discourage us. We confidently believe that God in his own time will make his truth effectual unto salvation. We are endeavoring to convince the Burmans by our conduct, that our religion is different from theirs."*

Then, just when they felt their cup of sorrow was full to overflowing, more trouble appeared. Adoniram's health was deteriorating. His headaches were intense, and the pain in his eyes was constant. Ann could see his agony growing day by day, and she was alarmed. What was happening to her beloved?

150

Reinforcements 1816–1817

Picture of Sule Pagoda. Sule is 2,000 years old and stands just about one block from Rangoon's large Immanuel Baptist Church.

ANN WAS WORRIED. MR. J SEEMED to be having more and more headaches, often so severe that he could not see to read. Occasionally Ann would stop what she was doing and read aloud to him for a while so that he could rest his eyes while still managing to be productive.

His pain and her anxiety notwithstanding, July 13, 1816 was a day to be remembered. Exactly three years from the day they had sailed into Rangoon's harbor, Adoniram completed the first-ever Burmese grammar book, which he titled *Grammatical Notices of the Burman Language*. Little could he have imagined that two hundred years later it would still be in use. Just one week later, Adoniram painstakingly recorded in his journal, *"Completed Tract No. 1 in Burman, being a view of the Christian religion."* Now more than ever, the Judsons were excited about the eminent arrival of a printer.

But what should they do about the dreadful pain in Adoniram' eyes and head? Late one night, Ann talked with Adoniram about a plan of action. He needed help. "Mr. J," she asked quietly, "what on earth are we going to do?" Adoniram shook his head and winced at the pain he felt with that simple movement. "Dear Love," he paused before sighing, "I fear I may need to take a sea voyage to try to recover. As I am now, I feel useless." Ann suffered for his pain, and they prayed together for a long time, pleading with God to show them the right answer.

About this time, however, one of their friends and favorite sea captains, Captain Kidd (no relation to the infamous pirate of the same name!), arrived in Rangoon and stayed with them for a few days. God used this kindly man to provide some hope that Adoniram could leave on his ship when it sailed to Calcutta in a week or so. However, just three days later an exciting message arrived: George Hough, the missionary printer, and his family, who had been newly appointed by the Baptist board in America, were already in Calcutta and preparing to come to Rangoon. Furthermore, the amazing Serampore Three (Carey, Marshman, and Ward), who had been friends to the Judsons in those early years of great uncertainty, were sending along a printing press and type. Adoniram decided that he *couldn't* leave Burma at such a strategic time.

Captain Kidd then presented an alternative plan. He was a great believer in exercise, and his own healthy body gave evidence that he practiced what he preached. Kidd suggested horseback riding. Ann immediately picked up on the idea, although Mr. J was dubious as to how much it would help. The first few days, Adoniram found the movements of the gentle old horse jarring and painful, but as he persisted, the headaches lessened and the intense pain around his eyes abated. Within a week, Judson's improvement was noticeable, and before the month was over, he was back at his intensive study and translation work, although careful to allow some time every day for exercise. He and his horse became a common sight riding around the outskirts of Rangoon.

October 15, 1816, was another red-letter day for Ann and Adoniram, for they had the great joy of standing on the wharf at Rangoon Harbor and welcoming the first reinforcements to the mission, George and Phebe Hough and their two children. The Judsons happily moved the Houghs into their commodious mission house.

Together the Houghs and the Judsons prepared and endorsed a document outlining their ideas for translation and printing, covenanting to work as a team toward their mutual missions goal. Just having fellow believers actually on Burmese soil was healing medicine to the hearts of the Judsons, deprived for three years now of Christian fellowship. Phebe immediately began to learn how to run a Burmese home and free up more of Ann's time for study, translation, and teaching. And for her part, eight-year-old Emily was thrilled to have two other children with whom to study and play.

George Hough eagerly began typesetting and printing the material that Ann and Adoniram had so brilliantly prepared. He could not speak, read, or understand Burmese, but he was an excellent printer who knew his trade well, and to this work God had called him. Hough's first item off the new printing press was Adoniram's seven-page tract. It included the story of Adam and Eve and the Ten Commandments—and was written in flawless Burmese.

Next, George set the print for Ann's catechism, which he did by matching the sausage-like strings of circles in type, although their meaning he did not begin to understand. The booklet, which outlined the distinctive tenets of the Christian faith, was titled simply *Mrs. Judson's Catechism.* Upon the completion of this material, Hough began at once to work on Adoniram's translation of the Gospel of Matthew. Judson found himself wishing that he could translate as rapidly as Hough could print.

Meantime, Ann was assuaging her grief over the loss of their precious Roger by immersing herself in work. Thanks to Phebe, she had more time to follow her calling and use her talents. She quickly organized a small school for Burman girls. Boys could easily be educated in Burma, usually by Buddhist monks, but not girls. Ann was at home in a schoolroom, absolutely in her element. Adoniram rejoiced to see the frequent smile on her face these days, despite those vulnerable moments when he would see unguarded pain cross her lovely countenance. Such fleeting looks were usually followed by a sigh of resolution and a straightening of her shoulders, and then she would decisively return to the task at hand.

In no time, Ann had thirty pupils, and their mothers would often sit in the classroom and learn as well. With a brand-new catechism now in print, she not only taught her pupils the Good News, but she also seized the opportunity of getting to know more Burman women and telling them the precious truths of God's Word. Within weeks, several of the children had memorized the catechism.

In her spare time, of which there was little, Ann managed to translate the Book of Jonah. Sometimes she smiled to herself, thinking that surely folks would wonder why on earth she would choose that Old Testament book. However, she was a New Englander born and bred, and she had grown up around stories of the sea and great whaling ships. When Adoniram inquired about her choice of this particular Scripture, she smiled and raised her eyebrows a bit, responding, "Mr. J, it is actually one of the easiest books to translate, and not long at all." Then she added, "It rather makes me feel like I am accomplishing something of worth." Judson gazed deeply into her lovely eyes and assured her, "Dear Love, you are an amazing woman, and I never pass a day without thanking God for the gift of you as my helpmeet. You are surely God's special gift to me. Was ever a man so blessed?"

George Hough had already printed a thousand copies of Judson's introduction to Christianity and three thousand of Ann's catechism. While the two scholars continued translating as rapidly as they could, George began preparing the printing machine for Adoniram's next project. On May 20, 1817, Adoniram had the satisfaction of recording in his journal, *"Completed a Burman translation of the Gospel of Matthew."*

During these exciting days, a few Burmans began to request copies of the "holy books," as they called the tracts. Many Burmans loved to read, and this was new material. Both the Judsons were highly motivated in their zeal to accomplish their goal of reaching the hearts of their adopted people and were ever ready to use their time as wisely as possible. Even though his eyes still bothered him a bit, Adoniram began the arduous task of working on a Burmese-English dictionary. Ever a visionary, he realized how vital such a dictionary would be as a tool in the hands of future missionaries. The task was monumental, but determination and discipline were traits he and Ann had in abundance. Even the heartbreak of having been in the country for nearly four years and not yet seeing a single convert did not prevent them from doggedly working and looking with eyes of faith to the day they would see fruit.

Then one night a well-dressed Burman gentleman, accompanied by his servant, arrived at the mission house and promptly seated himself on the mat beside Adoniram. By way of greeting, he asked, "How long will it take me to learn the religion of Jesus?" Judson was astounded. This was the first true seeker in these many long months! Thoughtfully, he replied, "Such a question cannot be answered easily. If God gives wisdom and light, the religion of Jesus is soon learned. Without that help, a man may study as long as he lives and make no progress."

Then Adoniram asked if the man had seen any writing concerning Jesus, and his visitor answered, "He is the Son of God, who, pitying human creatures, came into this world and suffered death in their stead." Judson was stunned. These were the very words he had written in his tract explaining Christianity. When he offered his guest a copy of his tract and Ann's catechism, the man, whose name was Maung Yah, exclaimed, "I've seen them before!" His face alight with excitement, he turned to his servant and declared, "This is the true God, the right way." Judson felt such joy to discover an inquiring heart that his eyes welled with tears. Before Maung Yah left that night, Adoniram was able to present him with the first five printed chapters of Matthew. For Ann and Adoniram, the visit itself was a gift, a reassurance that their work was not in vain and was indeed going to bear fruit.

By this time, with the exception of her footwear, Ann had adopted Burmese-style clothing. Sweltering climate notwithstanding, she remained determined to wear her New England half-boots, somehow not quite able to bring herself to put on open sandals as did Burman women. By the standards of nineteenth-century New England, Burmese dress would seem somewhat immodest, but on Ann it looked beautiful. With her tall and regal bearing, the blouse, called an *aingyi*, fit well with her *lungyi*, a long skirt made of brilliant flowered silk, with yards of fabric tied in a knot at her waist. The Burman women loved seeing her in their garb and felt a new sense of identity with the "beautiful foreign lady," as they called her. They considered it a compliment that "the teacher's wife" wore the same type of clothing as they. In contrast, Adoniram stuck with his unvarying black suits, despite the humid climate, but he too was happy to see Ann in Burmese dress.

Not only had Ann started a school; she also began holding Sunday meetings with the women. Her new friends always listened attentively but would usually remind her at the end of their sessions that they had no wish to give up their Buddhist beliefs. One morning a faithful attendee confessed that she would rather spend eternity in hell with her own ancestors and family than go to heaven with a lot of strangers!

Both Ann and Adoniram frequently wrote to family, as well as to friends and churches in America, asking for their prayers and explaining their situation in Burma. Judson told people at home not to get discouraged because they were not yet seeing any fruit, reminding supporters about how slow the beginnings had been in India as well. To friends in America, he wrote, *"If any ask what success I meet with among the natives, tell them, as much as that there is an Almighty and faithful God and he will perform his promises . . . beg them to let me stay and make the attempt and if we live some twenty or thirty years, they may hear from us again."* Adoniram concluded his plea for patience by stating that if he and Ann were to desert this field, the blood of the Burmans would be on their hands, so deadly serious were they about their call.

Ann wrote to Mary, a friend back in Massachusetts, telling of the depth of their concern: *"O my dear Mary, if we were convinced of the importance of missions before we left our native country, we now see and feel their importance.*" She continued by explaining to Mary about Buddhist beliefs: "*Their system of religion has no power over the heart. . . . It is like an alabaster image, perfect and beautiful in all its parts, but destitute of life.*"

In August 1817, Adoniram wrote a letter on the subject of baptism to his former church in Plymouth, the church where his venerable father was still pastor. His letter even had a title: "A Letter to the 3rd Church in Plymouth Mass." Much to his amazement, a number of months later Adoniram the son received the news that Adoniram the father had been immersed, become a Baptist, and resigned his Congregational pastorate, all this following the letter his son had written about baptism. When the news reached Rangoon about his father's decision, Judson dissolved in tears at the workings of Providence in his own family. After reading the letter, he found Ann and handed it to her without a word. Alarmed at the strange look on his face, she quickly read the letter and began weeping herself. Her tears, like his, were tears of joy.

Shortly before Christmas that year, Ann and Adoniram sat down to plan a definitive strategy for presenting the gospel to the people. Things were coming together to the point that Adoniram was eager to begin. The Burmese language had become so familiar to him by this time that he was ready to give preaching a try. He and Ann deliberated over various possibilities for introducing the gospel message. Adoniram's idea was that if even one Burman Christian could stand with him and explain in his native tongue to his fellow Burmans the wonder of God's love, it would be far more powerful. For Adoniram as well as Ann, when an idea became firmly set in their minds, there would be no stopping their attempts to carry it out.

Judson had learned that in the port city of Chittagong, India, lived several converts who had been won to Christ through an English mission group that had worked there years before. One or two of these Indian believers could speak Burmese. Judson's plan was to make the twelve-day sea voyage to Chittagong and persuade one of the converts to return with him. He finally located a ship called *Two Brothers* sailing to Chittagong, and on Christmas Eve 1817, Adoniram would set out with high hopes for the beginning of a spoken ministry to the beloved people of Burma.

Ann was dreading Christmas without her Mr. J but excited to think about the possibilities ahead for their work. Furthermore, she was pleased that he would be going to sea, which surely would help mend his tired body as well. The horseback riding and exercise had helped for a time, but for most of the past two years, Adoniram had continued to suffer acute pain due to the close study of the intricate and puzzling Burmese characters. The result of this intense, unremitting devotion to the task was severe eyestrain. Christmas Eve arrived, and with expectations high, the Judsons prayed quietly in their room before he left for the ship. They kissed each other good-bye, expecting this to be a short journey of recruitment and recuperation.

Neither one of them could have imagined the trail of disasters that lay ahead, not just at sea or in India, but also right there in Rangoon. *How could this happen?* Ann would ask herself many times in the weeks and months to follow.

Seven Months of Suspense 1818

CATECHISM AND VIEW.

Ann Judson's catechism was the first such translation into Burmese.

AS ANN WATCHED THE Chittagong-bound *Two Brothers* sail off into the Bay of Bengal, she was confident that in or a matter of weeks, two months at most, Mr. J would be sailing back into harbor, accompanied this time by a Burmese believer. She determined to handle their separation with as much grace as she could, meanwhile giving thanks for the company of the Houghs. Their presence meant she was not alone in the mission, as Adoniram had been when she had gone to India for medical help. After returning to the mission house that evening, Ann wrote to her good friend in Boston, *"Pray much for us, Mary, for we know not the trials and distresses that await us."* These would prove to be prophetic words indeed.

For several weeks, life progressed on an even keel, and Ann was thankful for each busy moment of the day that prevented her from fretting over the absence of Mr. J. The two of them had been so completely dependent on each other for these five lonely years that this separation was a wrench to her heart, especially in moments when she had time to dwell on her solitude. Ann's heart was lifted, however, the day their first inquirer, Maung Yah, returned to the mission house, apologizing for his long absence. He had been made governor in the Pegu country east of Rangoon and had not had a chance to return. Now he wanted more books.

Ann was thrilled with his interest and courteously asked, "Are you to the place of being ready to become a Christian?" Maung Yah responded, "Not yet, but I am thinking deeply and reading so that I may become one. But I cannot destroy my old mind." Maung Yah then entreated, "*Mah Yoodthan* [*Yoodthan* is the Burmese pronunciation of the name Judson], tell the great teacher when he returns that I wish to see him." Ann was moved by his sincerity and decided to give him the rest of Adoniram's translation of Matthew. The stately Maung Yah was delighted and assured Mrs. Teacher that now that he was governor in Pegu, he wanted the teacher to come and preach to the people there. After he bowed himself out, Ann slipped to her room to fall on her knees and thank God for the listening heart of this learned Burman man.

Changes came quickly in Rangoon that first month of Adoniram's absence. The elderly viceroy had been ordered back to Ava, and the former viceroy was now back in his old position. However, his vice-reine had not yet returned, so if Ann needed help from the authorities, she was going to face a problem. By Burmese custom, a woman could never approach a government official directly, and Ann was feeling quite vulnerable with Mr. J gone. What if there were an emergency requiring special favors during these weeks? The account of Queen Esther lodged in her mind, and she began recalling the ways God had blessed Esther in trying circumstances.

About two weeks later, a small ship arrived from Chittagong bringing unsettling news. The *Two Brothers* had never reached that city. Ann felt a chill run down her back. She realized that ships were often blown off course, but this was disturbing news indeed. *Where on earth could her beloved be?* Visions of all sorts of disasters ran through her mind. Clearly, Adoniram would have no way of getting a message to her. Could his ship have been lost at sea? Ann refused to believe such a disastrous possibility.

Then, as if to compound her worries, George Hough was ordered to appear at the courthouse. His lack of language skills was an obstacle in such circumstances, and even with an interpreter, Hough was thoroughly unsettled by the summons. He was a gentle man and a skilled printer but not a man with the gift of leadership or eloquence. Court officials were trying to intimidate the newcomer, hinting that if he did not tell them everything about his work in Burma, they would "write with his heart's blood." Ann strongly suspected that this had nothing to do with orders from higher officials but came instead from underlings seeking to exploit political gain through a vulnerable foreigner. For two more nerve-wracking days, George was detained at the courthouse and ceaselessly questioned. Ann was fully aware that he did not have a clue about the intricacies of Burmese culture. Something must be done. Never one to lack courage, Ann took an unheard-of step for a woman: she approached the great viceroy on her own.

Ann and her teacher carefully wrote a petition, outlining Hough's dilemma for the viceroy, and off she headed for the official residence. In the midst of the viceroy's morning court, he looked up and caught sight of Ann. She immediately held up the petition and looked straight at him. The viceroy in turn asked a clerk standing nearby to read Mrs. Yoodthan's petition aloud. And that was the end of that; the governor at once commanded that there be no more harassment for "Mrs. Teacher" and her group. Hough was promptly released, and the beleaguered missionaries heaved a collective sigh of relief.

But pervasive danger was lurking on another front. In the midst of Ann's constant anxiety over Adoniram's fate, a virulent plague descended on Rangoon. Burma had never before faced cholera, one of the scourges of India, but now, without warning, Rangoon was hit with the deadly disease. The population went into a panic. People were dying all around them, hundreds a day. Moreover, it was the hottest season of the year, which made the disease spread all the more rapidly; a person might be perfectly well in the morning and dead by night. Day after day, night after endless night, the death drums beat, incessant reminders of the specter of eternity. To make matters worse, the drumming noise was magnified by the mad din set up each night by the populace of Rangoon, who believed that by making loud noises, they could expel the evil spirits that were striking down men, women, and children indiscriminately. Yet, while all around the mission house people were dying, cholera did not touch one person in the missionaries' home. Ann took courage anew each morning.

Not as easy to put from her mind was the constant fear of what could have happened to her beloved. No definitive news was coming from any ship entering harbor, and Ann could only imagine the worst while praying for the best. Where in this vast part of the world might Mr. J be? What could have happened to his ship?

As if this were not enough over which to fret, rumors of war were growing daily. England was said to be at enmity with Burma and on the verge of bombarding the capital. Could this be the explanation for no ships from English ports arriving? And might this be the reason that few vessels of any kind were in the harbor?

George Hough was also living in fear, having been thoroughly intimidated by his experience at the local court. Amid the churning rumors, he was convinced it was time to leave Burma. With each passing day, he grew more frightened, and each morning he went to the harbor, trying to find a ship on which to leave for India and relative safety. He insisted that Ann and Emily also leave, declaring that a lone woman and child (for Emily was not yet eleven years old) should not remain.

Ann was in a quandary. Already stretched to the limit by concern for Adoniram, she now faced a dreadful predicament. Was Mr. J alive? Sick? Dead? If he were in India, maybe she could find him there. On the other hand, he might come back and find her gone and the mission deserted. Then what?

The Houghs were begging her to leave, so with the greatest reluctance, she packed some bags. Taking Emily by the hand, and with a

162

heart heavier than the luggage she brought aboard the ship, Ann climbed the gangplank to board the vessel. Then circumstance intervened. Shortly after the ship set sail, it had to lay anchor, delayed because of a leak. There was no choice but to wait for repairs. This was enough of a sign for Ann Judson. Immediately she ordered her bags ashore and returned to the desolate mission house with Emily. The Burman friends and servants who had remained in the mission house were overjoyed to see their beloved "Mrs. Yoodthan" back. Despite war, rumors of war, pestilence, or death, Ann Judson was back to stay. She wrote to family at home, *I know I am surrounded by dangers on every hand and expect to see much distress; but at present I am tranquil and intend to leave the event with God.*

Adoniram had now been gone seven months, but Ann still refused to believe he was lost to her. He must come back. And she would be waiting when he did.

She could never have envisioned what had actually befallen her precious husband. Winds had been totally unpredictable and contrary, and his ship was not only blown off course but became completely unmanageable. For an entire month it drifted helplessly at sea. Since the ship was unable to reach Chittagong, the captain headed instead for Madras. That too proved impossible for the crippled vessel, and they limped toward the closest Indian port of Masulipatam.

To exacerbate the whole situation, hardly had *Two Brothers* set sail than the pain that had plagued Adoniram off and on for years had returned with a vengeance, forcing him to stay in his bunk. As if that weren't enough, Adoniram came down with a raging fever and was in dire straits. Filthy, starving, and lying half dead in his hard bunk, he was on the edge of complete despair. After twelve unbelievable weeks adrift at sea, the disabled ship finally tottered into port at Masulipatam.

Adoniram summoned all his remaining strength and managed to pencil a note addressed to *any English resident,* pleading for *a place to die on land,* and gave it to a steward who promised to send it ashore. Later that morning, Judson managed to crawl to the porthole and saw a small boat on its way toward their ship. He saw aboard the red coats of British solders and the white coats of other Englishmen. They appeared to him as angels, and he collapsed on the floor sobbing, tears streaming down his unshaven cheeks. The Englishmen who entered the cabin were shocked to find a filthy, unshaven scarecrow of a man, so weak they had to carry him ashore.

Meanwhile Ann waited and prayed, with no way of knowing where her beloved might be, how he was, or even if he was still alive. Throughout each and every day she prayed for Mr. J's safety wherever he might be, for his speedy return, and that her faith would not falter. Over and over in her mind echoed the words of Romans 12:1: "Present your bodies a living sacrifice, holy, acceptable unto God." She cried out for mercy and implored that the Lord would accept their sacrifice. Again and again she prayed, until it became something of a litany, "O God, give me courage, give me courage." One long day followed another, but never did she lose all hope.

Ann's determination in the face of deadly peril was more vital than she possibly knew. Her decision to stay in Rangoon likely saved the mission and made possible the great future of Judson's work for the many years to come.

Even as Ann was attempting to remain positive in the face of possible disaster, Adoniram was recovering enough strength to begin making plans to somehow get home to his dear Ann and to his mission. No ships were headed that direction from Masulipatam, however, and he was forced to travel three hundred miles by land to Madras, finally arriving there April 8, 1818. Crushing disappointment awaited him: it would be several months more before a ship was leaving for Rangoon. Adoniram could do nothing but try to be patient, something that was always in short supply for the headstrong and determined Judson. Furthermore, there was no way to get word to his beloved; God grant that she be able to rest her heart and trust Providence. So must he; there was no choice.

Meanwhile in Rangoon, just two days after Ann and Emily had returned to the mission house, a long-lost vessel sailed into harbor. It was the *Two Brothers*, the very ship on which Mr. J had sailed six months before. Ann rushed to the harbor and learned from the captain what had happened to the ship, discovering that Adoniram had been forced by his precarious health to leave the ship and head to Madras, trying to recover sufficiently to get back home. Ann's heart sprang with joy at the news that he was still alive. *Alive.* The beautiful word echoed in her mind, and tears streamed down her cheeks. God had spared his life.

A few days later, she had another surprise when the Houghs returned to the mission house. The ship on which they had been to sail for India had been detained in port for weeks. Happy to have the Houghs back, Ann resumed her schedule as normally as she could without Mr. J. She wrote to family of the need to continue her daily program of study and translation: *"This, I find the best method to avoid dejection; besides, my conscience will not permit me to sit idly down and yield to those desponding feelings in which a Christian should not indulge."* Nonetheless, Ann would often weep herself to sleep, agonizing far into the wee hours of night over the predicament that must have engulfed her Mr. J. Each morning brought a new sense of hope, only to be followed by another night of grieving and conjecturing.

Wonder of wonders, the morning of August 4 dawned bright and hot, and joy followed the months of anxious sorrow. An English vessel had arrived in harbor, and yes, Teacher Yoodthan was on board. The news after seven months fraught with peril was nearly too much for even the amazing fortitude of Ann Judson.

Donning her brightest silk and with pounding heart, Ann hurried to the harbor, and there on the deck was Mr. J! Ann and Adoniram held on to each other as if they could not bear to let go ever again. They rejoiced that God had spared his life; God had spared the mission; and surely God would make a breakthrough in hearts in their beloved Burma.

Both Judsons wrote to family and friends in the United States, updating them on their dramatic year. Both were deeply aware of their dependence on prayer. Adoniram wrote to Luther Rice and others, *"We desire, humbly, to repeat to the Board, what the first missionaries from the Baptist society in England said to their friends. We are like men going down into a well; you stand at the top and hold the ropes. Do not let us fall."*

In a letter to a Mrs. Carleton in Boston, Ann beseeched, *"Pray much for me, my dear Mrs. C., O pray that I may be faithful unto death. I have many trials of a spiritual nature. O could you see my heart, my little devotedness to that dear Redeemer, you would feel that I was very unworthy of the high privilege of living among the heathen."*

Meanwhile, Ann continued studying and teaching, while also learning Siamese and somehow finding time to translate her catechism, Adoniram's tract, and the Gospel of Matthew into that new language. Those were the first portions of God's Word and truths ever translated into the language of the millions of people of Siam, a sizable number of whom lived in Burma.

The Houghs were never quite able to cope with the conditions and trials of life in Rangoon and set sail again for India, where George planned to continue printing portions of Scripture as the Judsons were able to translate them. Reinforcements were already on the way, and on September 19 the Judsons joyfully welcomed two young couples, James and Elizabeth Colman and Edward and Eliza Wheelock, quickly making room in the mission house for each couple to have their own room and a measure of privacy.

However, a major problem was instantly apparent. Edward Wheelock and James Colman, both young and inexperienced, were full of courage and zeal but neither possessed good health. They had scarcely settled in when both began spitting up blood, a symptom of tuberculosis, with Wheelock appearing to have an advanced case. Ann and Adoniram tried to make the anxious new arrivals as comfortable as possible, but there was no medical help or medicine to counteract the deadly effects of the disease that was wasting their bodies.

Gentle and gracious Elizabeth Colman immediately pitched in to help Ann in any way she could with the household. It was a different story with Eliza Wheelock. Eliza was a new bride, just twenty years old; she had sailed with lofty ideals and dreams of the glory of being a pioneer missionary. Reality was a far cry from glory. Her husband was pale, weak, and apparently dying before her eyes. Everyone else tried to help the failing Edward, but Eliza angrily refused the assistance. She would not even let the others into their room to talk with him. Unable to face the inevitable, Eliza became obsessed with taking her husband back to Calcutta, although poor Edward had developed a morbid fear of traveling on a ship after their nightmarish voyage out. Eliza insisted that they leave, however, and the Judsons sadly made the necessary arrangements.

To make a troubled situation even worse, Eliza was painfully jealous of Ann—the older, more mature and seasoned missionary. Everyone deferred to Mrs. Judson, but Eliza felt the attention should be hers and made no bones about her disdain for Ann, who herself was only twenty-nine years old, although she often felt twice that age as so much had occurred in the past five years. She was acutely aware of the vicious looks and cutting remarks young Eliza made about her at frequent intervals throughout each day. Ann, usually not loath to express her opinion and let problems see the clear light of reasoning, judiciously held her tongue and sought to give no offense. Sometimes Adoniram would start up at some cutting remark Eliza would make to his dear love, preparing to come to her defense. Ann would look into his eyes and place a quieting touch on his arm. Words would not help this situation. Sometimes as she tried to make excuses in her mind for Eliza's deliberate rudeness and spiteful behavior, the thought would come to mind: *But our precious Harriet was even younger, and she never displayed any spirit but one of love and gentle caring.*

As the Judsons and Colemans saw the Wheelocks off to Calcutta, they despaired of the difficult situation and of ever seeing Edward alive again. Instead of dying of tuberculosis, Edward Wheelock fell

167

overboard in the midst of high winds just thirteen days out to sea, and a rescue could not even be attempted. The Judsons and Colmans were horrified when the news reached them. (The widowed Eliza did reach Calcutta but never returned to the mission; she soon married again, an English businessman in that city.)

The good news was that James Colman's health was beginning to improve, and he and Elizabeth eagerly began studying the Burmese language. The young couple were a welcome balm and genuine encouragement to Ann and Adoniram after their unfortunate experience with the Wheelocks. James and Elizabeth, with their loving attitude and willing spirits, seemed to be a godsend to the two veteran missionaries.

Long before Ann and Adoniram had reached the shores of Burma, they understood that the Bible in the heart language of the people would be essential for a lasting ministry. Without God's Word, hearts could not be reached, and their translation work was well under way. But ever in Adoniram's heart and mind was the longing to preach, which was his first love. The years of painstaking preparation were for the most part behind them, and now the "real" labor of sharing the gospel could begin at long last. The question facing them now was how to do this "real" work. They had no pattern to follow; they would have to be the ones to establish the mold. Neither Judson had ever shied away from a challenge, and they weren't about to begin now.

The Harvest Begins 1818–1819

Maung Nau, baptized in 1819, was the first Burman convert to Christianity.

FROM THE MOMENT THEY ARRIVED in their adopted country, Ann and Adoniram determined to adjust to the culture in every way possible, feeling this must surely be the best way to reach Burmans and speak to their hearts. If they could somehow proclaim Christ in a "Burmese way," that was exactly what they wanted to do. Late into the night they would talk over various ways and means, and then decide on which idea might work. Studying both the culture and religion, the Judsons became aware of the way a Buddhist *zayat* (zee-yaht) functioned as a place of worship and learning. Zayats were small, wooden wayside structures where pilgrims stopped to listen to the monks or simply rest. Consequently, the Judsons decided to build a zayat and use it to share the Good News with all who stopped there.

One night as they began finalizing plans, Adoniram suggested they buy a small piece of property adjoining their mission. This site faced onto the public road leading to the great Shwedagon Pagoda, so hundreds of people walked past the choice spot every day. What better location to be visible and share the message of hope?

"Just think, Mr. J," Ann reminisced, "it has been more than seven years since we sailed from Salem. It almost seems like forever. But then," she concluded, "there's no time like the present to make a start." Adoniram looked uncharacteristically dubious when he responded, "I wonder, my love, if my voice still knows how to expound on the Scriptures? It has been silent so long." But Ann was all confidence. "Mr. J, you have just been saving that powerful voice for such a time as this. Let's get our zayat built. You'll see," she assured him. "I'm convinced your silent voice will assuredly wake up."

A sense of excitement coursed through the tiny mission group as the new wooden structure began to take shape. It was a simple affair and did not take long to construct, being about thirty feet long, twenty feet wide, and sitting on four-foot-tall stilts. Across the front was a porch where Adoniram would sit and preach. Behind the porch was an enclosed room for public worship. Behind this was a room that opened into the mission garden, where Ann planned to teach women and children.

April 4, 1819, was a day they would not forget. Burma's first-ever Christian worship service was held in a Burmese-style zayat, and the message of salvation publicly proclaimed. The inaugural worship included some fifteen adults and an assortment of children, plus a lot of disorder, inattention, and noise. This type of worship was entirely unknown to the people of Rangoon, and something so foreign to their experience would take some getting used to. Later in the week, Ann and Mr. J decided to visit a popular Buddhist zayat nearby in order to observe their style of service and learn some cultural niceties. When they first entered the enclosure, a Burman woman commented in a loud whisper, "It's those wild foreigners." Her companion corrected her, saying, "Oh no, just look. They are removing their shoes like civilized people do."

Gaining insight from their personal visit to a Buddhist service, Ann and Adoniram incorporated some new ideas into their zayat meeting on the following Sunday. This time more people were in attendance, and they managed to have an orderly service. Adoniram began by telling the story of redemption in very basic terms, realizing that Burmans had no concept of a living God who was actively concerned for them. The listeners were intrigued by the strange story told by the foreigner with the deep voice who spoke in clear and educated Burmese. Every Burman loved a good story, and they listened with keen interest. As the missionaries walked back to the house following the gathering, Ann's eyes sparkled as she grasped his arm and smiled with satisfaction. "Mr. J," she told him, "your silent voice has wakened and is quiet no longer!"

During the subsequent weeks, the two of them spent long hours in the zayat, conversing with all who called: Mr. J with the men, Ann with the women. Ann met with several women every Wednesday evening as well. She often used her blackboard when instructing both women and children. It was an exciting and optimistic time, as the couple finally felt like they were doing what God had called them to do. Both Judsons had a new spring in their steps.

After observing the forms and customs common in Buddhist zayats, the Judsons began to implement some of the ideas that had occurred to them. At Ann's suggestion, Adoniram decided to employ the compelling voice with which he had been blessed to attract passersby. Most days he would begin the hours in the zayat by calling out: *Oh yay gnat thaw thu ah boung doke, yay sheet tar those lag kyat law* ("Ho, every one that thirsteth, come ye to the waters"). These words of Isaiah 55:1 had always been a favorite of his, and what better way to introduce the reality of eternal life? The Judsons also provided fresh water for weary pilgrims passing on the road, making the meaning of the passage more tangible by presenting Jesus as the water of life. It was a fulfilling experience to finally be able to share the story of God's love in the heart language of the Burmans.

Ann had discovered that when a packet of mail from America arrived, it was always a mixed blessing: there was the thrill of news from dear ones, making them seem a bit closer, but it somehow seemed to exacerbate their isolation and aching loneliness. She often wrote back as promptly as possible. On the next to last day of April, a tired but happy Ann sat down to write home. She sometimes wrote all the family together, though often addressed one member or the other, knowing all would share in the news. Mary (Polly) was the recipient this particular evening:

> *"Though it is seven long years since I left my native land and scenes of my earliest years, they are as fresh in my recollection as though it were but yesterday; and the wound then inflicted every now and then opens and bleeds afresh. I believe very few females who have left their native country have had it in their power to make such sacrifices as myself."*

Ann wiped a truant tear from her face and wondered anew if she was *truly* being the kind of sacrifice that pleased her Savior. Fully opening her heart to Mary, Ann confided:

> *When I think of my pleasant home and dear Bradford friends, the sources of enjoyment which I left, I am often led to wonder how I was ever made willing to forsake them. But, my dear sister Mary, a little sacrifice for the cause of Christ is not worth naming; and I feel it a privilege, of which I am entirely undeserving, to have had it in my power to sacrifice my all for him who hesitated not to lay down his life for sinners.*

Readily acknowledging her own unworthiness to represent Christ, she further lamented, *"Mary, I do at times feel almost ready to sink down in despair, when I realize the responsibility of my situation and witness my short-comings in duty."* Ann explained how, as she grew in grace, she became even more aware of what she called *"my unspeakably wicked heart."*

And yet the very next day, a breakthrough in their seven years of service occurred. It became known as a "gold star" on the chart of Christianity in Burma. This was the day when the first serious inquirer came to the zayat, the one who blazed the trail for millions who followed in the years and centuries to follow. Maung Nau was a quiet and reserved young man. ("Maung" is a courtesy title used for young man, "U" for older men.) What was noteworthy about the thirty-five-year-old inquirer was that he was actively seeking hope. That first day he just listened, sitting very still but with keen focus. The next day he returned. Adoniram felt a rising sense of excitement. Obviously, the Lord had touched this seeker's heart. This second day, Maung Nau asked a few simple questions. He was a man looking for an answer, not an argument.

Adoniram was excited later that evening as he told Ann about his hours with Maung Nau. "Dear love," he eagerly recounted, "here is a teachable and humble spirit. It may well be," and he took a deep breath before continuing, "that the grace of God has reached his heart." The two stopped right there and prayed together for wisdom, even as hope and encouragement filled their hearts. Later in the week, Adoniram wrote in his journal, *It seems almost too much to believe that God has begun to manifest his grace to the Burmans; but this day I could not resist the delightful conviction that this is really the case. PRAISE AND GLORY BE TO HIS NAME FOREVER-MORE.* For many long years, the Judsons had been pursuing this moment and could scarcely allow themselves to believe what was happening. That very next Sunday morning, Maung Nau openly professed his belief in Christ. Pure joy overflowed in the long-suffering missionaries' hearts!

Maung Nau was hired by a timber seller and needed to leave on a trip. Just three days later, however, he came back to the zayat to report that he had discovered the seller was not to be trusted. He did not want to go, and certainly the missionaries hoped he wouldn't have to leave at this critical juncture in his spiritual growth. Judson solved the problem by giving Maung Nau a job copying pamphlets. The job was a double blessing for this new believer, for not only would he have employment, but he would also become grounded in Scripture as he painstakingly copied passages by hand.

A little more than a month after his first appearance at the zayat, Maung Nau quietly handed Judson a letter. For the benefit of the

Colmans, who were just learning the language, Adoniram translated Nau's letter:

> *I, Maung Nau, the constant recipient of your excellent favor, approach your feet. Whereas my Lord's three have come to the country of Burmah, not for the purpose of trade, but to preach the religion of Jesus Christ, the Son of the eternal God. I having heard and understood, am, with a joyful mind, filled with love. . . . I believe that the divine Son, Jesus Christ, suffered death, in the place of men, to atone for their sins. Like a heavy-laden man, I feel my sins are very many. The punishment of my sins I deserve to suffer. Since it is so, do you, sirs, consider that I, taking refuge in the merits of the Lord Jesus Christ, and receiving baptism, in order to become His disciple, shall dwell one with yourselves, a band of brothers, and therefore grant me the ordinance of baptism.*

It was a holy moment for the missionaries who had struggled so long and so hard for just such a moment. But before they could make plans to grant his request, political upheaval appeared on the horizon and spread throughout the nation. Ominous news had come from Ava: the emperor of Burma, the Golden One, was dead. His grandson Bagyidaw, the heir apparent, was now seated on the throne. The official edict read, "The monarch enjoins on all to remain quiet and wait his imperial orders." It further declared, "It appears that the prince of Toung Oo, one of his uncles, has been executed, with his family and adherents, and the prince of Pyee placed in confinement." With the new emperor eliminating all relatives who might threaten his claim to the throne, the entire nation was uneasy.

The little mission band decided to let the political climate cool a bit before proceeding. A month later the momentous Sunday arrived: the occasion of the first baptism in Burma. That morning a calm but elated Maung Nau stood before the group of worshipers and answered Mr. Yoodthan's questions about his "faith, hope, and love." Then everyone walked about half a mile to a nearby pond. While a crowd of curious Burmans watched from a hill close by, Adoniram led Maung Nau into the water and, as Ann wrote later to the Baptists of America, *"We administered the ordinance of Christian baptism to the first Burman convert."*

On the heels of this joy, a week later the Judsons wrote home about another high moment: *"We have had the pleasure of sitting down, for the first time, with a converted Burman, to administer the Lord's Supper in two languages."* The harvest was finally beginning, and even Ann and Adoniram, at their most optimistic, could not have envisioned what God would do in their beloved Burma in the years and even centuries to follow.

The mission house had a new sense of life and purpose about it now. The Colmans were hard at work on the language, and James was slowly regaining strength as his lungs showed improvement from his bout with tuberculosis. Elizabeth looked up to Ann as a beloved older sister and was quickly acquiring language skills in addition to learning the Burmese housekeeping style. After the painful experience with Eliza Wheelock, Elizabeth's presence was pure balm to Ann.

Maung Nau infused the small mission with fresh enthusiasm and zeal. There was a difference as well in those coming by the zayat every day now. These weren't just curious visitors wanting a look at the strange foreigners but inquirers genuinely interested in finding hope for their hearts. The local custom was to set up a house wherever one pleased and stay awhile. Several Burman inquirers, accordingly, built little bamboo huts in unused parts of the mission garden and stayed to learn from the Judsons.

Maung Thalah was one of these, along with his sister, Mah Baik, and her husband. Maung Thalah eagerly listened and quickly learned, and Ann spent a portion of each day teaching Mah Baik, who was clearly interested in understanding the message of a true and loving God. Ann often reminded herself that the very concept of a God who was concerned with mere human beings, and with each person individually, was far removed from any thinking found in the

Burman culture. Mah Baik had another big hindrance to her under-standing, for she was addicted, not to any substance found in a bot-tle or a pipe, but to quarreling. This was a challenge indeed for Ann, for Mah Baik's favorite activity was arguing about anything and everything. It didn't take much to send her into a rage, which Ann observed that Mah Baik seemed to thoroughly enjoy.

During the long summer days, a young fisherman who was a friend of Maung Nau, began visiting the mission. Maung Ing was poorly dressed and unassuming. The Judsons could have no way of know-ing that this humble fisherman would be the means God would one day use to literally keep them alive. Adoniram learned from the diffi-dent young seeker that the newly baptized Maung Nau had shared his new faith with him. Maung Nau had then given Maung Ing a copy of the Gospel of Matthew, and the fisherman's reading of it prompted many questions. That first night, Adoniram excitedly told Ann, "He says he wants to know more of Christ, that he may love him more. Oh, my Dear Love," he said with earnest eyes, "may the Lord Jesus give him saving knowledge of his loving self."

Each day more seekers came to the zayat, and between sharing the gospel one on one, meeting new inquirers, and still finding time to translate and study, neither Ann nor Adoniram had a spare moment. It was a good kind of busy, and they thrived on the challenge. For this they had come to the "Golden Shore."

Most of the seekers who showed up were average citizens, but one day a man appeared whose soul had the same needs but whose mind instantly appealed to Judson's own towering intellect. As Ann record-ed in her journal, Maung Shwa-gnong was "a learned teacher of con-siderable distinction." He was an immediate challenge both to Mr. J's mental acuity *and* to his missionary heart. Of all the Burmans that "Yoodthan" would meet and come to love, none did Adoniram enjoy more than the brilliant Shwa-gnong.

On September 11, 1819, Judson recorded, *"Maung Shwa-gnong has been with me all day. It appears he accidentally obtained the idea of an eternal Being about eight years ago, and it has been floating about in his head, and disturbing his Buddhistic ideas ever since."* As they talked seriously throughout the day, Judson concluded, *"He is certainly a most interesting case. The way seems to be prepared in his mind for the special operation of divine grace. Come, Holy Spirit, Heavenly Dove! His conversion seems peculiarly desirable, on account of his superior talents and extensive acquaintance with Burmese and Pali* [the sacred language of Buddhism] *literature. He is the most powerful reasoner I have yet met with in this country.*

One night their conversation lasted so long that Shwa-gnong's followers left, and Adoniram noticed that the man's skepticism seemed to depart with his followers. Shwa-gnong then pleaded with Judson to teach him. When the learned Burman scholar left late that night, Shwa-gnong amazed Adoniram by prostrating himself. This had never happened to him before! This Burman *sheeko* was an act of obeisance a Burman rarely made, and then only to a recognized superior. Adoniram knew that only God could have done this kind of work in Shwa-gnong's heart.

As Adoniram and Ann lay talking far into the sultry night, they concluded by earnestly beseeching the almighty Father to complete the work of grace in Shwa-gnong's seeking heart. Who would have thought, just a few of months ago, when all was dark and they were separated and the death drums of cholera were beating each night, that the light of God's love would now be breaking through and they could begin seeing the work God was doing in hearts around them?

Two views from ancient Ava, from more than 200 yeats ago, and the other taken in the twenty-first century.

To the Golden Feet
1819–1820

BOTH THE JUDSONS CONTINUED TO USE ALL THE TIME THEY COULD find for the exacting and demanding work of translating the Scriptures. Adoniram translated directly from Aramaic, Greek, and Hebrew into Burmese, and Ann was busily translating the English Scriptures into Siamese. A large contingent of Siamese citizens lived in Rangoon, to say nothing of the millions in Siam who had never seen any portion of the Bible in their heart language. All the while, the one-on-one outreach to each seeker was pure joy to Ann and Adoniram, leaving them with a feeling of hope and encouragement each night when they fell exhausted into bed.

Their Burman guests were still in residence in the mission garden in their bamboo huts. Adoniram taught Maung Thalah, while Ann spent some time each day with his sister, Mah Baik. Thalah was a quiet and gentle man, just the opposite of his argumentative sister. Ann tried hard to explain that Christians *should not* quarrel; if Mah Baik wished to believe and accept Christ, she would have to control her tempestuous emotions. Mah Baik's face was long as she admitted that "Mrs. Teacher" must be right, but that was asking too much. On the other hand, her brother Thalah came to saving faith and was awaiting baptism, as was Maung Byaay, who had also come to reside in the mission garden. Byaay was about fifty years old, and unusual for a Burman, he could not read. However, under Judson's expert tutelage, he quite quickly acquired the skill and could read God's Word for himself.

At the same time, trouble was brewing politically. One of the Buddhist leaders had caught wind of the interest in the "foreign religion" of the scholarly and wealthy Maung Shwa-gnong and had been threatening him. This in turn sent a wave of disquiet through all the inquirers. Thalah and Byaay, the two men who had recently professed their faith, asked to be baptized after dark, for, as attendance at the zayat grew, so grew governmental suspicion. The Judsons could understand why their new friends were apprehensive. They personally might be in some danger as foreigners, but not the kind of danger facing a Burman subject, who risked prison, torture, and even death.

Maung Ing, the fisherman friend of Maung Nau, had become a believer as well, but his work required him to leave temporarily, so he was to be baptized when he returned. On the night the little group observed the sacrament of baptism for the second time, Adoniram recorded the event: *"The sun was not allowed to look upon the humble, timid profession. No wondering crowd crowned the overshadowing hill. We felt, on the banks of the water, as a little, feeble, solitary band. But perhaps some hovering angels took note of the event. . . . and perhaps Jesus looked down on us, pitied and forgave our weaknesses, and marked us for his own."*

In the following weeks, every day was colored for Ann and Adoniram by the dark possibility of persecution. The more successful they became in reaching the hearts of the people, the more precarious became their safety. The new converts faced not only government persecution but also possible death. Long into each night, Ann and Adoniram prayed for guidance as to what best to do. Emperor Bagyidaw was not a mere puppet ruler nor a gilded figurehead in Ava; he was the lord of life and death in Burma. After all, he had executed his uncle and all his family simply because they were a threat to his throne. The latest gossip said that the emperor was now encouraging the Buddhist priests in their domination of the people. Each time a new rumor floated around, attendance at the zayat dropped off for several days. The Judsons felt deep compassion for their new friends and knew they must be sensing great danger.

One night as the couple deliberated over what they could possibly do, Adoniram suggested that they needed royal sanction. Ann agreed, but how on earth could they obtain such a thing? Nothing that they had heard about the royal presence was encouraging. Adoniram gave a deep sigh and concluded, "Dear Love, I think I must visit Ava and seek to obtain permission to share our faith, or at least ask for tolerance." Ann's eyes widened, and taking a deep breath, she replied, "Mr. J, in that case, if you go, I feel I should go as well." Adoniram objected to the danger, and thus began a lengthy discussion of their opposing views.

Not often did the Judsons have strong differences of opinions, but this one was real indeed. In vain, Ann reminded him of the success she had experienced at the court of the viceroy simply because she had the novelty of being a foreign woman. It might work this time as well. Adoniram could not see that line of reasoning, and it was a moment that saw the clashing of two strong wills. Ann did not often exhibit a strong temper, but she bordered on it now. Then with the greatest reluctance, Ann acquiesced, but she could not rid herself of a feeling a deep foreboding. This trip would be fraught with peril.

Just four days before Christmas, Ann Judson and Elizabeth Colman watched their husbands board a little boat Adoniram had hired for the trip. Ann's eyes filled with tears as it pulled away from the dock and disappeared into the early morning mist. This would be a Christmas Ann never wanted to repeat, yet another Christmas without her Mr. J. As she and Elizabeth turned and walked slowly back to the mission house, Ann's mind rang with the words of that first verse of Romans 12: "Present your bodies a living sacrifice"— *and this might well be just such sacrifice,* she thought as a sob caught in her throat. The women would have no way of learning what was going on while their husbands were away. Ann tried not to let the younger woman see her anxiety as the two of them waited week after long week with no news.

It was the last week of January before the little boat finally reached Ava. And on the very next morning, Adoniram called on Rangoon's former viceroy, their old acquaintance Mya-day-men, who had now been promoted to the exalted position of *wung*yi (prime minister). The vicereine immediately wanted to hear about her dear "Mrs. Yoodthan," and it gave Judson a pang to explain that she had not been able to accompany him. Since Mya-day-men now held such an important position in the capital, he was able to obtain permission for the two foreigners to have an audience with the emperor, or the "Golden Presence," as he was often called.

Maung Ing had accompanied the missionaries to Ava—a brave move, considering the disdain the Golden Eyes had for any foreigners. That disdain might well extend to the Burman who came with them to the capital. Judson and Colman had decided to wear white surplice-like robes to the royal court, and they had prepared a handsome Bible written in English, in six volumes, and covered with expensive gold leaf, symbolizing royalty. Sleep was hard to come by the night before the royal audience; both Americans were far too nervous. They had been traveling for six weeks, and now the goal was near.

Upon arrival at the palace gates, the foreigners' permits were examined before Maung Zah, the high official known by his title, the Atwinwun, deigned to allow them to enter and present their request for an audience with the Golden One. The audience hall was teeming with officials, major and minor, and most were seated according to rank and importance. The Atwinwun condescended to tell "Yoodthan" that he would deliver their petition to the Golden One.

Judson and Colman could have no way of knowing that this was less than a propitious day for an audience with Emperor Bagyidaw. The emperor was preoccupied with a celebration of a recent victory. Furthermore, while all foreigners were viewed as potential enemies, the Westerners' situation was made even more precarious by the bad blood brewing between Britain and Burma. There was trouble over borders and disputed territories, none of which would incline the Golden One to listen with favor to petitions made by mere foreigners.

High official Maung Zah was still in the midst of reviewing Judson's petition himself when the announcement came: "The Golden One is approaching." It was too late now to wait for a likelier day. Everyone in the audience hall knelt, Judson and Colman as well, and all but the foreigners bowed their heads to the ground. Judson's eyes were focused instead on the emperor, which immediately drew his attention to these foreigners with their pale faces and long white gowns.

The monarch then marched into the hall. After all he had heard about the Golden Presence, Adoniram was surprised at his actual appearance. Bagyidaw was a little man, just over five-feet tall and quite bowlegged. He strode in with the *proud gait and majesty of an Eastern monarch*, and Judson thought his age to be about twenty-eight. His forehead was slanted, a characteristic inherited from a distant ancestor, and his long black hair was enclosed in a turban-like headdress. One part of his costume was magnificently elaborate, an ornate sword in a golden sheath.

The Golden One stopped in front of the white-clad strangers and demanded, "Who are these?"

"The teachers, Great Emperor," replied Judson in flawless Burmese.

Bagyidaw stared at Judson and peppered him with questions: "What? You speak Burmese? When did you come? Where are you from? Are you teachers of religion?"

Judson answered every question thrown at him. Then Maung Zah crawled forward, as was the custom, to the Golden Feet and read Judson's petition for the Golden Ears. It simply stated their request to preach their religion and requested tolerance for Burman converts. Bagyidaw seized the petition and barely spared it a glance before contemptuously handing it back. Next, Judson handed Maung Zah a copy of his tract *A View of the Christian Religion.* Bagyidaw reached out for the tract, reading aloud the first few lines: "There is one Being who exists eternally—besides this, the true God, there is no other God." Bagyidaw immediately threw down the tract, even as an assistant crawled up and opened one of the beautiful gold-bound volumes of the Bible, holding it up for the royal eyes. The emperor paid no attention and moved on in disdain. Maung Zah put into words what was already painfully obvious: The Golden One did not deign to listen and had no intention of giving permission to foreigners to preach their religion in *his* kingdom.

A wave of crushing defeat flooded Adoniram's heart. *Now what?* He and Ann had so longed for a positive reception from the emperor, thereby affording protection for the believers. Now he wondered if danger would be even more imminent because of this visit. Judson felt overwhelming despair, and Colman could not help but pick up some of the same disappointment consuming the veteran missionary. Adoniram was usually positive, but this was a blow to his normal demeanor.

By the next morning, however, some of Judson's natural optimism reasserted itself, and he had recovered enough equilibrium to face the new day and the challenges ahead with confidence in what the heavenly Father could do, recalling that God could work miracles in spite of human failures. All the same, Adoniram wanted badly to talk this through with his dear Ann. It was like a deep ache in the heart that no one but Ann could soothe. He had already suffered many misgivings by insisting that she not come to Ava with him. Her heart was going to be broken over his failure.

The trip home seemed agonizingly long. On February 18, 1820, the little vessel finally made it back to Rangoon. News of its impending arrival had preceded them, and Ann and Elizabeth hurried to the docks. One look at Adoniram's face, and Ann knew the news was not good. Waiting until they reached the privacy of their room, Adoniram took her into his arms and began weeping. Ann quieted his sobs as the story tumbled out. Together the two knelt and prayed for wisdom and mercy. They desperately needed guidance to determine their next step in the face of possible persecution, not only for themselves but also for the Colmans and their beloved Burman believers.

"Mr. J," Ann suggested when they were finally able to sit and talk calmly about their next move, "let's gather the believers together and honestly lay before them what has happened. That we *must* do." She took a deep breath, and clasping his hands tightly, concluded, "We have done it before, and we can do it again. We will simply trust God and take courage." Long into the night, the two prayed for a strengthening of their faith and the courage to follow whatever path God had in mind.

Consequently, early the next day the Judsons called together the three baptized believers. Adoniram was brutally honest in reporting the events of Ava. Seated nearby, James Colman listened gravely as Judson proposed to the believers that he, Ann, and the Colmans might move to Chittagong. Situated between Arakan and Bengal, the city was under British rule and was home to many Burmans; the missionaries need not fear the Golden One there. If they remained in Rangoon, when word of the emperor's rejection of the missionaries' request for tolerance leaked out, open interest in Christianity would be all but dead, and the new believers would be in grave danger.

But as the believers began responding, their reaction to the proposal was not what the Judsons had been expecting. "No," each of the three declared. "Stay," they pleaded, adding, "at least wait until there are eight or ten believers." Maung Byaay spoke up boldly, "Then not even the emperor can stop God's work." Ann's eyes filled with grateful tears as she thought of the patriarch Abraham bargaining with God to spare the cities of Sodom and Gomorrah. The Burman converts' faith, zeal, and steadfastness amazed and humbled the mission-aries. As if to reaffirm their response, Maung Shwa-gnong reap-peared at the compound and astounded Judson by saying, "I believe in the eternal God, in his Son Jesus Christ, for the atonement which Christ had made, and in the teachings of the apostles, as the true and only word of God." Here stood the man with the most to lose. Shwa-gnong, highly educated and well known, would be an instant target for persecution.

The courage of the new converts strengthened the hearts and wills of their teachers. Ann and Adoniram, along with James and Elizabeth, talked for long hours and prayed even longer, seeking just the right decision. Their conclusion was the one all four embraced as difficult but feasible: The Colmans would go to Chittagong and establish a beachhead there, while Ann and Adoniram would remain in Rangoon. In March 1820 the Colmans left for Chittagong.

Eight years. After eight years in Rangoon, once more Ann and Adoniram were the lone missionaries in Burma. Emily Von Someron found it very quiet around the mission house now. The bright twelve-year-old continued to be a source of companionship and encourage-ment to Ann and Adoniram, and sensing their loneliness, she did her part to help them any way she could.

Encouragement continued to come from the Burman believers as well. Maung Nau, the first believer, had always seemed reserved and submissive, but not now. He expressed such devotion and zeal that they began calling him "Peter" in the group of believers. Maung Thalah was showing an astounding aptitude for memorizing Bible pages and talking with seekers who came to the zayat. His cousin, Maung Shwa-bay, became a believer as well.

A question mark was Maung Shwa-gnong. Although two of his wealthy, upper-class friends requested baptism, Shwa-gnong himself hesitated. Ann and Adoniram could understand; for someone of his position and public standing such an open commitment meant sure persecution, and possibly even death. Adoniram admitted to Ann, "My heart is wrung with pity. Just think of the iron maul," he said with a sigh. "I have a strong suspicion that if I were in his situation, I would have no more courage than he."

Meanwhile, Ann was deeply involved in reaching out to a Burman woman who had appealed directly to Ann's heart from the first morning she visited the mission house. Mah Men Lay was a lovely, soft-spoken woman around fifty years of age, exceptionally well-educated and articulate. Her brother, Mah Myat-lah, and his wife, Mah Doke, came with her, and they were earnest inquirers within just a handful of days. As Maung Shwa-gnong had appealed instantly to Adoniram's heart, so did Mah Men Lay appeal to Ann's. This gracious woman of many talents always had a group of friends who followed her leading and loved to have tea with "Mrs. Teacher Yoodthan."

Ann quickly realized that Mah Men Lay was afraid of what might happen to her family if she openly believed. One day she startled Ann by confessing: *"I am surprised to find this religion has such an effect on my mind as to make me love the disciples of Christ more than my dearest natural relatives."* Coming from this culture, such an admission was no small thing. In Burma then and now, relations are the most important part of life—meriting the greatest love. Clearly, the Holy Spirit was at work in Mah Men Lay's life.

Adoniram was closely watching the growing faith of this learned woman, and he hoped for several reasons that she would come to saving faith. Not only was he praying for her salvation, but he also longed for Ann to experience the joy of bringing the first Burman woman to belief. His eyes sought out his wife's expressive face in moments when she was unaware. Because Judson knew his beloved's face so well, he soon observed that something was clearly wrong. Each day the dark circles under Ann's once-sparkling eyes were growing deeper, and her beautiful complexion was turning quite sallow. His heart sank within him; these were all-too-familiar signs of a recurrence of liver disease. He could not bear to think of her having to leave the country. *Dear God,* he silently prayed each day, *what are we to do?*

Time of Dilemma 1820–1821

Immanuel Baptist Church in Rangoon stands just two blocks from where Ann and Adoniram Judson first stepped ashore in 1813.

ANN AND ADONIRAM STOOD hand in hand on the dock at Rangoon's harbor, waving as James and Elizabeth Colman sailed off for Chittagong and out of their lives. Ann brushed away an errant tear as it escaped down her cheek; Elizabeth had become as dear as her own sisters. Now she was losing this special companion. Both of the Judsons realized the importance of establishing a stable base of operations in a comparatively safe spot like Chittagong, but that did not make parting with their friends any easier. At the same time, they felt right about remaining with the faithful Burman believers and helping expand the mission in Rangoon. If they didn't, who would? No one else who had attempted a start in this ancient land had lasted more than a year or so. This work of missions was a lifelong business, a mission for life. Neither Ann nor Adoniram doubted it.

Unfortunately, the Judsons no longer felt free to conduct worship services in the zayat. It was too public an exposure in the current political climate. Instead, inside the mission house, they turned the Colman's recent living quarters into the "new zayat." They could have quiet evening services here without attracting undue attention.

All the while, Adoniram was closely observing Ann's condition. The dark circles under those magnificent eyes were deepening and her energy seemed to be draining away by the day. Fearing that this heralded the return of her liver problems, they tried a home treatment of salivation, which involved Ann taking mercury pills to produce an unnatural and abnormal continuous flow of saliva. In fact, they tried two such regimens, both long and sickening, but neither seemed to help, only adding sore gums and mouth to Ann's ailments.

Ann tried to conceal her tiredness and pain from her Mr. J. Sometimes, lying beside him after he fell asleep, she allowed the tears to trickle down her cheeks in silent sorrow as she prayed for mercy and help. Adoniram needed her; the work needed her. *O God,* her heart cried out, *let me know what to do.* For his part, Adoniram grew more concerned with each passing day as he thought of the dreadful possibility of another grave placed next to that of little Roger. God grant that not happen.

Late one night, realizing that Ann was still not asleep, Adoniram reached out a gentle hand and took hers: "Dear Love, we must do something. You need help, and you need it now." Ann's voice caught on a sob. "Oh, Mr. J, I can't bear to leave you and go to Calcutta alone. I just can't," and the tears flowed in earnest. Long into the night they considered what might be done, finally reaching the conclusion that they would go together to seek medical help, and God willing, together they would come back to Rangoon and the first Burmese Christians as swiftly as possible. Within days, Adoniram found a vessel preparing to leave soon for Bengal, so Ann and Emily quickly prepared the household for the trip.

It was difficult to tell their Burman friends, but to a person, each convert stood firm, insisting they must quickly go and get help for their beloved "Mrs. Yoodthan," and just as quickly come back. Two more applicants petitioned for baptism that same week, and once more they had a joyous time of baptism in a small pond near the mission house.

And then came another significant moment of joy, when the stately Maung Shwa-gnong came back to the mission house declaring, "I desire to receive baptism." Adoniram was astounded. "You say you are desirous of receiving baptism. May I ask *when* you desire to receive it?" Shwa-gnong answered immediately, "At any time you wish to give it. Now—this moment if you please?" Judson's face was alight with joy. "Do you wish to receive baptism in public or in private?" Shwa-gnong replied without hesitation, "I will receive it at any time and in any circumstances that you please to direct." Judson stood in awed silence. Then, to this distinguished man who so uniquely appealed to his heart, Judson said, "Teacher, I am satisfied that you are a true disciple. I reply, therefore, that I am as desirous of giving you baptism as you are of receiving it."

The bold profession of the scholarly Shwa-gnong galvanized the believers and inquirers alike. Nobody was surprised that the learned man was now a believer; the astonishing thing was his courage in making it public and allowing a foreigner to baptize him. This might well jeopardize his life. The one so close to Ann's heart, Mah Men Lay, stood with her arm supporting her dear, frail "Mrs. Yoodthan," and whispered in her ear, "Ah! Shwa-gnong has followed the command of Jesus Christ, while I remain without obeying. How can I sleep? I must go quickly and consult my husband," and off she hurried into the darkness of the evening.

Ann and Adoniram had hardly settled into bed that night when a knock came at the door. Mah Men Lay insisted on being baptized that very night, before her beloved teacher left for India. At once Ann and Mr. J, lantern held high, walked through the dark silent streets to the waters of the little pond, and Mah Men Lay triumphantly professed her faith through baptism. Thus July 18, 1820, was forever etched in the minds of Ann and Adoniram. Maung Shwa-gnong was an open believer, as were two of his followers, and Mah Men Lay had become Burma's first female convert, and Mah Doke soon followed her example. The dream of ten Burmese believers wasn't just a dream anymore.

Early the next morning, Ann and Adoniram, together with their dear Emily, headed to the harbor. Rangoon's summer sun was already scorching as they stepped into the little boat taking them out to the ship headed for Calcutta. The debilitating effects of the liver condition caused Ann to cling to Adoniram's arm and lean on it heavily. His step was firm, but the pain in his eyes that still persisted was intensified by the sun's torrid glare.

Standing on the dock were all the new disciples and many inquirers, waving their last good-byes. The women were crying aloud, not only a good Burmese custom but also a reflection of their genuine grief at seeing the "Yoodthans" sailing away. As Ann and Adoniram stood at the rail, too moved to speak, they waved back as long as they could see their faithful friends standing there. Ann and Adoniram exchanged a glance as both recalled another July morning, exactly seven years earlier, when they had first looked on this city, so foreign to their eyes—the city which was now home, holding as it did those who had become dear to their hearts.

It took a month for the vessel to reach Calcutta, but they found it discouraging that the weeks at sea had not seemed to improve Ann's condition. Immediately upon arrival, they found an eminent doctor to care for her. Dr. Chalmers gladly treated Ann and would take no compensation. It was disheartening, however, as one day she appeared to improve, but then the next, her condition faltered again.

The weary couple decided the weather in Serampore might be more beneficial, so they settled with Emily for two restful months in that city with George and Phebe Hough. Thankfully, the pain in Adoniram's eyes had begun to subside, affording him great relief. On the other hand, Dr. Chalmers felt that returning to Rangoon's climate would be a death sentence for Ann. That was not what either one wanted to hear. However, a Dr. McWhirter, equally as qualified and proficient as Dr. Chalmers, studied Ann's case closely and felt that some prescribed medication could allow her to return to Rangoon with Adoniram. That is what they both wanted to hear. Therefore, a hopeful Ann took the latter doctor's suggestion.

During the two months in Serampore, Ann's strength began to return, and her resolve had not faltered the entire time. She *must* get

back to the work she loved. They added on one month of recuperation in Calcutta, and on Thanksgiving Day, 1820, Ann and
Adoniram gave thanks and sailed home with Emily to Rangoon.
They were expecting a short and restful trip aboard the *Salamanca*,
but their voyages were seldom destined to be either short or restful.
The passage was stormy, with ferocious winds, squalls, and the worst
thunderstorm either had ever experienced. Out on the open seas, it
seemed a miracle that a lone small ship could escape the lightning that
flashed all around them. The expected two weeks at sea stretched
into six. Their hearts flooded with relief to finally see the shoreline of
Rangoon's dingy harbor appear in the misty distance. Scraggly and
unprepossessing as it might be, it was now home, and they were
grateful to be back.

What a change from their arrival in Rangoon seven years earlier!
On this January morning, Ann seized Adoniram's hand. "Mr. J," her
voice holding a smile, "just think. This time there are fellow
Christians waiting here to meet us. Look!" She pointed in excitement
at the tall figure of Maung Shwa-gnong, his hand raised high in greeting, and at the other believers clustered around him. As they came
down the gangplank, the converts crowded around excitedly, each
one with a tale to tell their beloved "Yoodthans." News soon spilled
out about the thirty-thousand troops on the way to war with Siam.
It was troubling.

However, Shwa-gnong had good news. Everyone had been anxious
about the repercussions of his baptism. There had been a conspiracy
by a leading Buddhist monk to have him persecuted, but the viceroy
May-day-men had nipped it in the bud. The Judsons were delighted
to hear that May-day-men, the elderly viceroy who had first befriend-
ed them, was back. He had been returned to authority in Rangoon,
and the Buddhist leader had sent word that "the teacher Shwa-gnong
tried to turn the bottom of the priests' rice-bowl upwards," suggesting the new believer was undermining their livelihood. The viceroy
cut him off quickly with, "What consequence? Let the priests turn it
back again." And that ended the threat.

There was more good news. Mah Men Lay, so radiant in her new-found faith, had opened a school for boys so they would have an alternative to the Buddhists priests' instruction. Every time Ann watched her friend at work teaching and sharing her faith so joyfully, her own heart gladdened. Seeing the transformation in this friend who had come to mean so much to her, made every struggle, every tear of the past seven years worth the pain. Mah Doke, sister-in-law to Mah Men Lay, had witnessed the change in her relative and began coming daily with Men Lay. Within weeks of their return, she had trusted Christ and sought baptism as evidence of her newfound faith. Men Lay was radiant that evening as she watched her dear sister-in-law follow Christ in the waters of baptism.

A steady flow of inquirers was coming to the mission house now, and Adoniram and Ann were both busy meeting with them, as were several of the new believers. Both Judsons used the remainder of each day in translation work, eager to get as much of the Bible into Burmese as quickly as they could. Translation had taken on a special satisfaction now that Adoniram had Maung Shwa-gnong to help him. Shwa-gnong's knowledge of the language and culture were of immense assistance in concise translation. Shwa-gnong gained new insight into Scripture on a daily basis. Ann wrote her family:

> *Maung Shwa-gnong is an invaluable assistant. He is one of the most indefatigable persons in the world; he sits with Mr. J from 9 in the morning till 5 at night, in which time they get through only 10 or 12 verses, as he will not let a sentence pass unless the meaning is conspicuous. How great is the mercy of God, raising up a man of his talents and influence to assist in perfecting the translation of the word of God.*

Then came even more good news! Maung Ing was able to come home to Rangoon and immediately came to the mission to request baptism. All the time he had been away, Ing had been busy sharing his faith—he who was to become Burma's first home missionary.

However, something else happened in March. There had been no way of hiding the prominent Shwa-gnong's conversion from his home village. The jealous village chief accused him before the viceroy of having embraced, as he called it, "ideas subversive to the Buddhist religion." It was so open an accusation that the viceroy could not simply ignore it. Rather than follow the normal procedure and issue a death penalty, the viceroy deliberately dragged his heels. Shwa-gnong heard the news, went immediately to Adoniram, got a supply of tracts and Scripture portions, and headed upriver, away from both Rangoon and his own village. There he settled and quietly evangelized the residents, effectively utilizing his great teaching skills in a new district. Thus the gospel message continued to spread in spite of open persecution.

Judson persevered in translating, although it took longer without his brilliant assistant. By mid-July he had completed the Gospel of John and much of the Book of Acts, in addition to the Gospel of Matthew. Next he undertook the three Epistles of St. John. There was never a day long enough, and Adoniram felt like he would need several lifetimes to accomplish all the tasks he felt needed doing.

Ann was also at her peak of productivity. Her language skills in both Burmese and Siamese were formidable, and she was constantly involved in translating, counseling, and teaching at her school for girls. By this time, Emily was a great help in the schoolroom, not just learning new skills herself but also able to help younger Burman girls. Ann was deeply grateful for the loving child who had become such a special part of their family. Emily was fast growing up and would soon be thirteen.

Often during the long and humid nights, Ann would wake up thinking of what needed to be done the next day. She was only too aware of the fragility of her health. Many a night, a tear would trickle down her cheek at the memory of their little Roger, and she would wonder why she had not been able to have another child. The liver condition was barely staying under control; her heart of hearts told her it was only a matter of time before she would have to take some sort of drastic measure for her health.

Then late in July, cholera hit both of them. Ann and Adoniram lay deathly ill in the same room. Thirteen-year-old Emily nursed both of them with great devotion, feeling a sense of satisfaction in finally being able to do something for the two people who were so dear to her. Adoniram slowly recovered, but the attack of cholera was devastating for Ann because the liver condition had already made her vulnerable body weak. When Adoniram was finally able to get up for a few hours, he wrote home: *"We are now in a convalescent state. Mrs. J, however, is suffering severely under the liver complaint that is making such rapid and alarming advances as to preclude all hope of her recovery in this part of the world."*

Ann knew she was failing quickly. There was no way she could hide the seriousness of her condition, much as she wanted to. His dear love was desperately ill, and it darkened his every waking hour. For so many years, these two had had only each other to confide in and lean on. To whom else could they turn? What could they possibly do? The exhausted and perplexed couple could find no easy answers. Time and again, late into the night, they would grip each other's hands and weep and pray together for wisdom and direction.

An Ocean Apart 1821–1822

ANN WAS DYING IN FRONT OF HIS eyes. Adoniram could no longer fool himself that there was any way his dear love could regain her health in Rangoon's climate. Desperation led to their inevitable decision: she must go home to America to recuperate. As husband and wife, the two were uniquely one, and the very thought of being separated again was heartwrenching. Nonetheless, the alternative was worse: Ann would die. In fact, she was so weak that Adoniram and Emily needed to do most of the packing.

Judson's great-grandson, Dr. Stanley Hanna, stands with the author at the site of Burma's first baptistry, located on the mission compound in Moulmein.

Emily was dreading the inevitable separation. The three talked for hours over what they could do, and they reached the painful decision that Emily would return to the Von Someron family in Madras. Ann smiled tenderly at Emily and patted her hand, "My precious Emily, I can nearly look into the future and see you teaching a band of Indian children, sharing with them the faith you have come to embrace." Emily clung to her beloved Miss Ann, knowing that she would never forget all the years spent with her Judson family.

That Monday night, August 20, 1821, both Ann and Adoniram struggled to maintain composure, each mindful of the agony the other was experiencing. As was their nightly custom, they finished the day with prayer. Facing together an unknown future, they prayed that old prayer from their earliest days in Rangoon: *"God grant that we may live and die among the Burmans, though we never should do anything else than smooth the way for others."* Before leaving the privacy of their room Tuesday morning, Adoniram gently took Ann's hollow cheeks between his hands and, looking into those beautiful eyes so glazed with pain, spoke a benedictory prayer: *"May God grant to watch over thee each moment that we are apart, and allow us to be together once more as soon as he sees fit."* The two held each other for endless agonizing moments, well aware that this could be the last time they saw each other on this earth. With a sob, Ann finally turned and, with Emily at her side, headed for the door, her eyes clouded with grief.

As the ship bearing his beloved wife and precious Emily sailed out of Rangoon's harbor, Adoniram resolutely turned his face toward the mission house and, prior to beginning the usual full day, wrote a sad letter to his missionary coworker George Hough in India, explaining their circumstances and Ann's desperate condition: *"I feel as if I was on the scaffold, and signing, as it were, my own death warrant. I have been occupied in making up my mind to have my right arm amputated, and my right eye extracted, which the doctors say are necessary in order to prevent a decay and mortification of the whole body conjugal."*

The ship was barely out to open sea when Ann became violently ill, and both she and Emily wondered if she would even reach Calcutta alive. The faithful girl nursed her Miss Ann diligently, and by the time they arrived in Calcutta, Ann had recovered a bit of strength, although her sunken eyes and jaundiced skin gave chilling evidence of her precarious condition. Then came the wrenching separation from Emily, both realizing that likely they would never be together again on this earth, but each thankful for the love their hearts felt for each other. Just before Ann fell into an exhausted slumber that night in the home of missionary friends in the bustling city, she reflected that practicing good-byes never made them get easier. Tears came easily now in her weakened condition, and her longing to be with her Mr. J was a palpable ache in her heart that never went away, nor was there any medicine that could ease the hurt.

If Ann had hoped for another option from the doctors in Calcutta, she was certainly disappointed. The physicians in that Indian city were adamant: go to a cooler climate if you want to survive. There was no acceptable alternative. To Ann's dismay, however, she could not find a ship going to America that had room for a passenger. They were all full of cargo. Only one captain offered to take her home— for the staggering price of fifteen hundred rupees. There was no way she could pay such an exorbitant amount. But at this point, Ann became aware yet again of the hand of Providence. A kind chaplain's wife knew of a ship sailing for England with three children returning to school, and Ann could share their cabin for a minimal fee. Furthermore, even that amount was paid by the grateful father of the three children, honored to have them in the company of the already legendary Ann Judson.

It was a shock to Ann to learn that she had become a woman of note, both in India and also in England, as the exploits of the young American missionary couple were told and retold. Ann arrived in England, astounded to find herself a heroine. She was also mortified, knowing how far from the truth that was, so conscious was she of her every fault and blemish. Couldn't people see that? Nonetheless, she quickly learned that the struggles and exploits of Ann and Adoniram Judson in Burma were common topics of conversation in Christian circles in England and Scotland. Joseph Butterworth, one of Parliament's most prominent members, was a devout Methodist. He and Mrs. Butterworth immediately welcomed Ann into their comfortable home, becoming her friends and sponsors. Leading Christians in London hastened to make the honored Mrs. Judson comfortable and do all they could to help her recover.

The biggest problem for her recovery was how to get desperately needed rest. There were still far too many demands on her time.

Everyone wanted to meet her, to talk to her, to learn about Burma. While in London, Butterworth introduced her to the famous William Wilberforce, that member of Parliament who, more than any other, brought about the abolition of slavery. Wilberforce and Ann Judson bonded immediately, and she wrote at length to Adoniram about the timely meeting.

The Butterworths had procured the best medical care for Ann but were increasingly conscious of how draining it was on Ann to meet so many people and take part in any social function. In order to recover her health, she *must* have rest and quiet. For years, Ann had been in correspondence with a Mrs. Deakin in Scotland, and the Butterworths felt a trip to stay with that fine lady might afford Ann an opportunity to truly rest and recover.

Mrs. Deakin made it her mission to keep Ann in quiet and serene surroundings, and this served as balm and medicine. Ann was only thirty-two years old, but most days she felt twice that age, so precarious was her health. Soon after reaching Scotland, Ann heard from the Baptist board in Boston, suggesting she secure passage on the America-bound *Packet*. Her friends in Scotland went a step further, however, and purchased Ann a passage on the larger and more comfortable ship, *Amity*.

Ann woke the morning of August 6, 1822—the day she was to sail—and realized it had been a year since she left Rangoon and her Mr. J. It seemed like an eternity, so deeply did she yearn for the companionship of the one who held her heart. She could not have any pleasant experience without a pang of regret that Adoniram was not there to share in the moment. The sting of separation would not go away. Ann had not received any news from Mr. J, and it was agonizing to picture him in this place, or that spot, with this believer or that inquirer, and to feel the aching loneliness that had to be his as well.

Scottish friends had become dear to Ann long before she boarded the *Amity* that August day, and this departure meant more goodbyes. After the shoreline of Scotland faded into the mists, Ann went to the stateroom and wrote in her journal:

Should I be preserved through the voyage, the next land I tread will be my own native soil, ever loved America, the land of my birth. I cannot realize that I shall ever again find myself in my own dear home at Bradford amid the scenes of my early youth, where every spot is associated with some tender recollection. But the constant idea that my husband is not a participator in my joys will mar them all.

One part of her felt hopeful, however, as her health was decidedly better. She was determined that she would be able, as soon as possible, to get back to her beloved and to her cherished work. This resolution was her driving motivation.

Meanwhile, Adoniram was assuaging his intense loneliness in constant work. It was a subtle pressure, perpetually wondering what the government might do about this foreign religion in their midst. He learned to be flexible and to discover what winds of persecution might be in the air that day. When there appeared to be no signs of problems, he would focus his energies on teaching in the zayat. But when a hint of danger came, he threw himself into translating. He could not bear to waste time.

Even under the pressure of impending persecution, Adoniram's essential optimism asserted itself. He wrote frequent letters to Ann, even though he realized very few of them had much chance of finding her somewhere in the world. He sat down to write shortly after she left Rangoon, and his words revealed some of the emotions he was experiencing in his lonely work:

Life is short. Happiness consists not in outward circumstances. Millions of Burmans are perishing. I am almost the only one person on earth who has attained their language to such a degree as to be able to communicate the way of salvation. How great are my obligations to spend and be spent for Christ! What a privilege to be allowed to serve him, and to suffer for him. Soon we shall be in heaven. Oh, let us live as we shall then wish we had done!

This letter finally did reach Ann, and it made her heart race with a fervent longing to get back home to Mr. J and Burma as soon as possible.

In December Adoniram wrote to Ann of a different source of encouragement: the arrival of reinforcements, namely, Dr. Jonathan Price, his wife, and their little daughter. Price, a New Englander, was not very polished or accomplished, but he was a utilitarian kind of medical doctor who especially liked to remove cataracts. He quickly learned enough Burmese to get along in conversation, not caring a whit that his accent was awful or his grammar atrocious, as long as he could be understood. But with stunning rapidity, tragedy struck. Not five months had passed before Mrs. Price took ill and died. Her body was laid to rest in the little garden near the grave of baby Roger. Memories haunted Adoniram that night like a dark specter.

Dr. Price sent his daughter to live with the Lawsons, missionary friends in Calcutta, and just about the same time, the Houghs returned to Rangoon. George could still print faster than Adoniram could translate, and by now he also had a better command of the language. The senior missionary, Judson, could not find enough hours in the day for all he hoped to accomplish, while constantly longing for his beloved wife and partner in ministry to return. Judson reported in a letter to Ann in February that half the New Testament was finished, and his desire to finish was a driving force that sped him through each day.

As if what he was already doing were not enough, Judson was determined to get a start on providing some hymns for the new believers, messages in music that would strengthen their faith and encourage their spirits. One theme kept running through his mind. The people of Burma focused on gold as a symbol of wealth or prosperity. Gold was a symbol of the royal family and was used prominently in their temples and pagodas. Judson began to weave a lyrical poem around gold and the wonders of heaven, where the great street of the holy city was pure gold. Recognizing that with Ann's severe illness, he was so often thinking about heaven, Adoniram wrote his first hymn in Burmese centered on this personal vision: *Shwe pyi kaungin sonlo gyinle* ("I Long to Reach My Golden Shore"). The first verse seemed to flow from his pen:

> *We shall taste the bliss of Heaven;*
> *We shall see the Savior's face,*
> *And in gladness without leaven*
> *Praise the riches of His grace.*

God willing, he would soon be able to share his hymn with the one closest to his heart.

The same week in August that Ann sailed from England for America, Adoniram baptized the eighteenth convert, for a number of the inquirers whom Ann had taught had now come to saving faith. He joyfully wrote about the event to Ann that night.

Then a new dilemma presented itself. The Golden Ears had heard about the strange foreign doctor who could restore eyesight, and the emperor now issued an order for Dr. Price to report to Ava. Adoniram was deep in translation of the New Testament and hated to interrupt the process. He was constantly aware that he was the only person alive who was capable of giving the Burman people the Bible in their own language. However, a royal order was a royal order, and there was no way Dr. Price could handle the situation in Ava without Judson to smooth the way with the volatile emperor.

At about this time and without warning, illness again ravaged Adoniram's body—first a violent fever, followed by a second bout with cholera. The devastating effects were slow in subsiding, and it took his body weeks to recover. Then, before the two men were finally able to leave for Ava in late August, devastating news from Chittagong reached the mission house in Rangoon. The brave young James Colman had lost his grip on life as the tuberculosis defeated his body. It was a crushing blow, and Judson knew this tragedy would be heartbreaking to Ann.

Meanwhile, Ann had no idea what was happening in Burma. As the *Amity* crept closer to the shores of New England, she continued to focus her energy on recouping her strength. Her courage had never faltered, though her body did not always cooperate. The nights were the longest. Ann soon adjusted to the gentle rocking of the vessel, but she frequently awoke during the endless nights, reaching out to put a hand on Mr. J's arm. Finding only an empty space next to her, the tears would begin again. By day she gave thanks for her returning strength and remained convinced that a period of time in her native land's air would complete her cure. She must get back to her beloved and to her people. Nothing else motivated her like this overwhelming yearning.

"Land ho!" came the call, and Ann hurried to the deck to catch her first glimpse of America in ten and a half years. Her mind harked back to a blustery cold February morning in 1812, when she and three other young and idealistic missionaries had begun their trip to the other side of the earth. Ann had been twenty-two years old, Adoniram twenty-three, Samuel Newell slightly older, and Harriet only seventeen. Now both Harriet and Samuel were dead. By God's grace, she and Adoniram had survived thus far and been able to establish a mission in Burma, and other missionaries had been able to join them for various periods of time. Ann had never expected to see her native land and her family again.

As the shores of New York slowly grew closer, Ann's beating heart seemed like it would burst from her chest. How would she bear the anticipation and excitement? She had never felt anything like it.

The ship docked on September 25, and word quickly reached the captain that yellow fever was rampant in New York. She dared not risk exposure to the deadly fever, not in her fragile condition. Ann immediately boarded a steamboat for Philadelphia, where she garnered her strength by resting a few days before boarding a stagecoach bound for Bradford and Mama and Papa.

Ann wondered if her parents would recognize her, their long-absent daughter. Ten years ago, the beautiful and vibrant Ann had been bubbling with life and vitality, her eyes sparkling with anticipation and joy. This Ann was painfully thin from the ravages of the disease—her "Indian constitution," as she jokingly labeled it—that had invaded her system and darkened her skin. Her heart and spirit had deepened, however, drawing on spiritual resources she had scarcely tapped a decade earlier. Her magnificent eyes were lovely still, though haunted by the lingering touch of jaundice. Shiny black curls now appeared dimmed by her condition and lay close to her wan cheeks.

Home. Ann's mind could scarcely wrap around the word. It just did not seem possible. She had never expected such a day to come. Hour after hour, the horses clip-clopped along, seeming interminably slow to her eager heart. Every glance out the window revealed a burst of glorious fall color. Each beautiful view caused a mixture of pleasure and pain, because her Mr. J was not here to share these moments with her. Refusing to give in to her sorrow in his absence, she concentrated on the blessed thought of seeing her precious parents once more. Gripped in the vise of that excitement, how could she bear the joy of it?

A fragment of original wallpaper and plaster from Ann Hasseltine's birthplace, Bradford, MA.

A World Away
1822–1823

BRADFORD AT LAST. OCTOBER IN BRADFORD WAS A RIOTOUS DISPLAY of fall foliage, but Ann Judson had no eyes for anything but the blessed faces of Mama and Papa. John Hasseltine was so choked with emotion that he could not speak. Rebecca clasped her youngest daughter to her heart and kept repeating, "Oh my Honey, my Honey, I thought I would never see this day." Tears streaming freely, Rebecca breathed, "My Honey rambled home this time." As for Ann, she was absolutely beyond words, feeling like she could never let Mama out of her arms. Then Polly hurried into the room, and the sisters fell onto each other's necks. Within minutes, Abby, the dignified headmistress of Bradford Academy, tumbled through the front door in undignified haste to grasp her beloved little sister to her heart.

The Hasseltine home was so filled with excitement that no one was able to sleep much that night, and thus began a week so full of joy that it threatened to overwhelm the fragile Ann. Sister Becky and Joseph came from Beverly, and with their children: daughter Nancy had grown into a vibrant teenager, and their son, Luther, who had been only fifteen months old when his Aunt Ann saw him last, was now a tall, slender twelve-year-old. Then began the stream of visitors: relatives, neighbors, church members—the numbers seemed unending, everyone wanting to see the daughter who had returned, as it were, from the dead.

Rebecca and John Hasseltine felt like they *did* have their child home from the dead, and they thrived on the joy of this unexpected blessing. One morning Ann addressed the pupils at her alma mater. Abby, who now led Bradford Academy, proudly watched as her sister held the students' attention, entranced with her tales of distant Burma.

But the price of joy was high. Ann wrote in a few weeks to her friend Mrs. Chaplin in Maine:

> *I had never fully counted the cost of a visit to my dear native country and beloved relatives. I did not expect that a scene which I had anticipated as so joyous was destined to give my health a shock which would require months to repair. During my passage, my health was most perfect, but from the day of my arrival, the idea that I was once more on American ground, banished all peace and quiet from my mind and for the first four days I never closed my eyes to sleep!*

She went on to recount that for the entire first six weeks at home, she had not had one quiet night of sleep. By late November, Ann realized that unless something changed, she would never gain enough strength to return to Mr. J and Burma. Her kind brother-in-law, Elnathan, had a helpful suggestion, even if it meant not being at home for Christmas. He proposed that she go to Baltimore, for the rigors of a cold New England winter after more than a decade in the tropics could well be more than Ann's body could handle. Baltimore's warmer climate would be less taxing on her body, and she would have the added benefit of rest and quiet, away from those who loved her deeply but were unaware that her body was using up energy it could ill afford. Furthermore, as a noted physician himself, Elnathan could procure for his sister-in-law the best physicians in Baltimore.

Ann wrote again to Mrs. Chaplin in Maine, explaining how the attentive doctors, much-needed rest, and a milder climate in Baltimore were all helping her regain her strength. Ann discovered that studying and meditating were not as taxing as the energy expended on family and friends, even though those times had been joyous. She fought against a feeling of idleness and began to think about the Baptist leaders, family, and friends who had been urging her to write about the beginning of work in Burma. This might be her best chance to do so; when would she ever again have such an opportunity? Ann wrote Mr. J about her plan, hoping that he might receive the letter at some point, and hoping even more that she would be back with him before the letter reached him.

Ann was ever hard on herself. There were not many in whom she confided, but Mrs. Chaplin was a trusted confidant. Ann confessed to her friend that she felt spiritually exhausted and in desperate need of this quiet time of renewal. She poured out her heart as she explained her feelings:

> *Your kind hint, relative to my being injured by the lavish attention of our dear friends in this country, has much endeared you to my heart. I am well aware that human applause has a tendency to elate the soul, and render it less anxious about spiritual enjoyments. Since my return to this country, I have often been affected to tears, in hearing the undeserved praises of my friends, feeling that I was far, very far, from being what they imagined; that there are thousands of poor, obscure Christians who are a thousand*

times more deserving of the tender regard of their fellow Christians than I am.

Sheer determination allowed Ann to complete her book, *An Account of the American Baptist Mission to the Burman Empire.* Ann's purpose in writing the account was to share the story of God at work in her beloved Burma, and it achieved her purpose far beyond what her imagination could have conceived. She could not have known how far-reaching the influence her book would become on the cause of missions, as the name "Ann Judson" came close to being a household word in the United States as well as in England. Furthermore, the events of the following three years would make hers a name known around the world. Ann was destined to become a missionary heroine, the likes of which America had not before known.

While Ann was convalescing in Baltimore, family members and friends insisted she have her portrait done. That was not at all on her own list of things that needed doing, but she agreed at the urging of her loved ones. The eminent Rembrandt Peale painted a beautiful portrait of her in oils, with Ann wearing one of the dresses given to her by solicitous friends in Scotland. She would personally have much preferred to be wearing one of her bright Burmese skirts. Today Peale's portrait of her hangs in the Peabody-Essex Museum in Salem, Massachusetts, just a mile from the wharf from which she and Adoniram first sailed in 1812.

Although grateful for the gift of reunion with loved ones at home and the opportunity for rest and writing, Ann's goal was unwavering. She would recover her health and return to Mr. J and their work together in Burma. The problem facing her was that the great majority of her doctors were adamant that she must not return to the climate of Burma. That would be a death warrant. In the 1820s, very little was known about how to treat liver disease. The wisest doctors of the era felt that body fluid needed to be "balanced." Several treatments were used to encourage this balance, including salivation (which Ann had suffered through in Burma years earlier), calomel (mercuric chloride) purges, and bleeding by using leeches. One of the miracles in Ann's case was that she was able to survive her treatments. She was bled so frequently that she was in almost total exhaustion. But Providence intervened, and Ann's body somehow began to regain strength.

In Ann Judson's mind, there was no other option. She would return to Burma. She *must* return. Doctors, family, friends, denominational leaders, all pleaded with her to recuperate for another year. However, Ann did not waver. She was returning *now*. Her heart was already there, both with Adoniram and with the people of Burma, whom she loved so deeply. Elnathan, who had been so solicitous of his sister-in-law's health, recognized the hopeful signs that Ann's body had begun to mend. He could see it in her improved skin tone, in the renewed sparkle in her eyes, and even in her hair, which had regained its beautiful sheen.

An unforgettable meeting—the Triennial Convention of the General Missionary Convention of the Baptist Denomination in the United States of America for Foreign Missions—took place in Washington, DC, that May of 1823. Ann was able to attend one of the sessions, and Baptist leaders from around the nation met this woman of whom they had heard so much. Here was Ann Hasseltine Judson in person, and they were awed.

One personal encounter, however, exceeded all others. Ann walked into a room of Baptist leaders, and one of them stood up immediately and came forward, first grasping her hand in a fervent grip, and then embracing her with scarcely contained emotion. It was Luther— Luther Rice, the Judsons' treasured friend and coworker. Words tumbled from them as they tried to catch up on ten years apart and what God had wrought in their lives in the intervening time.

Rice especially relished being able to tell Ann about the women's missionary societies springing up in several states—from the first one in Boston to the low country of South Carolina. Those devoted groups of women read with joy regular letters from the Judsons that were printed in the missionary magazine. Much of Ann and Luther's conversation centered on the one who could not be present and what it would have meant to Adoniram to experience this moment with them. Their emotions were overflowing as they parted, knowing that they were unlikely to meet again on this side of eternity.

Ann returned to Bradford for her final month in America, and her heart cherished these remaining days with family and friends. At the same time, she already looked on the past year as a moment out of time. After all, when she had left these shores in 1812, she had thought she would never be able to return. She would simply be thankful for the extra blessing with which God had touched her life. As Ann wandered through the rooms of her childhood home during her last days in Bradford, she would pause in Mama's parlor and once again run her fingers over the delicate little pink blossoms in the wallpaper. That memory remained forever crystal clear in her mind.

The morning Ann left Bradford, Rebecca looked into the amber eyes of her youngest daughter: "My dear, dear Honey, God speed your rambling this time as you hasten to follow his call." Mother and daughter embraced one last, eternal moment that each would treasure for the remainder of her years. Ann wept as the carriage pulled out of the town and headed toward Boston, reflecting yet again on the new meaning of words of Romans 12. There were so many ways in which one could give herself a living sacrifice. This angst of separation from those so dear must surely be one of those ways.

Upon arriving in Boston, Ann learned that she need not travel alone this time, for a promising young couple, Jonathan and Deborah Wade, were headed to Burma with her. The three boarded the *Edward Newton* the morning of June 22, 1823. Ann recalled kissing her Mr. J good-bye more than two years earlier in Rangoon. It seemed an eternity since she had seen his dear face. Ann had received painfully few of the letters that Adoniram had written. The majority never reached her, so she had only sketchy accounts of what had been happening to the one so near to her heart but so far away from her presence.

Meanwhile, Adoniram, having recovered from his most recent bout with fever, traveled to Ava with Jonathan Price, arriving there the last week in September 1822. They found that the official attitude toward foreigners was now quite friendly. In fact, it was the wish of the capricious emperor for the foreign doctor and his friend who spoke such fluent Burmese to remain in Ava.

Adoniram realized that this could change quickly at the whim of the Golden One. Between several more bouts of illness, he managed to accomplish intermittent bursts of translation work. By the end of January 1823, he had actually been able to lease land in Ava on which to build a house. Who would have thought there would ever be a mission house in the heart of the Burman Empire!

Then Adoniram headed back to Rangoon, having explained to the Golden Ears that he was awaiting his wife's return. The Golden One promptly declared that when Mrs. Judson arrived, the teacher was to bring her to Ava. Emperor's orders. With hope in his heart, Adoniram anticipated his Ann's return so that the two of them could endeavor to plant a mission in the capital. Ann in Ava. Adoniram liked the sound of that.

Judson reached Rangoon in February and settled down to complete the translation of the New Testament while awaiting her return. Although he never let his heart doubt for long that she would find a way to come back, the months dragged by with no word from America. Day after dreary day he would check for mail. No letters. Each day he went to the docks to hear of any ships that might be arriving. Even the optimistic Adoniram Judson could feel the heaviness of his own heart. *What if Ann didn't get back?* He couldn't allow himself to think of it.

For his part, Adoniram stuck tenaciously to his meticulous verse-by-verse translation, never satisfied with any phrase that did not seem 100 percent perfect. He spent long hours writing a summary of all the main prophecies concerning Christ. And finally a day of rejoicing: On July 12, 1823, Adoniram recorded in his journal, *"Completed the translation of the New Testament into Burmese, together with an epitome* [summary] *of the Old."*

This was the main bright spot in a world that was lonely and bleak for Adoniram. He spent most of his remaining time encouraging and discipling the faithful group of believers who had bravely remained with the mission. However, his dear love was far away; he did not even know if she would be able to return. Her first letter had taken more than a year to reach him, and not one letter since then had managed to make its way across the seas to his hands.

Despite his moment of celebration, the situation of the young church in Rangoon had become discouraging. Some of the members had left the area to escape constant persecution. Some had been denounced by their families and their huts destroyed. One had died. Only three or four remained at the mission. One of the most faithful was Mah Men Lay, who had proved to be an anchor of strength. Each time Judson saw her teaching with such skill and enthusiasm, he gave thanks for the special blessing of this first woman Ann had brought to Christ.

The morning of December 5, Judson awoke with the usual thought: *Could this be the day my dear love returns?* And as usual, these past few discouraging months, he would say again to himself: *But what if she can't come at all? What if she can never come?*

While Judson was waiting and trying to maintain hope, Ann's voyage from Boston to Calcutta was proving to be surprisingly easy, and certainly less eventful than most voyages she had experienced. She delighted in the Wades' company and introduced them to the Burmese language as the comfortable ship made its way toward Calcutta. The Wades were excited to get a head start on learning the Burmese language and understanding of the culture of its people from one who had such rich experience. But the three reached Calcutta only to be told that war between Burma and Britain was imminent. They would be well-advised, wise heads told them, to wait in Calcutta and see. Not Ann and not the Wades! They located the first ship headed for Rangoon, and early in the morning of December 5, 1823, they saw the glistening spire of the massive Shwedagon appear on the horizon. Ann's heart was about to burst within her. A smiling Deborah Wade put a steadying hand on the arm of her excited friend. Ann felt as thrilled as a child on Christmas morning. Burma, right in front of her. Mr. J, just moments away now.

On shore, Adoniram did exactly what he had been doing every morning for the past six months since his return from Ava, going to the docks to see if any ships might be arriving. It had become a routine. To his amazement, on this bright Friday morning he spied a vessel approaching the harbor. Calling out to one of the dockhands, Judson asked, "Where is this vessel from?" "Calcutta," came the reply. Adoniram strode to the edge of the wharf and gazed intently at the horizon. As the vessel drew closer, he could make out the figures of three people standing by the rail and waving in his direction. *His direction?* Could this possibly be?

Adoniram saw the joy of his heart after the longest two years and three months of his life. As the ship drew up to the dock, the vision of Ann standing next to two other Westerners grew clearer, and his eyes flooded with tears of elation. As he wrote home later, he "saw the Ann Hasseltine of other days" coming toward him, and his heart was nearly overcome. It was never their habit to embrace in public, but this moment was different. "Oh Mr. J, I thought this day would never come," Ann repeated over and over again as they held each other. "I'm home! I'm home!"

A couple of days later, Adoniram wrote to Thomas Baldwin at the Baptist Board, *"I had the inexpressible happiness of welcoming Mrs. Judson once more to the shores of Burmah."* In the rapture of reunion, the agony of long separation slowly faded. It would have been difficult for either to evaluate the true worth of her convalescent period, for they could not view it from the vantage point of history. Ann had written in a recent letter, *"I know not the designs of God toward me, and it is well I do not. I trust, however, he will prepare me for all."* In this golden moment, they were flooded with joy. Neither could have conceived of what lay ahead for them in the two years to come.

CHAPTER 27

Author stands with Judson's descendant Dr. Stanley Hanna on the spot in Ava where his ancestor lay in prison chains.

Rumors of War
1824

ADONIRAM WAS ELATED TO SEE ANN SO RADIANT AGAIN. WHAT A change from the fragile, wan woman who had sailed away over two years ago! Ann actually felt stronger upon her return than did her husband. The constant burning that plagued his eyes and recurrent attacks of cholera had left him weakened. Only the discipline of daily exercise had kept his body and mind strong enough to endure these chronic ailments.

Ann and Adoniram felt they would never be able to catch up on each other's news, but Mr. J assured her that on their trip to Ava they could reminisce to their hearts' content. He explained what was taking place in the capital, telling her of the emperor's command to "bring your wife to Ava." He had not been able to get fresh news from Jonathan Price in several months, however, so he was uncertain about events at the palace and the intrigue of the royal court, and he knew that ongoing rumors of impending war with Britain might affect their plans.

Jonathan and Deborah Wade were a welcome addition to the mission house. Their unanticipated arrival with Ann meant the Houghs would have help in Rangoon while the Judsons proceeded to the capital. Adoniram had planned for months that as soon as his dear Ann arrived, they would head up the Irrawaddy to Ava; in fact, Ann did not even unpack her trunks and baggage. They were taken directly to a boat being prepared for the trip ahead.

In the brief interval before departing, Ann told Mr. J about a new rocker and worktable that Elnathan had given her in Baltimore, and she was eager to unpack after arriving in Ava. Adoniram was anxious for them to go as soon as possible, for with such a capricious monarch, the winds of acceptance might quickly shift back toward antagonism.

Nonetheless, the current state of the mission in Rangoon was quite encouraging. The Judsons would be sent off by an enthusiastic church of eighteen Burmans and four missionaries. The very thought made them smile. Ann's reunion with Mah Men Lay had brought both of them to tears, and Ann was doubly thankful that while she was away in Ava, the faithful Mah Men Lay would continue to teach her school boys and witness to the many women who regularly came to the mission.

Maung Ing, the fisherman convert, was going with them to Ava, along with Koo-chil, the Bengali cook Ann had managed to talk into accompanying them to the capital. Maung Shwa-bay asked that Ann take his two little girls to instruct them. His wife had become deranged and could not care for them. Ann's tender heart enfolded the two Burman youngsters. To the delight of the children, she gave them English names—Mary and Abby—in honor of the teacher's sisters. Thus, it was quite a merry band that set off up the Irrawaddy in a small boat that Ann euphemistically called their "floating conveyance." The vessel was very narrow, although about fifty feet in length, and got up the river mainly by means of their boatmen walk-ing on the banks and pulling the boat along with ropes. Sometimes the current was so strong that the boat rocked precariously in the muddy waters.

After their long separation, the reunited couple had plenty of time to catch up on events, both major and minor, as they traveled up the river. Adoniram filled Ann in on the emperor's apparent change of heart and the intrigues of the court, but he had no idea what had hap-pened after his departure. No news had come from Dr. Jonathan Price for months. Even had he managed to write from Ava, Mr. J explained, the well-intended doctor was still clueless about the Burman mind-set.

Adoniram explained the difficult situation with this missionary colleague she had yet to meet. Dr. Price had operated on a Burman woman's eyes, and rather than helping, she was now completely blind. Jonathan had then insisted on marrying her, even though Judson tried to talk him out of such a rash move. Next, Price said that he would make her his common-law wife if he didn't have benefit of clergy. Mr. J shook his head in dismay as he described the ceremony he had performed for the most ill-suited couple he had ever seen.

Ann was wide-eyed on the leisurely trip up the mighty river that cut through the heart of Burma. This was her first chance to travel north, and she wrote letters to Mama and Papa describing the wonders of life along the Irrawaddy. Mother Nature, usually stingy with her favors, had smiled on them this journey with cool breezes and pleas-ant evenings. The river did host thousands of pesky mosquitoes, but this was a small price to pay in exchange for the thrill of their reunion and quiet time together.

The Irrawaddy sprang from the Himalayas in the north and wound more than thirteen hundred miles down to the Andaman Sea. Along its lush banks, the countryside looked permanently abandoned to nature. For a young woman who had grown up in the cultivated order of a settled New England, it looked like the jungle primeval. Either side of the river was thick with reed and brush, much of it teeming with wild animals. The travelers would frequently pass tiny villages of scattered huts half hidden in the thick foliage of clinging vines and trees. Tales of tigers, snakes, and alligators were enough to make the two Americans willing to look but never venture too close to those impenetrable thickets.

Slowly the jungle changed to plains and a river delta. Occasionally their vessel would pull to shore so they could stroll in a village. Ann loved writing home about their "village moments." One night she recounted:

> *In one instance, we seated ourselves down, when the villagers as usual assembled, and Mr. Judson introduced the subject of religion. Several old men entered into conversation, while the multitude was all attention. The apparent school-master of the village coming up, Mr. Judson handed him a tract and requested him to read, and, the master remarked that such a writing was worthy of being copied. Mr. Judson informed him he might keep the tract, on condition he read it to all his neighbors. We could not but hope the Spirit of God would bless those few simple truths, to the salvation of some of their souls.*

Ann also wrote Mama and Papa about the fascinating scenes along the riverbanks:

> *The Arah-wah-tee is a noble river; its banks every where covered with immortal beings, destined to the same eternity as ourselves. We often walked through the village; and though we never received the least insult, always attracted universal attention. A foreign female was a sight never before beheld, and all were anxious that their friends and relatives should have a view.*

Her parents could no doubt picture Ann smiling as she told them what happened so frequently. *"Crowds followed us through the villages,"* she wrote, *"and some who were* less *civilized than others, would run some way before us, in order to have a* long *look."*

About a hundred miles before reaching Ava, their boat was confronted with a spectacle such as they had never seen. The forces of the famous Burmese general, Bandula, were making their way to the coast, confidently expecting to fight and defeat the armies of Britain. Bandula had an army of some thirty thousand and a vast flotilla of golden warships. The sight was more than enough to confirm their fears about the likelihood of war, which suddenly seemed a menacing rather than remote possibility. Ann wrote home that night: *"War boats are continually passing us. We know not what effect this war will have upon our mission, or how much our own lives will be endangered from the suspicions that we are English. But we always have the consolation that God reigns, and that the greatest, as well as the smallest events, are under his direction."* The Judsons could not know that they were sailing into a dangerous situation.

Their boat reached the banks of the capital on Friday, January 23. Jonathan Price was there to meet them with disquieting news: Foreigners were now out of favor with the Golden One. Rumors of war with the hated British were racing throughout the city. After all the emperor's earlier words of welcome and requests for the "teacher's wife" to hasten to the capital, now foreigners were under the gravest suspicion. Furthermore, having arrived in Ava, there was no escape, for one must have royal permission to leave the capital.

The emperor treated Judson coldly when he appeared at court, not deigning to even notice him. And the queen, who had expressed such eagerness for Ann's coming, paid her no attention whatsoever. The best the Judsons could hope for was to build a house on their plot of land in Ava and quietly begin their missionary endeavors. Ann was eager to get started with her school for girls, beginning with Mary and Abby, both of whom were excited about learning to read and write, and learning how to sew as well.

In Ava, everyone was talking about the new palace and the fabulous dedication day when the Golden One and his empress would take possession. Ann wrote her family:

> *I dare not attempt a description of that splendid day when majesty with all its attendant glory entered the gates of the golden city and amid the acclamations of millions, I may say, took possession of the palace. The viceroys and high officers of the kingdom were assembled on the occasion, dressed in their robes of state and ornamented with the insignia of their office. The white elephant, richly ornamented with gold and jewels, was one of the most beautiful objects in the procession. The king and queen alone were unadorned; they hand and hand entered the garden in which we had taken our seat. All the riches and glory of the empire were on this day exhibited to view. The number and immense size of the elephants, the numerous horses, and great variety of vehicles of all descriptions, far surpassed any thing I have ever seen or imagined.*

Although the queen (empress) did not express any interest in seeing the foreign lady, those of the royal family living outside the palace were friendlier and more accessible. Several of the wives of princes frequently invited Ann to visit them, and she tried to be as discreet as possible when calling on the women. Under the current climate, she and Adoniram had no wish to attract attention.

Despite swirling rumors and lack of favor at court, the Judsons went to work, building a modest house on the property Adoniram had been allowed to purchase the year before. It was constructed of bamboo and raised by stilts some four feet off the ground, with three small rooms and a verandah, as was the custom. Maung Shwa-bay's little girls were excited to be learning to read and write and diligently applied themselves to their daily lessons. In addition to teaching them, Ann was also working tirelessly to make their little house on stilts into a home. The tall and beautiful foreign woman walking through the streets of the capital and shopping in the market excited no small amount of interest. However, with the situation at court so tense, no one dared venture more than a small smile in greeting. Since the court had set up in the grand new palace, the Golden Lips decreed that all foreigners were forbidden at the royal residence.

The Judsons quietly set about their daily endeavors of translating and teaching. Jonathan Price had built a small house across the river in Sagaing, and each Sunday Ann and Adoniram took a little rowboat across the water and worshipped at their home. Only a handful of foreigners lived in the capital, Price and the Judsons being the sole Americans. Captain Laird, a Scotsman, was a lumber agent, and a Spaniard named Lanciego collected duties at the port in Rangoon. He had just recently come to Ava with the amassed funds. Arakeel, a young Armenian merchant, lived alone in Ava, as did Constantine, an older Greek man who was afflicted with leprosy. Two Englishmen also lived in the city. The elderly Mr. Rodgers, who had fled to Burma more than forty years earlier to escape trouble in England, had been in the service of the emperor ever since. The young Englishman Henry Gouger, was the only foreigner sympathetic to the missionaries. Just twenty-four years old, he was a brilliant and gregarious man who loved to visit the Judson home each evening for tea and a visit. His arrival was usually the signal for Adoniram to stop translating for a time and enjoy the fellowship.

Henry became a regular in attendance at the Sunday services. As a child, he had attended church with his parents but in recent years had shown no interest in spiritual matters. Such was the influence of Ann and Adoniram on his heart and thinking that this began to change. Gouger was an enterprising businessman and had great language skills. In fact, Judson's Burmese grammar book had proved invaluable to Henry. He also displayed an incisive understanding of the Burmese mind-set and learned even more by associating with the Judsons and gleaning bits of insight from their years of experience.

219

The three new friends relished exchanging stories of adventures, some unusual and others downright ridiculous. The other foreigners in Ava considered Henry a bit of a rogue, but the Judsons found in him an innate sense of honesty and common sense that was endearing. He loved talking about his early days at the Burmese court, when the Golden Eyes had looked kindly at him. Henry's adventures along the Irrawaddy were fascinating, and the Judsons shuddered at violent encounters he or his friends had had with such varied hazards as poison springs, at least one man-eating alligator, and even a voracious tiger.

Some of the best stories revolved around foods eaten and some that they wished they had not. All had learned not to inquire about the origin of certain delicacies. Gouger had both Judsons laughing and shuddering as he described a favorite court dish. As a guest, he had had no choice but to eat it:

> *Being already a favorite, I was permitted to gratify my curiosity by tasting one of the most suspicious-looking dishes. It was a kind of sand-cricket fried crisp—nice enough, except in name. Another favorite insect is one with which I would not offend the stomach by calling it a maggot, if I could find another word equally appropriate. It somewhat resembles a nut-maggot, magnified to three or four inches long. When fried and spread on toast, it is not to be distinguished from marrow, though I never could overcome my repugnance to its shape and its large black head, with which it was brought to table entire in undisguised hideousness.*

In a more serious vein, the three discussed at length the tense situation to which they awoke each morning, never knowing what might happen that day. Gouger shared his insights into the "royal" mind, feeling that the possession of power spelled ruin for what he called "the Burmese character." Gouger had actually met the mighty

General Bandula and described him as "beside himself with pride." In all his observations, Gouger concluded that the worst habit of the Burmans was their utter disregard for truth when an object could be gained by lying. The Judsons agreed but shared with Henry that the Burman converts had found divine help in getting rid of this troubling habit.

The little group that gathered each Sunday saw the political situation deteriorating by the day and sadly reached the inevitable conclusion that the war was about to begin. Worse, the Burmans seemed totally ignorant of both their own weakness and England's strength. This could only be a recipe for disaster for Burma. Many years later, Gouger would write a penetrating book about the prison months that each of the foreigners would soon endure. The book reveals his deep admiration and respect for the Judsons. Until meeting them, Gouger had held a cynical view of missionaries. Shared sufferings radically changed his views, and the influence of Ann and Adoniram permanently changed his relationship with God.

The foreigners in Ava had no way of knowing what had happened in Rangoon. Even had they known, they could have done nothing to aid their distant friends since they were under constant surveillance in Ava. The English had already attacked Rangoon, and the two missionary couples there—the Houghs and Wades—were immediately arrested by Burman authorities and marked for execution. Through a harrowing set of events, the four miraculously escaped with their lives and sailed for Bengal and safety. George Hough wrote to missionaries in Calcutta to say that they had not been able to hear from the Judsons or Price in three months and could not predict their fate. He wrote, "*We tremble whenever we think of them. We can only pray that God, who has delivered us, may deliver them also.*"

On Sunday morning, May 23, 1824, the usual group of worshippers in Ava were in prayer when the door burst open and a breathless messenger blurted the chilling news: the British fleet had reached Rangoon, bombarded that city, and captured it. They were gripped by fear and immediately began to pray for wisdom and guidance. Gouger knew that his presence as an Englishman meant danger for all the foreigners, and they agreed not to be seen together again. Being Americans might help protect the Judsons, but the couple knew that every hour was still fraught with danger.

Ann and Adoniram stayed close to home with Koo-chil, their loyal Bengali cook, Maung Ing, and Mary and Abby. Soon an ominous new rumor began to spread that all foreigners were spies. The invidious power of the Golden One was like a snail crossing the road, leaving a trail in its wake and tainting all who could not avoid its effect. What possible means of escape from the emperor could there be?

CHAPTER 28

Henry Gouger, the young English businessman imprisoned with Judson, made this sketch some twenty years after their release.

The Death Prison 1824

THE AIR FELT HEAVY AND STILL IN THE MISSIONARY HOUSE ON STILTS, as Ann and Adoniram Judson attempted to remain calm and draw no attention to themselves or their fellow foreigners. The veteran missionaries understood all too well that the emperor's power was absolute and that he led a court that was ignorant in the ways of the world and arrogant. Bagyidaw had a reputation for being swift in changing from smiling monarch to vicious executioner if he were crossed in any way. The lives of others were mere toys to him, and most vulnerable and expendable were foreigners.

One by one, the foreigners in Ava were questioned by the emperor's officials. First in line were Rodgers and Gouger, the hated Englishmen. Gouger was a special target because he was known to be wealthy, making him a perfect quarry for corrupt leaders. The insidious whispers had already spread through the streets of Ava: "All foreigners are spies." Among Gouger's papers were the records of business transactions showing that the funds for the missionaries' salaries came from Bengal through Gouger and his bank account. To greedy eyes, it was damning evidence of collusion between Gouger and the Americans.

Late on a steamy Tuesday afternoon, June 8, 1824, Ann and Adoniram had just sat down to their evening meal when the royal summons reached their door. They heard an insistent banging on the door above the usual din of children at play. Ann stared at Mr. J, her eyes widening, and opened the door to the terrifying sight of "Spotted Face," the dreaded chief jailer of Let Ma Yoon, the death prison. With him stood a band of prison guards. Ann's heart was beating so loudly she could scarcely hear the fateful words he spoke: "Where is the teacher?" Adoniram stepped forward, declaring, "I am he."

Spotted Face spoke the dreaded words, "You are called by the emperor," and immediately threw Adoniram to the floor. Kneeling on top of him, he took a hard cord and slipped it around his arms above the elbow. The cord was as effective as a tourniquet, not only an instrument of control but also one of torture. If drawn too tightly, whether accidentally or by design, blood would spurt from the person's nose and mouth, and a prisoner could literally choke to death on his own blood.

Ann stood frozen in horror. The hour of terror was upon them. Their only recourse was absolute dependence on their sovereign God as they faced the dark pit of the unknown. Seeing Adoniram lying helpless on the floor galvanized an intrepid Ann, releasing her from the grip of fear. Clutching the chief jailer's arm, she cried out, "Stop! I'll give you money! Stop!" The jailer whirled around and stared at her, barking out a new command, "Arrest her as well—she's a foreigner too!"

Adoniram somehow struggled to his feet and begged Spotted Face to leave his wife alone. The jailer, seeming to forget his malice toward the foreign woman, dragged his bound victim out of the house as a crowd looked on in dread. From that moment on, the scene was chaos personified. Mary and Abby were screaming in terror, and Maung Ing and Koo-chil stood petrified at the insults heaped on their beloved Yoodthan. Ann ignored her trembling hands and the sinking feeling in the pit of her stomach and, grabbing a handful of silver, pressed it into Maung Ing's hands and asked him to follow Adoniram and bribe Spotted Face to loosen the cord before it dislocated his shoulder. While she waited for Maung Ing's return, Ann's keen mind was already at work thinking of what she might possibly do in the face of such terrifying circumstances.

It felt like forever to Ann before Maung Ing came hurrying back, despair written across his face. One look told Ann the news was not good. A bleeding Adoniram had been dragged through the streets, first to court, where the emperor's order was read before governor and city officials, and then to the most foreboding spot imaginable, Let Ma Yoon. Ann knew the translation of the term immediately—"Hand Shrink Not," from perpetuating any depravity. Thankfully, when the governor at the court saw the treatment accorded the teacher, he ordered the cord removed from Judson's swollen and bleeding arms. Maung Ing watched helplessly as his beloved Yoodthan was pushed into the inner prison and the door slammed shut. All was darkness at Let Ma Yoon, which stood right next to the emperor's palace. There could not have been a greater contrast in the two spots: one a palace, the other a prison.

As Ann listened in dismay to Maung Ing's account, her inner core quickly asserted itself. She might be confined to her own house, her husband thrown in prison, the two little girls and faithful servants waiting in dread and totally dependent on her, but no longer was her mind paralyzed by fear. She had no time for tears or terror. Ann managed to calm the children and set them to a simple task. Then she slipped away to her room and fell on her knees beside the bed, calling on her sole and sure Refuge.

Not an hour passed before the city magistrate came hammering on the door, demanding that "Mrs. Teacher" come out and submit to interrogation. He kept shouting, while inside Ann rushed from room to room, destroying their letters and journals. Because they were being accused of spying, it would be suicide to have their correspondence fall into Burmese hands. Her mouth was dry with fear, but this was no time to collapse in despair. Ann stepped onto the verandah and submitted to questioning. The magistrate tried every possible method at his disposal to entrap her, but he found himself facing a far quicker mind than his own. She parried every question put to her with evasiveness but never with untruth. The magistrate went away, grinding his teeth in frustration and leaving a guard of ten men to prevent Ann from leaving the house.

Ann went inside and barred the door. Immediately the guard became suspicious and commanded her to come back out or they would "break the door down." In turn, she threatened to report them to the authorities in the morning. They took revenge by placing Maung Ing and Koo-chil in stocks. Ann could not bear that. She promised to give the guards a "gift" in the morning if the two terrified men were released. The Burmans lived by bribes, and Ann knew she could use such knowledge to her advantage. In the months to come, bribery became her mainstay in the battle to keep Adoniram alive.

Darkness now covered the city of Ava, although it had invaded Ann's heart hours earlier. She had heard the phrase "the dark night of the soul" countless times, but never had it been this real to her. The dreadful silence was deafening, and she was perilously close to hopelessness. *Was Adoniram still alive*? Anguish gripped her at so dreadful a speculation. She dared not consider the alternative. Ann knew she must garner her resources and seek divine power and wisdom beyond her own if they were to survive. She could only weep as she contemplated what terrors this night held for him who was dearest to her. Two years later she wrote about that infamous night: *"You may well imagine that sleep was a stranger to my eyes."* Ann lie staring into the darkness hour after hour; most of the time her prayers were nothing more than a refrain of *"Oh God, oh God, oh God, help!"* while the tears trickled unheeded down her cheeks, soaking her pillow.

Morning dawned, and with it a new determination on Ann's part to somehow, some way, help Adoniram. First, she prepared food for

Maung Ing to take to Mr. J, and then helped their friend slip away early to see what news he could learn at the prison. Ing soon returned with news both good and bad. Teacher was alive, thank God. However, he was in the inner prison and in three pairs of iron fetters. They would not let Ing see him. The blood drained from Ann's face, leaving her icy cold with fear. In that moment, the magistrate banged on her door, once again demanding answers to his endless questions. Ann begged permission to go and plead for help from a high government official. Still sulking from her evasions of the night before, the magistrate refused, giving as his excuse, "You might escape."

Now what? Then Ann thought of the emperor's sister; this princess had been most friendly and interested in Adoniram just the year before. Ann asked if she could send a note to the princess, and surprisingly the magistrate granted permission. However, a negative answer soon came back: the princess wrote that she "did not understand." It was painfully apparent that she feared approaching her brother, the emperor.

Now what? Ann feared that this might become a question she would ask herself repeatedly in days to come. That likelihood proved all too accurate. Her mind rejected first one scheme and then another. One idea was impractical, and another downright impossible. She decided that for now her best move was to befriend the guards. Her keen understanding of the Burmese culture put her in good stead. She served the guards tea and cigars, of which they were inordinately fond.

Reasoning that no self-respecting Burman could turn down a bribe, she sent a note to the governor asking permission to call on him with a gift. Her tactic worked, and with a flare of hope, Ann set off for the governor's residence. It would be the first of hundreds of trips that she would make in the months to follow, approaching all sorts of officials, pleading for the life of her husband.

The governor did not turn her away. Ann entered her plea for Judson and for Price, who had also been taken, stating that they were not English and certainly were not enemies of Burma. The governor informed her that it was beyond his power to have Judson released or the fetters struck off. He then referred her to his chief officer for

227

help in seeing what might be done to alleviate Judson's suffering. The scowling face of the officer was anathema in Ann's eyes. Predictably, he demanded a bribe and smiled to inform her that the prisoners were at his mercy. He demanded two hundred *ticals* of silver, about $100—a princely sum in that day. Ann did not have nearly enough money with her, but the official took all she had, and on a palm leaf wrote the governor's order to allow her to visit the prison.

While Ann was devising ways to come to his aid, Adoniram had been introduced to the foul spot that would be his home for many months. When he first arrived at the stockade, the ruler of the prison met him at the gate with a grin that was forever imprinted on Judson's mind, a look so happily malicious that it chilled his blood. The chief jailer and all the guards at Let Ma Yoon were convicted murderers, who were known as "Spotted Faces" because of the brand on their foreheads. He demanded immediately that Judson call him Father, *Aphe*, in a cruel twisting of the meaning of the word. Two guards grabbed Adoniram's arms and pushed him toward a block of wood. Aphe and the guards joked while one of the ruffians riveted three fetters to his ankles with an iron maul. Adoniram watched the dreadful process through a blur of sweat and tears. Just one errant stroke of that maul and he would be forever maimed.

The guards then prodded him to walk, but the steps Judson took could not be dignified with the term *walking*, for the chains linking the fetters on his legs were just inches apart. With his first attempt to move, Adoniram fell face first into the muck of the prison yard. The guards poked and prodded him into the shelter at one side of the prison area, forced him to the far corner of the building, and ordered him to lie down on the filthy floor. Judson could hardly see a thing in the faint light that managed to slip in between the chinks in the prison walls. With morbid humor, he quickly concluded that no self-respecting person would *want* to see anything in such appalling surroundings.

When Adoniram's eyes eventually adjusted to the gloom of the inner prison, he could see that he was in a room some thirty-by-forty feet. It was empty except for one piece of equipment: a gigantic row of stocks that could hold more than a dozen hapless sufferers at a time, like an alligator that opened and shut its jaws on its victims. In the weak light, Judson could make out the shapes of some fifty or more fellow captives. All were nearly naked; most looked more like skeletons than living men. He could also see insects of every description, shape, and size. The only bright spot that met his horrified eyes was a small hole in the roof where a rotten plank had been torn off. At least the hole allowed a bit of the fetid prison air to escape.

That air itself defied description. Let Ma Yoon had never been washed down, had never even seen a broom. Consequently, there was a strange sense of permanency about its overpowering odors. Adoniram's first impulse was to gag, then hold his breath, neither of which relieved his misery. Partial remains of long-decayed animals and vegetables, combined with the remains of the betel juice so universally chewed and spit out in Burma, were added to the odors emanating from scores of bodies that never had a chance to bathe. To top it off, daily temperatures exceeding a hundred degrees made the spot seem as close to an approximation of hell as one could find on earth. Such were the daunting conditions that Judson endured on that dreadful, fateful evening in June.

He soon recognized the faces of some of the other prisoners. There lay Captain Laird, and next to him was Rodgers, old and bent with age. Henry Gouger was also lying in chains, and in just a matter of minutes, the small door was pushed open yet again and Jonathan Price shoved inside. Poor leprous Constantine was added to the motley collection of unfortunate foreigners. Within days, two Armenians and the Spaniard Lanciego rounded out the number of non-Burmans. They were fated to be imprisoned together; for how long, they knew not. Furthermore, they were forbidden to communicate in English.

At night, the foreigners' conditions were worse. They were all forced to lie side by side, secured to a bamboo pole passed between their legs and hoisted up so that only their shoulders rested on the ground. In this torturous position, they passed the night, wondering if it were indeed endless or just seemed that way. Dawn eventually came, although in the dim prison light it was hard to see clearly. As soon as one and then another began to stir and stretch with a clanking of chains and moans and groans, the movement of their bodies aroused the repulsive vermin burrowed in their tattered clothing and sent them scurrying.

The grinning Aphe appeared and asked in mocking concern if the prisoners had enjoyed their rest. He lowered the painful bamboo until their feet were barely elevated. The blood began to circulate in legs that had long since become numb, and this in itself brought excruciating pain. Then they were taken, two at a time, outside to relieve themselves. The "comfort" break was five minutes at most and was the only one allowed each twenty-four hours. The sanitary problems that resulted inside the malodorous shed are best left to the imagination.

Judson, Gouger, and the other foreigners who could speak Burmese inquired about their need for food. A smiling Spotted Face informed them that the "government" allowed each prisoner a basket of rice per month, not one grain of which was ever seen by the prisoners. Without help from family outside, all the captives would have starved to death. (Some actually did.) That morning, Ann was still under house arrest, but she sent Maung Ing with food. He was horrified at his first look at Judson. In just a few hours, his honored Yoodthan had become so filthy and disheveled that he was scarcely recognizable. How could he possibly tell Mrs. Yoodthan how dreadful the prison was? Could she bear it?

After living through the longest night of her life, Ann's inner strength manifested itself. She was alive, and God willing, her beloved was also alive. She would somehow find a way to get through this nightmare. There was no other option. Ann Judson's deep faith and determination had never before been tested to this degree in life's extremities. With God as her strength, she would find a way to help Adoniram as well as care for her little Ava family. With renewed courage, she prayed, *"Oh God, I will bless your name."* Then she set about making plans.

Dr. Hanna, Judson's great-grandson, is pictured holding a rare copy of Judson's first edition Bible, housed in Aungbinle Church.

The Priceless Pillow
1824

ANN HAD NO TIME TO DWELL ON WHAT COULD NOT BE CHANGED. Desperate to find some way to help her husband, she began devising one plan after another, searching for any idea that might succeed. In the meantime, she tried to appear composed and kept the little girls busy studying, while also maintaining a calm demeanor in front of Maung Ing and Koo-chil. They were badly frightened by Adoniram's imprisonment and felt completely helpless. Both knew all too well that the emperor's word had the power of life and death.

At Let Ma Yoon, Judson and his fellow prisoners were fearful of what might happen next. Gouger was ordered outside first. Even as he waited to be interrogated, he was forced to watch the torture of a

231

young Burman who finally fainted from the pain. Gouger waited in his chains and tried to endure his terror. Mercifully, he was not tortured, but he was questioned exhaustively. The greedy officials, aware of his extreme wealth, wanted to get their pound of flesh.

Even in the face of such danger and misery, Judson's spiritual depth would not permit him to completely lose hope. He and Henry Gouger even exchanged a bit of gallows humor. The hours dragged by, and rumors began to run rampant through the shed that 3:00 p.m. was the daily hour of execution. As the hour approached, all conversation ceased, with only an occasional whisper. The great gong from the palace grounds pealed out the hour, and the single small prison door was thrust open. Spotted Faces entered and walked toward two men lying with the foreigners on the floor. Not a word was spoken as they were poked and prodded outside, the only sound the clanking of their ankle fetters. The remaining prisoners looked at one another and began to breathe again. At least for one more day, the great gong had not tolled for them.

Next to be questioned was Adoniram, and he, too, was forced to watch a Burman prisoner being tortured. When his interrogation began, Adoniram answered the endless questions about his possessions; afterward he slowly shuffled back into the dark hole of the prison shed. He and Gouger agreed that their situation looked beyond hope, certainly beyond human help.

As soon as she possibly could, Ann headed in the direction of Let Ma Yoon. This morning, in the face of such peril, she wore the bright Burmese outfit given her by the governor's kind wife in earlier, calmer days. With her erect carriage and fine figure, her dark hair combed back and adorned with a flower, she attracted many stares along the uneasy streets of Ava. Ann noticed none of this attention, being intent only on getting to Adoniram. She clutched her precious permit tightly in her hands while her heart raced with apprehension, dreading what she might find.

She never forgot the moment when the guards, after reading the governor's orders, went to bring Adoniram to the gate to see his wife.

Ann looked in horror as the haggard, filthy form of her beloved emerged from the malodorous shed, dragging his iron fetters as he stumbled across the prison yard. In the short time he had been imprisoned, her vigorous, perfectly groomed husband had turned into a filthy, unshaven shadow of himself, his vermin-infested rags making him almost unrecognizable. Many years later, Gouger, who was at that moment hobbling across the stockade yard to receive food from a baker friend, described the sight of Ann at the gate: *"Two nights of restless torture of body and anxiety of mind had imparted to Judson's countenance a haggard and death-like expression, while it would be hardly decent to advert in more than general terms to his begrimed and impure exterior. No wonder his wretched wife, shocked at the change, hid her face in her hands, overwhelmed with grief."* Gouger concluded, *"For though more than thirty-five years have since passed away, the moments reverts* [sic] *to me with all the freshness of a scene of yesterday."*

Ann nearly collapsed. She had already faced the possibility that her Mr. J might have been tortured, even killed, yet this degradation defied her imagination. But her spiritual resources were deep, as was her devotion. Ann swallow the lump in her throat, raised her head, and the two whispered snatches of plans and possibilities. Ann was wracked with pity and a sense of helplessness because she was unable to alleviate his terrible suffering. For his part, Adoniram was beyond grief, knowing he had no way to protect this woman he loved so dearly.

Then suddenly, the Spotted Faces commanded Ann to leave. Turning from an anguished good-bye, Ann, in her brightly colored garments that defied her mood, began the two-mile walk home. With each step of the journey, however, her mind was at work figuring out what she could do now to relieve some of her husband's suffering. Into her mind came the words of Proverbs 12:10: "The tender mercies of the wicked are cruel." It took on a whole new meaning for her that dreadful morning.

If only she could have known that her valiant efforts were already having results! Before the sun set, Adoniram and the other foreigners were moved out of the dark shed into the open enclosure of the stockade. At least for a little while each day, they would be allowed respite from the worst of the filth and sludge of the inner prison. Those wretched men gave silent thanks for the indomitable courage of Ann Judson.

Even against the background of utter degradation that surrounded Adoniram in the death prison, he refused to give up hope. For years he had studied the writings of Madame Guyon, the French mystic, and committed to memory many of her verses. They stood him in good stead in his present dire circumstances. Over and over, his mind would repeat the lines: *"No place I seek, but to fulfil, In life and death, Thy lovely will, no succor in my woes I want, Except what Thou art pleased to give."* The words gave comfort to his heavy heart.

Ann could not forget, even for a moment, the dreadful conditions her dearest one suffered. *What more could she do to help?* Not shy by nature, Ann discovered that her husband's plight was enough to make her even bolder than usual. She decided to go in person to the prince's wife, since his sister was the empress and consequently bore influence at court. Off she went to the residence of the princess, obligatory gift in hand.

Ann would describe how she found the royal wife "lolling on her carpet," but the determined Mrs. Judson minced no words, immediately telling Her Highness the terrible conditions in which her husband found himself, through no fault of his own but simply because he was a foreigner. *"What can Your Highness do to help right this wrong?"* The piercing question startled the royal wife, and Ann wrote later: *"The noble answer came: 'This treatment is not unusual. All foreigners are treated the same.'"* Not quite able to meet Ann's penetrating look, the princess defended herself: *"I am not the king; what can I do?"*

"Place yourself in my situation," Ann countered. "Were you in America, your husband, innocent of crime, thrown into prison, in irons, and you a solitary, unprotected woman, what would *you* do?"

The princess did not answer immediately, but Ann refused to withdraw the question. It hung in the silence of the room as if roasting over a spit and getting blacker by the second. Reluctantly, the princess finally replied, "I will present your petition. Come again tomorrow." Ann stood for a long moment, then spun on her heels and walked out of the royal presence. As she returned to her lonely house, she felt no confidence as to what tomorrow's answer would be and began to plan her next move.

News greeting her at home was scarcely encouraging. A notice had been delivered that as soon as the foreigner Gouger's possessions had been inspected and confiscated, the Judson household would be next. Realizing she must retain some valuables or she would not be able to buy food or have funds for the essential and endless bribes, Ann went to work at once. The silver and valuables had to be protected, so she wrapped most of them in cloth and, as soon as darkness fell, buried them in the backyard—but only after she buried the most precious bundle of all: Adoniram's New Testament manuscript, the work of ten demanding years. As she dug a hole for the priceless document, copious tears watered the ground as she remembered those optimistic times when they had rejoiced to be able to bring God's Word to the Burmans. That already seemed a lifetime ago.

The burials hadn't been a moment too soon. Early the next morning, the royal treasurer appeared at her door with some fifty men, apparently expecting the foreign woman to be sorely intimidated. He had picked the wrong target. Ann Judson, with that marvelous force of personality and unerring people skills, was equal to the moment. She greeted the small army at the door as if they were the parson in Bradford coming to call, and she personally served hot tea and refreshments to all those who could crowd into the little room. It was the power of Ann's presence that dominated the morning, not that of the high-ranking royal treasurer.

The treasurer's first question concerned her gold, silver, and valuables. Ann looked him straight in the eye and told him she had no gold or jewels, but handed him the key to the box that held the remaining silver. He immediately began examining, counting, and weighing, having brought along scales. Ann did not intend for the men to feel comfortable while they did their ugly work. As they counted, she informed them that this money had been given by disciples of the Christian faith in America. It was sacred money, whereupon the treasurer squirmed a bit and suggested that they would list it and maybe it would later be restored. Then he boldly asked if that was all the silver she had. Not willing to lie, she responded with composure, "You are free to search the house as you wish." The search turned up nothing more, and thus the buried treasure remained untouched. Ann's eyes flashed when the greedy officials started fingering the clothing left in the Judsons' bedroom. She shamed them all by observing that surely it would offend the Golden One to be handed someone's used clothing. That ended the pilfering. After what seemed a small eternity, the army of inspectors trooped out, leaving an exhausted Ann to collapse into the nearest chair, the strength drained from her legs. They wouldn't have held her erect at that moment if her life had depended on it. When she felt recovered enough to function again, Ann left for her next trip to Let Ma Yoon. She stopped along the way to check on her petition with the princess, only to learn that her plan had failed: the princess would do nothing, and the prisoners would remain as they were. For Ann, this was nothing other than a momentary setback. She was already working on other strategies, most significantly a plan to protect the New Testament manuscript.

Arriving at the prison and knowing that she would have only a few moments with him, Ann held back tears at the sight of her beloved's haggard face. Together they quickly devised a plan. Ann would bind the manuscript papers tightly together and then figure out a way to cover them. Adoniram suggested she could paint on a lacquer coat to form a hard pillow such as was common in the country. Their hope was that they could then bribe the avaricious guards to accept silver in exchange for allowing the prisoner to have the small comfort of a pillow.

It took several days, for she had to wait for the lacquer to dry, but the scheme worked. Ann arrived at the prison one afternoon with the crude pillow tucked under her arm. When the jailer brought Adoniram to the gate, Ann slipped several pieces of silver into the jailer's waiting hands, her heart pounding so rapidly she feared the man could hear its beating. But when Spotted Face walked away to brag about his largesse, Ann and Adoniram looked at one another in perfect understanding. It was the supreme irony: disguised as Adoniram's headrest, the only existing copy of the Scripture written in Burmese would be protected right under the eyes of the enemy. Ann clasped his hand as their hearts took courage once more. The Holy Presence was in their midst in this most unholy of spots.

CHAPTER 30

The emperor's watchtower is the only extant structure from the palace in Ava.

The Heart of Darkness
1824

NIGHTS IN THE DEATH PRISON WERE THE MOST ABSOLUTE DARKNESS Judson had ever experienced. They felt tangible enough to be cut into sections: early darkness, midnight black, and that dreary darkness before dawn that seemed to stretch until it screamed. The sounds of misery were unceasing, from the clanking of chains to the groaning of souls in constant torment. Yet even in the throes of such unremitting misery, Adoniram gave thanks for the priceless pillow, right there under the enemies' eyes, inches from their treading feet.

One night about a month after Adoniram's imprisonment, Ann lay in her solitary bed and, as had become her habit, pondered schemes for the next day, wondering what she might contrive that would help her beleaguered Mr. J. A sudden thought pierced her mind: *something is different.* She had been tiring so easily, and her stomach seemed in a constant state of turmoil, as well as her mind and spirit.

The realization struck her with chilling force: *I'm pregnant. Oh, dear God, a baby. A baby now? It couldn't be.* Even as Ann tried to convince herself it wasn't so, she knew she was carrying a child.

Tears welled in her eyes, and she was soon weeping helplessly. For these past seven years, ever since little Roger had died, she had longed for a baby. But now? Her baby's father was in the death prison. Repeatedly she prayed, "Oh dear God, help me bless your name whatever happens." Her hands curved protectively about her body, thinking of the little one to come. "Dear Lord," she whispered, "somehow keep this baby safe. Grant me grace to handle each day." Once again she thought of the verse from the Book of Romans that had been her mainstay these dozen years: "Present your bodies a living sacrifice"—but surely she had never thought of conditions such as this. Within an hour, she had wept herself into the welcome oblivion of much-needed sleep.

Hurrying to Let Ma Yoon the following morning, Ann determined not to give the news of her pregnancy to Mr. J. He was already grieving terribly, and knowing that he was helpless to aid her in her condition would merely increase his already heavy burden. Walking along, she began reciting the words of Deuteronomy 33:27 that so frequently brought solace to her hurting heart: "The eternal God is thy refuge, and underneath are the everlasting arms." How desperately she needed those arms to hold her up!

Glancing up from the road, Ann noticed a young woman coming toward her and recognized her noble status as evidenced by the richness of her dress. She had seen this woman nearly every day as she walked back and forth the weary two miles to the prison. This morning, the lady fell into step beside her, saying timidly, "Excuse me, *Tsa-yar-ga-dau*," and Ann smiled at the woman's use of the same phrase by which the governor of the north gate addressed her: "eminent wife of the big teacher." Shyly the young woman thrust a small package into Ann's hands, saying, "Please, I know you go each day to see your honored husband. Let me help with a bit of rice and fish," and she looked at Ann with pleading brown eyes.

Ann was moved, and so raw were her emotions this morning that she was close to tears. Pausing a moment, she responded, "How kind of you. But I can do nothing in return for you, I fear." "Oh, honored lady," protested the younger woman, "I simply want to help." Deeply touched, Ann walked beside the kind woman and began to explain her reason for coming to live in Burma with her husband, the "big teacher": they wanted to share some special stories with friends in Ava. "I love stories!" exclaimed the courtier's wife, for such she was, her husband serving in the emperor's entourage.

And thus began a routine for Ann as she traversed the long and lonely route to Let Ma Yoon, day after long and sweltering day. The courtier's wife would join her for several minutes each day as she made her way to the local market, always with a gift of food for Ann to share with "Honorable Teacher Yoodthan." Over the period of the many prison months, Ann was able to share stories from Scripture with her, ranging from Creation to the cross of Christ. It was balm to Ann's aching heart to have an opportunity to feel like she was doing that to which she was called.

Ann and Adoniram established something of a routine, if the chaos in which they lived could be dignified with such a term. Each day had a bit of variation from the one that preceded it. The differences stuck out like little jewels against the black fabric of long hours of hunger, of walking, of pleading for help. Some days Ann would take meals to Mr. J, and other days she would send the food by Maung Ing. When food became harder to procure, Ann was so very grateful for the generous and compassionate courtier's wife.

Ann haunted the courts and the various palaces of the nobility, hoping and praying her silver and gifts for bribes would hold out. Who knew how long she would need them? Every week seemed like a month, and Mr. J's release from prison appeared a forever away. As she importuned on Adoniram's behalf, the officials would listen, shake their heads, and remind her yet again that there was nothing they could do. Occasionally a gift would open a door, and someone would pity her and send orders for some small and temporary relief for Judson and his fellow prisoners.

One unforgettable morning, a particularly malevolent court official made the nearly five-months pregnant Ann stand an entire morning in the hot sun with only a parasol for protection, awaiting her chance to talk to her husband. After finally condescending to hear her plea, he rejected it immediately. A weary Ann turned and started back down the steep steps, the reservoir of unshed tears in her heart threatening to overflow. "Wait!" called the official, just as she reached the bottom step. Turning with a new flare of hope, Ann waited for what he might say. Instead, he strode down the stairs, seized her parasol, and informed her with a malevolent laugh, "You are so thin," he announced, "the sun cannot find you!" Ann never forgot that blinding moment of vicious spite, nor the malicious look on the official's face. As she walked determinedly toward the prison without her parasol, she thought wryly, *If I were a teapot, I'd be steaming just now.*

Some days the guards at Let Ma Yoon would let her see Adoniram for a few minutes. Other days they refused altogether. Henry Gouger had a faithful servant who frequently brought him food, and Ann often brought Gouger and Price meals along with Adoniram's. Gouger had also found another way to obtain food: he speared fat rats that made themselves at home in the prison and traded them with a jailer's daughter for rice. She was infatuated with Gouger, and he in turn was thankful for a steady source of rice.

If they were in a particularly benevolent mood, the guards might allow Ann to bring some clean clothes for Mr. J, which were every bit as welcome to him as food. Sometimes when she was not allowed to see Adoniram, she would slip him messages, finding ingenious ways to hide them. One of her favorites was in the spout of the teapot she regularly prepared for him.

After the war with Britain finally ended, Ann wrote Elnathan about the horrors of those endless months:

> *During these seven months, the continual extortions and oppressions to which your brother was subject, are indescribable. Sometime sums of money were demanded; at*

241

other times, an order would be issued that the white foreign-
ers should not speak to each other and how many, many
times have I returned from that dreary prison at nine o'clock
at night, solitary and worn out with fatigue and anxiety, and
endeavored to invent some new scheme for the release of the
prisoners. Sometimes, for a moment or two, my thoughts
would glance toward America and my beloved friends there,
but for nearly a year and a half, so entirely engrossed was
every thought, with present scenes and sufferings, that I sel-
dom reflected on a single occurrence from my former life, or
recollected that I had a friend in existence out of Ava.

On rare occasions, Ann was permitted to spend an hour with Judson in the open shed. After a matter of months and numerous bribes, she was granted permission to build him a little bamboo lean-to where he could have a bit of privacy. It was tiny, about five by six feet, scarcely enough space in which to lie down. All too seldom, Ann was allowed to bring him a container of water for washing. That little treasure of a pitcher of water was like liquid gold to Adoniram. Cleanliness was the luxury Judson most craved. His distaste for anything not spotlessly clean that went all the way back to his childhood was so deeply ingrained that it made his suffering in the death prison that much closer to unendurable. Years later, it was still impossible for Adoniram to put on clean white garments and shiny shoes, or to take a bracing shower, without remembering what a privilege such a simple thing could be.

With the passing of each day, Ann realized she could no longer delay telling Mr. J about the baby. One afternoon in the little lean-to, she broke the news. Judson's eyes were a mixture of hope and horror. He came to tears, knowing that he was unable to be with her during such a vulnerable time. At the same time, Adoniram's heart swelled with pride at the inestimable fortitude of his wife, toiling now to walk the miles back and forth to Let Ma Yoon yet never faltering in her pleas on behalf of her husband. She continued to wear her bright Burmese *lungyi* and was a familiar sight in the streets of Ava as she went from one official to another, secretly respected and admired as she doggedly sought relief for the foreign prisoners.

One of the hardest things for Judson to bear was idleness. He longed to be up and doing, fulfilling his call. Enduring the enforced inactivity of prison was agonizing, and he tried to keep his mental faculties sharp by reviewing passages of Scripture and bits of literature he had memorized through the years. Another favorite mind exercise was translating an English passage into Burmese, or maybe Hebrew or Greek. One of Madame Guyon's memorized sayings took on new relevance in his imprisonment: "*If knowing answers to life's questions is absolutely necessary to you, then forget the journey. You will never make it, for this is a journey of unknowables, of unanswered questions, enigmas, incomprehensibles, and most of all, things unfair.*"

In their rare moments together, Adoniram would recount to Ann how he and the others managed to pass the long, dreary hours. He and Gouger were by far the most compatible and the most alike in intelligence and creativity. They managed to find scraps of bamboo and carve a chess set. While playing such a challenging mind game helped while away many hours, Judson longed for the relief of a few books. What a treasure a Bible would be! He was thankful to God for the countless passages he knew by heart. In truth, in these unspeakable living conditions that were the epitome of the heart of darkness, the precious truths of the Lord, the Light of the world, sustained his aching soul and brought a comfort beyond mere words.

As Judson struggled to maintain a grip on all that was good and pure, he consistently gained strength from Ann. Just being able to see the determination and tenderness written on her dear face gave him renewed courage. She spent her days devising some small thing to lighten his load or to cheer his weary heart. The food she was able to obtain was so monotonous and so nearly unpalatable that she was forever trying to find some way to improve it. She discovered that she could use some substitute ingredients to prepare a dish that closely approximated his childhood favorite, mincemeat pie. The morning she prepared it, however, she was detained by the governor, so she sent the treasured pie by Maung Ing. Years later, a friend described Judson's reaction:

> *When his wife had visited him in prison, and borne taunts and insults with and for him, when she had stood up like an enchantress, winning the hearts of high and low, making savage jailers and scarcely less savage nobles, weep; or moved, protected by her own dignity and sublimity of purpose, like a queen along the streets, his heart had throbbed with proud admiration. But in this simple, homelike act, this little unpretending effusion of a loving heart, there was something so touching, that he bowed his head upon his knees, and the tears flowed down to the chains about his ankles. Plymouth, Mother, home—the memories overwhelmed him. Ann's loving gift had touched an unprotected corner of his heart.*

Bandula was now the supreme commander of all Burma's armies and ruler of the nation in every way but one. As the war progressed, so progressed the treatment of Adoniram and the other prisoners. The captives came to understand the signal. Two blasts of a cannon meant the Burmans had won a battle. One blast meant a defeat. The foreigners quickly learned that their conditions varied depending on the signal. One blast and they were immediately confined to the inner prison, and it would be days before Adoniram was allowed to see Ann.

About this time, a new prisoner arrived at Let Ma Yoon and was placed in a barred cage. The foreign prisoners looked at one another. A lion? At Let Ma Yoon? Why on earth? King Lion, it came to be known, had been given to Emperor Bagyidaw by some faraway potentate and had been a favorite of the Golden Eyes. Then the emperor learned that the lion was the symbol of British power. To the Golden Ears, this sounded like a harbinger of bad luck. Thus the unfortunate animal was consigned to the death prison, with orders that no one was to feed him. The roar of the dying lion haunted the prisoners for months to come. However, when the poor creature finally died, the event indirectly benefited Judson. Ann was able to bribe Spotted Face, so eminently bribable was he, and Judson was permitted to spend occasional hours in blessed solitude and comparative cleanliness in the deserted lion cage.

Ann valiantly did all she could to prepare to deliver her own child. She grieved that she would have to go for several weeks without seeing her dear one. At the same time, she repeatedly gave thanks for the blessing of faithful friends like Maung Ing and Koo-chil, who stood in the gap when most needed. On Wednesday, January 26, Ann went into labor. Ing and Koo-chil, neither of whom knew a thing about childbirth, became willing assistants to help their beloved Mrs. Yoodthan. Tiny Maria Elizabeth Butterworth Judson, scarcely as long as her name, finally made her appearance.

Judson, to his dying day, recalled his first look at his beautiful daughter. He recounted the moment to his family many years later. There stood Ann, clothed in her bright Burmese silk, with her shiny black hair combed back and up—a lovely sight. In her arms was a tiny, blue-eyed, fair-skinned little mite wrapped in folds of plaid silk. Ann was not permitted to enter the prison door on that occasion. Maung Ing stood close behind her, and the diabolical old jailer was at one side, laughing and ready to order her away. Fettered as he was, Judson hobbled to the door and held out his arms for his sleeping babe. A family member asked how he would picture himself in that scene, and Judson responded, *"I suppose I should look like some poor convicted wretch bowing before a Madonna, for with all my efforts, I could not get above the knees."* There at the gates of the death prison, Judson looked with love at his newborn baby girl. What could the future possibly hold for her? Their first babe was under the sea, and little Roger lay beneath the battleground of Rangoon. Did Maria have any better chance than they of survival?

The memorial stone at the site of the death prison was ordered buried by the government in the 1980s. This 1919 photo shows the stone in its original form, and standing next to it is Judson's youngest grandson, Dr. A. C. Hanna, father of Dr. Stanley Hanna.

Facing Death
1825

AFTER THAT FIRST VIEW OF HIS PRECIOUS BABY GIRL, ADONIRAM spent the remainder of the day mentally composing a lengthy poem of twenty-four stanzas to welcome her into their family. Many months later, upon release from prison, he wrote it down from memory.

For the moment, however, his all-consuming goal was simply survival. One dreary month followed another, and while Judson constantly fought depression, he could not, by nature, stay disheartened. On afternoons when Judson was allowed in the open part of the stockade, he would seek the shade of the huge tamarind tree that grew just outside the stockade wall in one corner of the yard. From that vantage point, he could see the watchtower near Bagyidaw's palace. That tower reminded him of the watchful eyes of almighty

God, his own strong tower, who surely saw his wretched servant lying in the filth of Let Ma Yoon, as well as that servant's dearest love and newborn daughter, two miles away and far from reach.

Also clearly visible over the stockade wall were the golden spires of glittering pagodas dotting Maha Aung Mye Bonzan, the Buddhist monastery that had just been built near the palace in 1818. Judson was creative enough to find something positive even in such a heathen monument. Ever the optimist, Adoniram believed that the day would come when the spires of Christian churches attesting to the power of omnipotent God would adorn the skylines of Burma.

Fellow prisoner Gouger had a morbid sense of humor and was often heard saying, "Nothing is so bad that it can't get worse." Exactly. By March 1825, the foreign prisoners were occupying their little rooms in the prison yard and feeling about as comfortable as possible in such appalling surroundings. Any sense of optimism abruptly ceased that March afternoon when, without warning, a Spotted Face led each of them to the now-familiar wooden block. One after another was thrust to the stone and two *more* pairs of fetters added to the three they already dragged around with them. Not a word was heard as the prisoners looked at one another with apprehension. Still silent, the guards thrust them back into the fetid darkness of the inner prison.

It was one of their darkest nights. Judson could hear several of the Burman prisoners whispering that the foreigners were to be killed at 3:00 a.m. Adoniram's first thought struck anguish to his heart: he didn't even have a way to say good-bye to his dear Ann and their tiny baby. His next thought was, *"Christ is certain to win Burma."* As to the priceless manuscript, surely his intrepid love would manage to save it, as well as find a way to get through to the British forces that would protect her and baby Maria. In the face of imminent death, Judson reviewed in his mind several passages whose translation he felt he might improve upon.

The hand reaching out to him through the fog of utter despair surrounding that terrible night was a pierced one. The darkness of Let

Ma Yoon was smothering, but Adoniram's soul felt that divine touch. As the nearby pagoda bells sounded the three o'clock hour, the prisoners bowed their heads, and Judson lifted his voice in a prayer for them all. In that moment, an unearthly calm descended on that vile spot, and the prisoners awaited their fate. And waited. And waited. Wonder broke upon them like the morning light that finally penetrated the darkness of their prison. They were still alive.

The following morning, a breathless Maung Ing came hurrying back from the prison after taking breakfast to his teacher. Yoodthan was now in five pairs of irons. Whispered rumors spread of executions soon to come. A frightened Ann rushed to the prison, finding a deathly quiet about the place. Not even bribes could gain her admission. She hurried to the home of the north-gate governor. Ann later wrote of how she pleaded with him that day:

> *Your lordship has hitherto treated us with the kindness of a father. We have looked to you for protection from oppression and cruelty. You have in many instances mitigated the sufferings of those unfortunate, innocent beings. You have promised me particularly that you would stand by me to the last, and though you should receive an order from the king, you would not put Mr. J to death. What crime has he committed to deserve such additional punishment? The old man's heart was melted and he wept like a child, and he said, "I pity you Tsa-yar-ga-dau, a name by which he always called me. I knew you would make me feel; I therefore forbade your application. But you must believe me when I say, I do not wish to increase the sufferings of the prisoner."*

Ann recorded that the elderly governor spoke with sorrow:

> *When I am ordered to execute them, the least that I can do is to put them out of sight. I will now tell you what I have never told you before: that three times I have received inti-*

mations from the queen's brother to assassinate all the white prisoners privately, but I would not do it. I will never execute your husband. But I cannot release him from his present confinement, and you must not ask it.

Within days there was a sudden change in the capital. Mighty Bandula had won a victory. The guns boomed twice with the great news. Surely the British would soon be completely routed. Everyone was praising the glorious and mighty Bandula. But the fame of his victory was brief. In April Bandula was blown to pieces by a stray shell, throwing the armies of Burma into great disarray and erupting panic on the streets of Ava. In the vulnerable aftermath of Bandula's shocking death, his rival officer, the Pakun Wun, saw his opportunity. Going at once to the Golden Ears, he poured out his grandiose plans for quick victory, guaranteeing the frightened Emperor Bagyidaw that the hated British would soon become his slaves. The terrified emperor quickly made the Pakun Wun his new commandant. This signaled new danger for the foreigners, for the Pakun Wun hated Westerners with a passion. This would be his perfect opportunity to settle old scores.

As if the current atmosphere were not sufficiently forbidding, Adoniram fell ill with a violent fever, and Ann despaired for his life. The sorrowful governor took pity and wrote an order to move him to his tiny shed and allow Ann to see him. There she was able to bathe him with a cloth and give him medicine and pure cool water.

The next morning, May 2, when Ann arrived with food for breakfast, she discovered that Adoniram could not eat. The fever was consuming him. Even as she lingered to comfort him, an urgent message came from the governor, asking her to come at once. It alarmed Mr. J, but Ann went. Upon arriving at the north gate, she was puzzled. Apparently the governor only wanted to consult her about his wristwatch but detained her for quite a while. When Ann finally headed back toward Let Ma Yoon, she had only taken a few steps before she met a servant coming on the run, his frightened face telling of new disaster. "All the white prisoners are carried away!" he blurted out.

In horror, Ann turned back to the governor's residence. He knew at once why she had returned. "Yes, Tsa-yar-ga-dau, I heard of it, but I did not want to tell you." The distraught old man looked deep into her eyes: "You can do nothing more for your husband. Take care of *yourself.*" Those daunting words turned her blood cold with fear. Rushing back to the prison and arriving at the gate of Let Ma Yoon, Ann stared in shock. The prison yard was deserted. Not a prisoner, not a Spotted Face to be seen. *Oh God, oh God, oh God*, the despairing cry of her heart kept echoing through her frantic mind.

Panic propelled Ann through the streets of Ava, asking everyone she saw if they had seen the foreign prisoners. Some shook their heads in pity. Others scurried away in fear. Remembering the governor's warning to "take care of yourself," Ann later wrote:

> *It was one of the most insupportable days I have ever passed. Towards night, however, I came to the determination to set off the next morning for Amarapoora (where the prisoners had been taken). Never before have I suffered so much from fear in traversing the streets of Ava. I now suspected some design with which I was unacquainted. I saw also the governor was afraid to have me go into the street, and advised me to wait till dark, when he would send me a cart and a man to open the gates.*

Nearly paralyzed with anxiety, Ann finally reached their little house. She packed their remaining valuables in several trunks, and then thought to fill a chest with medicine. When darkness fell, she took them to store at the governor's residence. She may have slept two hours that dreadful night, spending her long wakeful hours weeping and praying. She could not even know if her beloved had survived the day. It seemed all too likely he had not, considering the fever consuming him just hours earlier.

With the dawn, Ann bade a tearful farewell to Maung Ing, who remained to guard the house and what little they had left. Koo-chil was determined to go with her and the children. With the governor's permit tucked carefully in a pouch that she had concealed in her *lungyi*, Ann set off for Amarapura, eight miles away, where the captives had been taken. Koo-chil, two little Burman girls, and Maria in Ann's arms filled the rickety little cart. She later recorded in her journal, *"The day was dreadfully hot. I procured a cart, but the violent motion and the heat and dust made me almost distracted."* In Ann's thirty-five years, she had made some difficult trips, but at that moment she could remember none this wretched. Maria cried constantly, and the jarring progress of the cart caused Mary and Abby to vomit repeatedly.

Ann's perseverance seemed close to running out when they finally arrived in Amarapura, only to be told the captives had been taken four miles farther, to Aungbinle. Forever afterward, Ann referred to it as *"that never to be forgotten place."* During those tortuous extra miles to Aungbinle, questions kept racing through her mind. Why Aungbinle? Was Adoniram even alive by this time? It seemed likely that the end of hope had arrived.

When Ann had hastened the preceding day to the governor's house in response to his summons, Adoniram had remained helpless in the shed, so hot with fever that he could not eat the food she had brought. The moment she left, a Spotted Face rushed to Judson and stripped off his outer garments and shoes, leaving him only a tattered shirt and trousers. Not a word was spoken as Spotted Face struck off the fetters and tied him with a rope to the Scotsman, Laird. Thus did the guards lead the foreign prisoners, bound two by two, through the streets of Ava. So poor was their condition that it turned into something perilously close to a death march. Ten groaning, filthy wretches staggered through the dusty roads beyond the city gate.

Burning up with fever, Judson suffered pure agony with his feet. For eleven months, he had persisted in wearing his shoes, such that the soles of his feet were not calloused and remained extremely tender and vulnerable. His now bare feet were soon torn and bleeding from the stones in the road. Every step was torment, and within minutes, his footprints were marked in blood. Laird, being both larger and stronger of frame, tried to bear some of Judson's weight, but a year in prison had weakened his constitution as well. Gouger later wrote about that unforgettable march. When they had passed near the edge of a gorge, Judson spoke in a low voice: *"Gouger, the parapet is low; there can be no sin in our availing ourselves of the opportunity."* But Adoniram was bound to Laird, so he would not do that to him.

Every prisoner was in sad stead by this point, with burning, bleeding feet and blisters that formed and burst. Gouger fared only a bit better than the others because of his youth and strength They had scarcely gone a mile when the leprous Constantine collapsed. No amount of prodding or yelling could make him move, and in disgust the guards thrust him into a cart. Within another mile, the feverish Adoniram was nearly as far gone. The bottoms of his feet were a mass of raw flesh.

Then, seemingly from out of nowhere, help came. One of Gouger's Hindu servants had heard the news of the march and came running to help. He took one look at Judson's feet and, not saying a word, tore off the turban that covered his own head, something unheard of for a devout Hindu. Tearing a long strip of its fabric into four pieces, he gave two of them to Gouger. He then took the remaining pieces and gently bound up Adoniram's bleeding feet, and then gave him his shoulder on which to lean for the remainder of the march. For the rest of his life, Adoniram never forgot that golden act of mercy in his hour of deepest need.

Nonetheless, by the time the hapless prisoners reached Amarapura, Constantine had already died. Judson himself was close to fainting from the scorching sun, lack of food or water, and relentless fever. He was, in fact, close to death. The prisoners were turned over to new guards, but no amount of yelling, prodding, and beating could get any of them to their feet. These guards were rough and calloused men, used to suffering, but they were not Spotted Faces. The pathetic prisoners were allowed to spend the night right where they had dropped. The wife of one of Amarapura's judges had followed the prisoners out of curiosity, but now, out of pity, she gave them some fruit and water.

Come morning, even the comparatively strong Gouger could not take another step. The compassionate wife of the judge fed them rice this time, and they were loaded onto a cart and taken the remaining four miles to Aungbinle. By late afternoon, the primitive cart had squeaked its way to a small, rough structure sitting on a grassy plain. The building had clearly been deserted for a long time, its thatched roof all but collapsed and tilting perilously to one side. Only one sign of its sordid past could be seen: a row of stocks in an advanced stage of rot. The exhausted prisoners noticed that in the space beneath the prison's stilts were stacks of piled wood. One commented that this seemed an odd place to store firewood. Horror dawned on several of their haggard faces, and one dared to voice their common fear: "Remember the rumor we heard in Ava that we were to be taken out and burned?"

All this time, Ann was trying to follow the prisoners to wherever they might have been taken. She felt close to defeat when, upon arriving in Amarapura, she learned that the prisoners were no longer there but had been taken on to a place called Aungbinle. At that point, the cart man refused to go farther. After waiting an excruciating hour in the burning sun, Ann was finally able to procure another cart and set off for four more miles of misery, dreading what she and her companions might discover when she got there. In the back of her mind was another grief—the priceless manuscript. God only knew what had happened to Adoniram's lacquer pillow. Lost forever. Helpless tears coursed down her cheeks just thinking of those ten years of diligent work now gone.

But before her lay a more immediate crisis. Aungbinle stretched in front of her, and she saw a shattered prison building with no roof. As her cart approached, she saw a dozen Burmans on top, trying to make a roof with leaves. Outside the prison, under a few scraggly trees, lay the foreigners, chained together in twos, almost dead with suffering and fatigue. In her letter the next year to Elnathan, Ann wrote: *The first words of your brother were, "Why have you come? I hoped you would not follow, for you cannot live here."* As if to emphasize the truth of what he said, Judson's eyes glazed over, and mercifully he fainted and remained unconscious for hours.

But Ann Judson had achieved at least one of her goals: she had found Adoniram, and he was alive. In their hour of such dire need, in a place that was an approximation of hell on earth, with no human resources on which to rely, Ann cried from the depth of her soul, "*Oh God, give me courage. I bless your name.*" Even as the salty tears ran down her flushed cheeks, she repeatedly sought mercy from the only Source she knew. "*Oh divine Master, grant me mercy; imbue me with courage. Mine is all used up.*" And to her broken heart came the assurance: "The eternal God is thy refuge, and underneath are the everlasting arms."

Judson Memorial Baptist Church is built on the site where Judson lay for the last months of his imprisonment. It was built as a memorial to Ann Judson.

From Aungbinle to Maloun 1825

NIGHT WAS FALLING. HER HUSBAND WAS CLOSE TO DEATH. THERE was no food, no shelter. An ordinary person would have given up in despair at such appalling circumstances, but Ann Judson was no ordinary person. Cradling her baby in her arms, Ann appealed to Koh-bai, the head jailer, asking for permission to put up a little shelter nearby. The jailer refused. It was not customary, was his immediate response. Then he looked into her dark eyes, weary with a fatigue that transcended words, and even his hardened heart was moved by pity. Standing just yards away was the tiny two-room house where his family lived in one room. Looking at the thin young mother drooping with exhaustion, he spoke: "The other room here, where I have grain. You and the little ones can use it." Ann gave thanks for that rare moment of mercy, knowing they would at least have a shelter over their heads. They still had no food, and they were out in the middle of nowhere, surrounded by a darkness unrelieved by moonlight. Thanks to Koo-chil, they at least had boiled water to drink, and everyone fell into exhausted sleep on the sacks of grain in the tiny, sweltering shelter.

Not far away in the rotting old prison, Adoniram was close to death and barely aware of his circumstances. The captives were put in the stocks, and the bamboo pole raised their ankles again above their heads. There was a difference, however, between these stocks and those at Let Ma Yoon. These at Aungbinle allowed the prisoners to be victimized by the army of mosquitoes swarming in from the surrounding rice paddies. The pesky insects feasted on the bleeding soles of their victims, and the pain was agonizing.

Dawn finally came, and a friend of Dr. Price who lived in Amarapura arrived with curry and rice for the captives. The jailer Koh-bai miraculously allowed Ann and the little ones to share the bounty. She was even blessed with a cup of tea, which to Ann seemed like a special gift. The jailer also permitted Ann to visit Mr. J.

Although Adoniram was slightly better after some rest, he could not get to his feet. For dinner that evening, Gouger's baker showed up with biscuits and salt fish. In the bright light of day, Ann looked about their tiny room and later described her feelings in her lengthy letter to Elnathan:

> I had not a single article of convenience—not even a chair or seat of any kind, excepting a bamboo floor. But our heavenly Father was better to us than our fears, for notwithstanding the constant extortions of the jailers during the whole six months we were at Aungbinle, and the frequent straits to which we were brought, we never really suffered for the want of money, though frequently from want of provisions which were not procurable.

Ann then proceeded to recount the subsequent development of events that occurred during the next dreadful months. She explained:

> The very morning after my arrival, Mary Hasseltine [the lit-tle Burman girl] was taken with the smallpox, the natural way. She, though very young, was the only assistant I had in taking care of little Maria. But she now required all the time I could spare from Mr. J, whose fever still continued in prison and whose feet were so dreadfully mangled that for several days he was unable to move. I knew not what to do, for I could procure no assistance from the neighborhood, or med-icine for the sufferers, but was all day long going backwards and forwards from the house to the prison, with little Maria in my arms. Sometimes I was greatly relieved by leaving her for an hour, when asleep, by the side of her father, while I returned to the house to look after Mary, whose fever ran so high as to produce delirium. She was completely covered with postules [sic] . . . and I knew Maria would take it; I therefore, inoculated her from another child. At the same time I inoculated Abby and the jailer's children, who all had it so lightly as hardly to interrupt their play. But, the inocu-lation in the arm of my poor little Maria did not take—and she had it the natural way. She was then only three months and a half old, and had been a most healthy child; but it was about three months before she perfectly recovered from the effects of this dreadful disorder.

Ann's fame spread through the village, and all the mothers wanted their children inoculated as well. It was a risky thing, for the inocula-tions might well fail, and she would be blamed. Nonetheless, she carefully inoculated the children of the entire village, and not one child contracted the deadly disease. Ann constantly looked for bright moments in the fabric of unspeakable hardships. This was one of them.

She and Mr. J gave thanks for the country air. The hot weather was suffocating, but the air in the countryside was clean and not laden with the incredible stench of Let Ma Yoon. All the foreigners rejoiced to discover that the wood stacked under the ramshackle prison had been put there to keep the rotting floor from completely collapsing. It was not for a prisoner bonfire. Within two days of arriving at Aungbinle, Ann had located a small market not far away, where she and Koo-chil could buy food. She was again grateful that she had been able to save some silver and valuables to trade. Otherwise they would have starved.

Meanwhile, Adoniram was finding his ability to concentrate weakening, and that frightened him. The daily anxiety of the unknown future and an ever-present sense of insecurity plagued his mind, especially because he could do nothing to ease his dear love's hardships. In fact, he only added to her burdens, as Judson realized all too well. Furthermore, his grief was multiplied by sorrow over the loss of the priceless New Testament manuscript. It was surely gone forever—ten years of loving labor. Over and over he prayed: *God, somehow give me the opportunity to do the translation again.*

However, there were other bright spots for which Ann and Adoniram were grateful. Above all, they thanked God for the absence of Spotted Faces. The prisoners from Ava had not been at Aungbinle very long when the jailer, Koh-bai, realized that these foreigners were not fierce enemies but simply weak, dejected mortals. Thus the prisoners were fettered in only one set of chains and— glorious news—given a little water for bathing. Ever so slowly, the soles of Adoniram's feet healed, and after about six weeks, he could hobble about the stockade to get some exercise. Adoniram was also thankful that, despite the mosquitoes, Aungbinle lacked the other nasty vermin of Let Ma Yoon. There was a new problem, however, because deadly snakes often slithered in from the rice paddies—a ghastly sight to the weakened prisoners, but miraculously none of the prisoners was bitten.

As for Ann, she gave thanks that Mr. J and the others had gained enough strength to move around again. Unfortunately, she had now reached the limit of her own physical endurance. Dysentery was almost always fatal to foreigners, and Ann's blood ran cold the morning she woke up and realized it had struck her. Her first thought was, *Oh God, I cannot die now. Too many depend on me,* and she could not stop her tears. That inner fabric of spiritual strength was straining under the pressure, and she cried out for mercy: "God, sift me clear of weakness, Lord. Make me strong."

Adoniram was appalled at her condition and agonized over his own inability to give her aid. In the letter Ann later wrote Elnathan, she recounted the harrowing dilemma that confronted her:

> *My constitution seemed destroyed and in a few days I became so weak as to be hardly able to walk to the prison. In this debilitated state, I set off in a cart for Ava, to procure medicines and some suitable food, leaving Koo-chil to supply my place. I reached the [mission] house in safety, and for two or three days the disorder seemed at a stand: after which it attacked me so violently, that I had no hopes of recovery left—and my only anxiety now was to return to Aungbinle to die near the prison.*

Ann finally managed to get to the governor's residence where her medicine chest was stored. Overcome with weakness, she crawled back into the cart and started back to Aungbinle, wracked by fear for Maria and the others. Occasionally she would take two drops of laudanum (a tincture containing 10 percent opium). The jolting cart ride nearly tore her weakened body apart. She later wrote, *"I had just reached Aungbinle when my strength seemed entirely exhausted. Koo-chil came out to help me into the room, but so altered and emaciated was my appearance, that the poor fellow burst into tears at the first sight."* Ann was in fact very close to death for two months. Faithful Koo-chil thrust aside his Hindu taboos about caste and did everything he could for his beloved Mrs. Yoodthan, never once complaining and receiving no wages for his care of the entire household.

During those perilous weeks when Ann was so ill, Judson used some of the hoarded valuables to bribe the jailer to allow him to hobble to the village with Maria several times each day to beg some kind mother to nurse his infant. Ann was so ill that her milk had dried up.

Miraculously, Ann lived, Adoniram lived, and tiny Maria lived. But about the time Ann was regaining a measure of strength, a new rumor reached the foreigners at Aungbinle. All had been curious to know why they had been transferred to this isolated spot. The new rumor spread that Aungbinle was also the birthplace of the great General Pakun Wun, and hearsay murmured that the plan was to bury the white prisoners alive as a good luck charm to ward off the approaching British. They would be an offering to the spirits of war. The mere thought was enough to chill their blood.

Whether it was true or not they never learned, because stunning intelligence arrived within a matter of days. Gouger's staunch baker stumbled into the prison big with news: Pakun Wun was dead. "Are you certain?" Gouger asked in amazement. The baker was absolutely certain, for he had seen it happen: The emperor had heard that Pakun Wun was plotting to seize the throne. Upon confirming the veracity of the conspiracy, Bagyidaw proceeded to have his own palace guards drag the general by his hair to the place of execution, where a wide-eyed crowd watched as Pakun Wun was trodden to death by elephants. Judson, Gouger, and the other prisoners could not help but rejoice. There would be no live burial after all!

But with the Burmese armies having no high commander and the British fast approaching the Golden City, panic reigned in Ava and rumors ran rampant across the countryside. Sir Archibald Campbell, the British commander, was said to have offered the emperor some form of treaty, but being highly suspicious of Westerners, Emperor Bagyidaw suspected this was a plot. Surely the British weren't *really* going to march on Ava.

Soon the Burman court realized that in order to get at the truth, they would have to deal with the despised British with words. Who could do that? They must have help. They must have an interpreter, a translator. One thoughtful noble recognized that there was only one person in all Burma who was qualified for such a task: the American teacher, the foreigner who spoke and wrote flawless Burmese. *The Golden One needed Adoniram Judson, the prisoner!*

The morning of November 4, 1825, as Ann emerged from their bare little room with food to take to the prison, a messenger from Ava came running up and thrust a note into her hand. Puzzled, Ann read the letter sent to her by their friend, the governor of the north gate. An order was even now being written at the palace for Adoniram's release. Ann could scarcely take it in. *Was this some kind of cruel joke? Freedom?* Even in the face of her doubts, a frisson of hope ran through her.

Sure enough, official word arrived that evening, and the following morning Adoniram's fetters were struck off. Then, incredibly, they were told that Ann could not leave. As a safeguard, the jailers would keep Ann there. They were both stunned. All the deprivations and sufferings of the past many months had not removed the power of Adoniram's presence, however, and he convinced the jailers to allow Ann to leave with him by promising them all the food and supplies she had hoarded there in Aungbinle. How could they have survived these agonizing months of captivity without the effectiveness of bribes?

About noon that day, a gaunt and emaciated man and woman, a tiny baby, two Burmese girls, and a Bengali cook climbed into a creaking old cart and headed off for the capital. They had only covered the four miles to Amarapura before Adoniram was taken by guard to the house of the city's governor. Surely the parting was only temporary, the two missionaries thought. Ann hired a little boat and took the others home to Ava and the welcome sight of Maung Ing.

Early the following morning, she went to her friend the governor, who had now been promoted to *Woongyi* (deputy ruler). He assured her that although Judson was still considered a prisoner, it was only until his translating work was completed. Ann, like her beloved

261

Mr. J, was very much a "doer," and to *wait* was a taxing exercise. Weariness finally overcame her, and she fell into exhausted sleep.

The next morning, Adoniram was allowed to stop briefly by their house. Many of their belongings had been looted in spite of all Maung Ing's efforts, but Ann was able to pack a mattress, blanket, and pillow for his trip to Maloun, where the work of translation would take place. Mr. J tenderly held little Maria and once more had to say good-bye to his dear love. This time, both thought, surely it would only be a brief separation.

Ann set about as quickly as her weakened body could manage, trying to get back to some semblance of normality. Thank God, they were home. Upon going to the market the next morning, she was puzzled not to see her young friend, the courtier's wife. She soon learned that the woman and her husband had disappeared some months ago, and no one had seen them since. Ann missed the kind face and the eager ears that had wanted to learn about the living God, and she hoped the compassionate young woman, who had been a bright spot on many dark days, was safe and might turn up again.

Meantime, Judson was given no time to recover from the ordeals of the past nearly two years. It was a three-day journey south to Maloun, and the boat in which they traveled was not even long enough to allow him to stretch out. By the time they reached Maloun, fever had made Adoniram nearly incoherent. The guards put him in a bamboo hut on the blinding white sand beach along the Irrawaddy River. Even realizing he was terribly ill, the guards continued to come every hour with papers for him to translate. This continued until Judson finally lost consciousness. The subsequent days were a tangle of wild dreams and delirium before the fever finally subsided.

Although Adoniram could scarcely move his body, his mind continued to work. It was obvious that the Burmese were now in mortal fear of the English. Their troops were painfully naïve regarding anything not Burmese, so Judson had to spend hours explaining to them what they needed to do, acting not only as translator of the treaty documents but as diplomat as well. With a wry inward smile,

Adoniram thought of this as a "school of negotiations." Burmans had no concept of giving up territory or paying reparations. Both Western means of negotiation were completely foreign to Burmese thinking. At any hour of day or night, Burmese officials would appear at his little tent and ask for advice.

Judson noted the fine irony of the situation: thirteen years ago the British had driven Ann and him from India, not even allowing them to remain there temporarily. Now the British were completely dependent on the good services of Adoniram Judson to effect a treaty on their behalf with an enemy bent on noncooperation.

At this point, the Burmese were entirely disbelieving the good faith of the British. They asked Judson if he would be willing to leave his wife and child behind to be put to death should the English take the money and still march to Ava. Absolutely not. Judson was adamant about protecting his family. After tense back-and-forth discussion, unreasonable demands, deals and counterdeals, a tentative treaty was finally drawn up. Provisions stated that Burma would have to give up four territorial areas and pay the equivalent of one million pounds of British sterling. The British commander, General Campbell, would then allow a fifteen-day armistice for the document to be signed by the emperor.

Fifteen days passed and no word came from the capital. Was Burma playing games? In disgust, Campbell began a march on Maloun. Several days later, on December 17, the Burmese decided negotiations were completed and sent Judson on a boat back to Ava. Shortly thereafter, the British stormed the stockade at Maloun, only to discover the original treaty document, still unsigned, lying on a table in a deserted tent. It seemed that no Burman had been eager enough to have his head separated from his neck by delivering such a treaty to the Golden One.

Adoniram had no idea that the treaty had never been delivered. His sole thought that December day was to get to Ann. Night had fallen before they reached Ava, but the guards led him right past his house. No matter how vociferously he protested, nothing persuaded his guards to allow him to stop there. In an outbuilding by the court-house, Judson was held under guard, sweltering in a humid, stifling room. One guard said he understood that "Teacher Yoodthan" would be returned to Aungbinle prison, which sent a shudder through Adoniram's body. Then late in the evening of his second day back in Ava, Maung Ing appeared in the doorway of the hut. En route to the north gate, he had encountered one of the men who had accompanied Judson from Maloun, and this man told Ing where his teacher was being held.

Maung Ing's face lit up at the sight of his beloved teacher, and he quickly told Adoniram that Ann had just learned that he had been brought back to Ava. "She asked me to go to the governor to see if Yoodthan could be spared from returning to Aungbinle," Maung Ing informed him. In answer to Judson's anxious query, Ing assured him that baby Maria was fine; the teacher was not to worry. Maung Ing then hastened to the governor's residence on his errand, leaving Judson's spirits buoyed by seeing his dear friend. Nevertheless, sitting in the evening twilight with nothing to do but think, Judson began reflecting on their conversation. Several times he had asked about Ann, and Maung Ing had been evasive. That was unlike him. The more Judson thought, the more worried he grew. Something was amiss, badly amiss.

Deadly Fever 1825

Daw Lone Ma, a convert who was baptized by Judson in the early years. She married Ah Vong, the brilliant Chinese-Burmese printer who printed Judson's first edition Bible. Their twelve sons became Baptist leaders across Burma. Picture courtesy of Harriet Bain, great-great-granddaughter of Daw Lone Ma.

ADONIRAM WAS RIGHT TO BE worried. just two weeks after he had been taken under guard to Maloun, Ann had been struck with "spotted fever" (spinal meningitis). Ann later wrote to Elnathan about the traumatic time:

I was seized with the spotted fever, with all its attendant horrors. I knew the nature of the fever from its commencement; and from the shattered state of my constitution, I concluded it must be fatal. The day I was taken with the fever, a Burmese nurse came and offered her services for Maria. The circumstance filled me with gratitude and confidence in God; for though I had so long and so constantly made efforts to obtain a person of this description, I had never been able; when at the very time I most needed one, and without any exertion, a voluntary offer was made. My fever raged violently.

Ann continued her account and then related the next miracle that came to her aid: *At this dreadful period, Dr. Price was released from prison; and hearing of my illness, obtained permission to come and see me. He has since told me that my situation was the most distress-ing he had ever witnessed, and that he did not then think I should survive many hours. My hair was shaved, my head and feet covered with blisters.*

Her neighbors gave her no chance of recovery. The Burmese women living near the mission house clustered sympathetically by the door while Dr. Price was working to save her life. One of the women shook her head in sorrow, saying, "She is dead. If the king of angels should come in, he could not revive her."

Miraculously, consciousness gradually returned to the shattered form of Ann, lying limp on her bed. The first thing to impinge upon her awareness was the faithful Koo-chil standing by her side, trying to induce her to take a little wine and water. Ann wrote to Elnathan:

> *I now began to recover slowly, but it was more than a month after this before I had strength to stand. While in this state, [Maung Ing] came in and informed me that his master had arrived and was conducted to the courthouse in town and it was reported that he [Adoniram] was to be sent back to the prison. I was too weak to hear such ill tidings of any kind; but a shock so dreadful as this, almost annihilated me. For some time, I could hardly breathe; but at last gained suffi-cient composure to dispatch Maung Ing to our friend, the governor, and begged him to make one more effort for the release of Mr. Judson.*

On December 31, 1825, immediately upon hearing the news of Judson's presence in Ava, their influential friend, the governor, came to the rescue, petitioning the highest court for Adoniram's release. The governor actually offered himself as security. That same morn-ing, Judson was released. The last day of the year was his first day of freedom in nearly twenty-one months.

Fifty years later, Judson's youngest son, Edward, wrote about that first day of his father's blessed freedom: "*With a step more fleet than for the last two years he had practiced, and in spite of the maimed ankles which sometimes almost refused their office, he hurried along the street to his beloved home. The door stood invitingly open, and without having been seen by any one, he entered."* Edward then described his father's shock at the sight that met his eyes:

> *The first object which met his eye, was a fat, half-naked Burman woman, holding on her knees a wan baby, so begrimed by dirt that it did not occur to the father that it could be his own. He gave but one hasty look, and hurried to the next room. Across the foot of the bed, as though she had fallen there, lay a human object, scarcely more recognizable than his child. The face was of a ghastly paleness, the features sharp, and the whole form shrunken. The glossy black curls had all been shorn from the finely shaped head, which was now covered by a closely-fitting, cotton cap, of the coarsest and—unlike anything usually coming in contact with that head—not the cleanest kind. There lay the devoted wife, who had followed him so unweariedly from prison to prison, ever alleviating his distresses. The wearied sleeper was awakened by a breath that came too near her cheek. Perhaps a falling tear might have been added; for, steady as were those eyes in difficulties, dauntless in dangers, and stern when conscience frowned, they were well used to tender tears.*

At that moment, Ann slowly opened her eyes, finding before them her beloved's face, and to her wondering gaze, it was like glimpsing heaven. For his part, Adoniram looked into her large brown eyes glazed by the ravages of months of fever and pain. As he saw her dawning joy as she recognized him, it was as if he were seeing into the very corner of her soul.

Ann whispered in disbelief, "Mr. J, is it you? Is it you? You are really here?" In that sublime moment of reunion, each could do nothing but weep. Ann looked close to death, frightening him mightily, but she was in fact slowly recovering. Those earlier weeks when her life hung in the balance, God had provided Koo-chil and Maung Ing. They had become the instruments of her survival.

Now, for the first time in nearly two years, Adoniram could do something to help this one so dear to him. He found great joy in being able to lavish care on his beloved Ann. She had expended everything within her to keep him alive, and now he could focus attention on her.

Several days after Adoniram had returned, Maung Ing came quietly into the room where Adoniram was helping Ann drink some nourishing broth, explaining that he had something for honored Yoodthan. He then placed in Judson's hand a tattered object. Ann and Adoniram gazed down in wonder at the hard inner core of the pillow Ann had made, the pillow on which Adoniram's head had rested those agonizing months at Let Ma Yoon. Judson was absolutely speechless. He had thought he would never see it again, yet here in his trembling hands was the priceless New Testament manuscript, ten years worth of single-minded dedication.

He finally found his voice and asked Maung Ing how on earth he had managed to save the manuscript. An elated Maung Ing explained that after Yoodthan had been dragged from Let Ma Yoon, he had gone to the deserted prison grounds to see if he could find any remembrance of his beloved teacher. Poking around in the bits of rubble scattered on the filthy ground, he had come across the remains of the pillow he had watched Mrs. Yoodthan lacquer and take to the prison. Evidently a guard had ripped off the outer cover, thinking it might be of some value, and had thrown aside the hard inner roll. There in the deserted prison yard, Maung Ing carefully picked up the core of the pillow and took it home, having no idea that he held in his hands such a prize.

That afternoon the Judsons and their friends were alight with rejoicing over the lost that now was found. Ann and Adoniram could not have had a more cherished gift, and Maung Ing was overjoyed to discover that he had unwittingly been the one to rescue such a treasure.

In the next nearly two months of waiting for a peace agreement to be reached, the Judsons were the guests of the governor of the north gate. Ann, Adoniram, Maria, and their two Burmese girls spent those weeks in the comfort of the nobleman's home, while Maung Ing and Koo-chil took care of the mission house and began packing what remained with the hope that soon they could return to Rangoon. It was a healing time for the reunited couple and a special joy for the governor. It eased the old man's heart to finally be able to show special kindness and attention to the courageous woman who had so valiantly spent herself to keep her husband alive. She had earned the Woongyi's lifelong respect and admiration.

Threats of renewed war and bumbling attempts at peace continued in the capital as uneasy negotiations went on. Ann slowly began to regain strength and was finally able to stand on her own. Both she and Adoniram were now treated with great respect by the Burmese authorities, and officials of the government and army were constantly consulting the honored Yoodthan. The Burmans spent weeks vacillating between negotiating and resisting militarily, still unable to grasp the overpowering might of the British armies.

With grinding reluctance, Emperor Bagyidaw finally permitted sufficient gold and silver to be collected to provide for the required indemnity and prepared for its release into the hands of the British. It was the most difficult task of all for the avaricious emperor to pay ten million rupees to the hated enemy. As part of his conditions for peace, Campbell demanded that, in the presence of both Burmese and British generals, each foreigner who had been imprisoned by Bagyidaw be asked if he wished to stay in Ava or to leave. Otherwise, General Campbell warned, there would be no peace agreement.

It was a tense situation, and the Burmese government was not going to lose Judson without a strong effort to persuade him to remain. Adoniram's language skills made him particularly valuable for future purposes. Repeatedly, the most influential Burmans among both the military and the emperor's court pleaded with him. Over and over he heard, "You must not leave us; if you remain, you will become a great man." Ann and Adoniram exchanged quick glances of perfect understanding. Thirteen years of acquaintance with the Burmese propensity for lying when it was expedient assured them of the weakness of such flattery.

In a strange twist of fate, Jonathan Price, the lanky New Englander who had early on become intrigued with the pomp of the royal court, decided he would stay in Ava. Although both shocked and saddened at his decision, neither of the Judsons felt it wise to attempt to persuade him of the folly of such a move. In contrast, Adoniram, when asked for his final decision, was careful to be diplomatic. He was keenly aware of the overweening pride of the Burmese nobility and did not want to exacerbate an already tense situation. Judson quietly but firmly informed the Burmese officials that his wife wished to go with the British and, of course, he would go with her and their child.

It was February 21, 1826, when Ann and Adoniram, baby Maria, and their little family entourage finally left the Golden City of Ava. The boats loaded with the gold and silver indemnities prepared to start down the river. Ann joyfully wrote Elnathan of the moment:

> We took an affectionate leave of the good-natured governor who had so long entertained us at his house, and who now accompanied us to the water side, and we then left forever the banks of Ava. It was on a cool, moonlight [sic] evening that with hearts filled with gratitude to God, and overflowing with joy at our prospects, we passed down the Irrawady, surrounded by six or eight golden boats, accompanied by all we had on earth. The thought that we had still to pass the Burmese camp would sometimes occur to damp [sic] our joy, for we feared that some obstacle might there arise to retard our progress. Nor were we mistaken in our conjectures. We reached the camp about midnight, where we were detained two hours.

The Burmese military at the camp could scarcely be brought to believe the British would keep their word, fearing that as soon as the English had received the money and prisoners, they would continue their march and destroy Ava. Once again Judson used all his powers of persuasion and was at long last able to convince the leery commanders that the honor of the British could be trusted, and the Judsons were allowed to continue with their trip. When the Burmese finally and reluctantly allowed their boat to pass on down the Irrawaddy, Ann and Adoniram heaved a huge sigh of relief. They could still hardly believe they were genuinely free at last. So much time had passed that they had nearly forgotten how freedom felt.

Ann remained gaunt, both from malnutrition and disease. Those two long years had taken a heavy toll on her body. She, whose skin had always had a healthy glow, was now dreadfully pale. A thoughtful British officer had arranged a comfortable cushion on which she could recline, her curls now just long enough to feather her head. Ann appeared more a wraith than a substantial woman, but a smile of relief revealed the joyful state of her heart. Maria was thirteen months old now but no larger than an infant of some three or four months, so meager had been her diet. Twenty-one months of prison life and a daily struggle to stay alive and sane made Adoniram appear an old man. He was now little more than half the weight he had been when in the full vigor of health, his wrists and ankles still an angry pink from the months of wearing tight fetters. Those reminders of Let Ma Yoon and Aungbinle would remain forever carved into the flesh of his wrists and ankles, but his character was of such remarkable depth that the scars were not etched into his soul.

Adoniram looked down at Ann as she reclined on the soft cushion, and he rejoiced that she could finally have some comfort. More than that, his dear love had the exhilarating sense of knowing that they were finally free. Ann glanced up and, seeing his tender look, reached up, touched his cheek, and softly said, "Mr. J, what shall we render to the Lord for all his benefits toward us?" Her eyes filled with wonder as she put into words what her heart was feeling. "Can you believe it? We are free. Just think, no more Spotted Faces, no more chains and fetters." She smiled in pure pleasure, finishing, "and plenty of food, and clean water at last," as she drifted off to sleep with a smile of contentment on her lips.

Adoniram sat watching her relaxed slumber and thought, as he had so many times these past two years, *"Oh Dear Love, what a gift the Lord gave me the day I first saw your beautiful face. God grant I can care for you at long last in the way you so deserve."* The thought became the prayer and the goal of the man whose life she had saved.

The only extant picture remaining of the original 1827 Baptist Church in Moulmein. The printing press was housed next door.

ပထမ နှစ်ခြင်း အသင်းတော်
ဖော်ဝယ်ပြုပြီ.

FIRST BAPTIST CHURCH
FOUNDED BY Dr ADONIRAM JUDSON
1827

Freedom
1826

THE JOY OF THAT NEXT MORNING, FEBRUARY 22, 1826—THEIR first full day of freedom—brought a feeling of relief beyond expression, like a grievous burden suddenly lifted. Ann wrote about the rapture of that memorable time to Elnathan: "*With what sensations of delight did I behold the masts of the steamboat, the sure presage of being within the bounds of civilized life!*" The sight that had greeted them was the English ship *Diana*, its masts shimmering in the bright morning sun. The massive vessel looked overwhelming to Burmese eyes; they had never before seen such a sight.

For their part, the British officers found Ann Judson awe-inspiring. The entire camp had heard numerous accounts of the intrepid American woman who had not only managed to keep her imprisoned husband alive for nearly two years but also to gain the grudging admiration of the Burman nobility. The British were astonished that a woman so fragile had endured such deplorable living conditions, to say nothing of sustaining her husband's life in the process. It sounded nearly beyond belief. Ann stood before them, still more wraith than substance, painfully thin and obviously fragile. A shining cap of short black curls topped her fine but gaunt features, and her pale skin appeared almost translucent. Mrs. Judson's most striking feature, all immediately noticed, was her remarkable warm eyes that took in the gleaming British ship and the officers in their immaculate uniforms, and frequently glanced down at the delicate baby in her arms.

Not one of those men ever forgot the power of Ann's eyes. They could only conjecture as to what horrors those eyes had seen, what suffering they had endured. That February day on the Irrawaddy, Ann Judson appeared to them like a bona fide angel, and that is the way they treated her. After two years of taunting, insults, and disrespect, the deference accorded her was refreshment to her weary heart and balm to her spirit.

The Judsons became the honored guests of Sir Archibald Campbell in the British camp. Ann wrote in her long letter to Elnathan:

> We feel that our obligations to General Campbell can never be cancelled. Our final release from Ava, and our recovering all the property that had there been taken, was owing entirely to his efforts. His subsequent hospitality, and kind attention to the accommodations for our passage to Rangoon, have left an indelible impression on our minds, which can never be forgotten. . . . I presume to say that no persons on earth were ever happier than we were during the fortnight we passed at the English camp.

Ann seemed unable to get over the glorious sensation of release from bondage, and she described it to her brother-in-law: "*For several days, this single idea wholly occupied my mind, that we were out of the power of the Burmese government, and once more under the protection of the English."* Ann found herself spending the leisurely hours during those days of recuperation thanking God over and over again for having preserved their lives and bringing them once again into the bright light of freedom. General Campbell, recognizing the vital importance of both Ann and Adoniram Judson in bringing about an honorable end to hostilities, went out of his way to afford them honor. He sent his own son to head the welcoming committee that boarded the *Diana* to bring the Americans ashore. He then proceeded to give the Judsons the largest tent in the camp and enlarged it with a comfortable verandah. To all this, he added a certain fatherly kindness and genuine interest in their welfare, making Ann feel as though she were receiving all these favors from a friend. At the same time, it made Adoniram's heart swell with pride and gratitude to see Ann receiving well-earned attention after the degradation she had endured for his sake.

Two days after their arrival in camp, the treaty of peace was finally signed by both the British and Burmese commanders. Campbell marked the moment by arranging a huge dinner party that included both the victors and the defeated. He decided this was going to be an affair with much pomp and circumstance. Whether it was his intention to intimidate the Burmese generals and officers, that is exactly what occurred. The entire camp became a mass of crimson and gold and floating banners, and a band played during the elaborate banquet.

When the hour for dinner arrived, the processional music began and the company marched in couples toward the tables, led by the general, who walked alone. When they reached the tent with the verandah, the music stopped and the whole procession stood still. While the awed Burmans watched the proceedings, wondering what was coming next in the drama unfolding before their eyes, General Campbell entered the tent. In a moment, he reappeared with a lady on his arm—no stranger to the eyes of the dismayed Burmese officers. It was none other than their former prisoner's much-maligned wife, Mrs. Yoodthan. For a long moment, no one moved.

Ann was beautifully dressed, painfully thin but standing erect. Adoniram immediately noticed the twinkle in her eyes, and reminded him of how they looked during their courting days, dancing with life and just a touch of mischief.

With Ann Judson on his arm, General Campbell approached the head table and seated her at his right hand, her husband at her side. The cowed Burmese commissioners slid lower into their seats, transfixed as if by a mixture of astonishment and fear. Campbell looked around at the shock written on the faces of the Burmese generals. He smiled at Ann, seemingly amused by what he was beginning to suspect, though he could not understand the reasons behind their fear. Campbell quietly remarked, "I fancy these gentlemen must be old acquaintances of yours, Mrs. Judson." He paused, nodded his head, and continued, "And, judging from their appearance, you must have treated them very ill." Ann smiled quickly as she thought of what those men had done to them in past months. The Burmans could not understand the general's remark, but they evidently considered themselves the subject of it, and their faces stiffened with trepidation.

Sir Archibald kept pursuing the subject: "What is the matter with yonder owner of the pointed beard?" he inquired. "He seems to be seized with an ague fit." Ann fixed her eyes on the trembling man, and with just a bit of mischievous enjoyment at his obvious anxiety, responded, "I do not know," and she paused a long moment, "unless his memory may be too busy. He is an old acquaintance of mine and may probably infer danger to himself from seeing me under your protection."

Ann then related the incident of the day when Adoniram was suffering from a high fever, with five pairs of fetters around his ankles, and she had walked several miles to this man's house to ask for a favor to ease her husband's suffering just a bit. She had left home very early but was kept waiting so long outside this man's door that it was noon before she could make her request. He had immediately refused, she explained, and she turned sorrowfully away, when suddenly this official's attention focused on the silk umbrella she carried in her hand. He then roughly seized it, whereupon she explained to him the danger of her walking home two miles without its protection. "Then he laughed," Ann told the indignant British commandant, "and told me I was too thin for the sun to find me, and he left with my umbrella."

Outraged reactions could be heard up and down the table as the British officers heard the galling story. All turned their glares upon the offending Burman who had treated their honored Mrs. Judson with such disdain. The poor man was clearly conscience-struck and feared the anger now directed at him. As Ann and Adoniram watched, perspiration began trickling down his trembling face. Ann Judson's inner spirit rose above any wish to be vindictive, and she could only pity him. Speaking softly in Burmese, Ann reassured the trembling man, "You have nothing to fear," and gave him a little smile. Back in their spacious tent later that night, Ann and Adoniram had a rare moment of laughter together, thinking of Pointed Beard and what the unwelcomed memory had done to his tortured and guilty mind. The celebration banquet had been immensely satisfying.

Ann had not sought the attention and praise heaped on her those two weeks in the British camp, but they meant the world to Adoniram. All she had done for him was a gift too rare to ever be repaid, but it thrilled him to the core to see her receive some justly earned honor and acclaim. Adoniram was honored by the British leaders as well, who clearly recognized that without his language and diplomatic skills, a peace treaty would never have happened. Not only had his work been remarkable; it had been done when his malnourished body was weakened and failing by living in brutal conditions. Only his spirit and courage had remained strong, ever the essential Adoniram Judson.

The time spent recuperating at the British camp was healing for both Ann and Adoniram. When lying in their comfortable bed at night, Ann would frequently turn to look at the sweet face of Maria, who slept on soft, clean blankets—something heretofore unknown to her. Ann's eyes would invariably fill with tears of gratitude that at last she had a chance to nurture their precious child, to spend time and energy on seeing that she was happy and content.

Meanwhile, General Campbell had personally arranged for his own gunboat to convey the Judsons home to Rangoon. Sailing downriver in quiet safety on board a well-equipped vessel was sheer bliss after two years of uncertainty, pain, torture, and loss. Ann and Adoniram could talk through their experiences, share feelings and impressions, and recount little details of the trying experiences they had improbably survived by God's mercy.

Adoniram would remember for the remainder of his life that leisurely cruise and the heartfelt joy of being together again. In his latter years, while some close friends were visiting him, several began recounting what people in different ages had considered the highest type of enjoyment in all of life, at least enjoyment from outward circumstances. Adoniram reflected:

> *Pooh! Those men are not qualified to judge. I know of a much higher pleasure than that: floating down the Irrawaddy on a cool, moonlight evening, with your wife by your side and your baby in your arms, all finally free! But you cannot understand it, either. It needs a twenty-one months' qualification, and I can never regret my twenty-one months of misery when I recall that one delicious thrill. I think I have had a better appreciation of what heaven may be ever since.*

For the first time in two years, Ann had the leisure to think about something other than surviving and protecting those dearest to her. It had been too painful during the torturous months of captivity to think about her New England home, to speculate about Mama and Papa and her precious family so far away. They must be in agony wondering what had happened to her and her husband, not even able to know if they were still alive. Ann would occasionally wake in the middle of the night, listen to the gentle lull of waves lapping against their sturdy vessel, and think back to moments at home in Bradford, of conversations with Mama, and often hearing her remark, "My Honey, you always seem to want to ramble." *What would Mama make of the ramblings of these last wretched years?* Then she would drift back to sleep, thankful they would soon be able to send letters home and receive news from their loved ones.

Along the route one morning, the British crew noticed a distress signal from the riverbank and drew closer to investigate. To their amazement, it was a wounded British officer, a Lieutenant Calder Campbell, left injured and bleeding by Burmese brigands. He was immediately helped aboard the British gunboat, and Ann dressed his wounds and cared for him. Years later Campbell, by then a major, recounted in a journal his fond memories of that rescue: "*My eyes first rested on the thin, attenuated form of a lady—a white lady! It was the first white woman I had seen in over a year. She was standing on the little deck of the boat, leaning on the arm of a sickly-looking gentleman with an intellectual cast of countenance, in whom I at once recognized the husband.*"

He continued his recollections of that day:

> *Later, she was seated in a large sort of swinging chair, of American construction, in which her slight but graceful form appeared almost too ethereal. Yet, with much of heaven, there were still the breathings of earthy feelings about her, for at her feet rested a babe—a little, wan baby, on which her eyes often turned with all a mother's love. . . . Her face was pale, with that expression of deep and serious thoughts which speaks of the strong and vigorous mind within the frail and perishing body; her hands—those small lily hands— were beautiful; beautiful they were, and very wan; . . . That lady was Mrs. Judson, whose long captivity and severe hardships amongst the Burmese have since been detailed in her published journals.*

279

The major concluded his account of that memorable time:

I remained two delightful days with them. Mrs. Judson's powers of conversation were of the first order and the many affecting accounts she gave of their long and cruel bondage, gained a heightened interest from the beautiful simplicity of her language, as well as from the certainty I felt that so fragile a flower as she in very truth was, had but a brief season to linger on earth.

In the remaining days of their trip to Rangoon, Ann and Adoniram spent hours planning what they might do when they arrived home and speculating on the fate of their faithful group of believers. It had been difficult to spend two years not knowing what might have happened to them. *Had they suffered? Had they escaped the ravages of war?* They named each one and prayed, as they had these many months, for God's mercy. Adoniram was especially concerned about the noble Maung Shwa-gnong, who had fled upriver to escape persecution, and Ann named the women converts, speculating on how they had handled the horrors of war. And how was the one so close to her heart, Mah Men Lay, who had given her allegiance to Jesus Christ on that joyful day? And ever in their speculations were their fellow missionaries Jonathan and Deborah Wade and George and Phebe Hough. What had been their fate? Had they survived the war?

As the days stretched into weeks on the month-long journey, their anticipation continued to heighten. At long last they were returning to the mission and their beloved friends. This was the work to which God had called them. Fourteen-month-old Maria had taken her first steps, and her rosy cheeks glowed with returning health. She was a beautiful child, with light hair, fair skin, and big blue eyes that lit up her face. Every evidence of growth brought joy to her parents' hearts. And the exhilarating air of freedom and a sense of hope for the future filled their hearts to overflowing with gratitude.

Her Golden Shore 1826

Amherst, Burma. The grave and memorial of Ann Judson. Dr. Stanley Hanna and the author stand with Harriet Bain and Joan Myint, great-great-granddaughters of Ah Vong, the first Burmese printer. In 2002 Dr. Hanna laid a plinth stone for the rebuilt church on the site.

ABOUT A WEEK AFTER LEAVING General Campbell and his troops in Ava, the British gunboat carrying them downstream stopped at Prome to resupply. Previously, Prome had been the site of a decisive English victory, and British troops still occupied the city. As their boat docked, Ann glanced at a small boat docked next to theirs, and then looked more closely at a Burmese woman walking across the deck of the neighboring vessel. Clutching Adoniram's arm, Ann exclaimed, "Mr. J, look!" She pointed to the refined Burmese woman. "That looks like Mah Men Lay. Oh my heavens, could it be our Mah Men Lay?" It was indeed the beloved first Burman woman to believe and be baptized! In excitement, Ann called out a greeting, and when the older woman turned and saw her beloved Mah Yoodthan, her face lit up with incandescent joy.

Once on the dock, the two embraced as if they would never let go, and their tears ran freely. Mah Men Lay related how she and her sister-in-law, Mah Doke, had escaped Rangoon just before the battle for that city began, and fled upcountry. Now they were preparing to head back to the mission house. The reunion of the two faithful women believers with their beloved Yoodthans was a golden moment for all of them. Each talked excitedly about how they might revive and continue their mission work and made plans to meet again shortly in Rangoon.

Ann and Adoniram could scarcely contain their excitement as home was drawing so near. They were hoping for more good news soon. Ann wrote to Elnathan about some of the second-guessing that ran through their minds as they looked back on the past two tortuous years. She concluded:

> All we can say is "It is not in man that walketh, to direct his steps." But two years of precious time have been lost to the mission, unless some future advantage may be gained. We are sometimes induced to think, that the lesson we found so very hard to learn, will have a beneficial effect through our lives, and that the mission may, in the end, be advanced rather than retarded. Pray, dear brother, that these heavy afflictions may not be in vain.

After weeks on the river, their gunboat reached Rangoon on March 21. The Judsons and their entourage began making their way toward the mission house, their minds awhirl, wondering what they might find there two years later. As the cart taking them from the docks drew closer, so grew the mixture of dread and excitement that had their emotions in a jumble. They rounded the corner—and there stood the mission house—intact, blessedly intact! All around, however, was devastation and disorder, evidence of the fierce battle that must have been pitched in the area.

The front door swung open, and the beaming face of Maung Shwa-bay appeared, joy written large across his countenance. His eyes fell on his two little girls, and tears began streaming down his thin face. His children had lived! His beloved Yoodthan and Mah

Yoodthan had survived! Long minutes passed before any of then were able to control their emotions enough to speak coherently. Shwa-bay had faithfully remained at the mission house, guarding it and doing all in his power to preserve the house and the zayat.

Ann and Adoniram had a hundred questions, one tumbling out after the other as they tried to find out what had transpired in their absence. Shwa-bay briefly recounted the hair-raising experiences through which the Houghs and Wades had gone, telling of their imprisonment and imminent execution by Burmese forces, and then of their rescue by the British expedition that arrived in time to save their lives. The two couples were now in Calcutta, waiting for hostilities to end. At the same time, Maung Shwa-bay learned of the tribulations through which they and his daughters had lived, scarcely able to take in how God had brought them through such unspeakable horrors and returned them to the mission.

As to the body of believers, Maung Shwa-bay could give them news about several. The fate of others was still unknown, for they had fled into the countryside to escape death. Four of the believers had already returned to Rangoon, and Mah Men Lay, Mah Doke, and their relatives were to arrive soon. Ann walked around the mission house, seeing what remained and what was now gone forever, simply happy to be there once more after spending many a wakeful night thinking she would never see it again.

Later that first evening, Ann and Adoniram walked through the tangled jungle of the mission gardens and found Roger's grave. As Ann stood there in tears, holding Maria close, the toddler reached up a little finger and wiped away one of her mother's tears, softly inquiring, "Mommy sad?" Ann hugged her more tightly and assured her, "Mommy is just so glad she has her Maria with her, safe and sound."

Ann and Adoniram continued to consider their next steps. Should they remain in Rangoon? That option presented a clear problem, as the city was only temporarily under British control. According to the terms of the treaty, Rangoon would soon revert to Burmese control. In exchange the British would control Arakan, the area to the west, bordering the Bay of Bengal, and Tennasserim to the south. With their all-too-personal knowledge of the Burmese mind-set in general and the Burmese emperor specifically, both knew the dangers of remaining in an area that would revert to Burmese control. A fresh mission field, now in British hands, lay before them in the southern part of Burma. Here they could preach and teach in safety and would have a far wider field of service.

Never one to take long to make decisions, Adoniram determined, after just a few days of consideration, that they should move south where the work could quickly flourish. Ann's eyes twinkled as she noted, "Mr. J, you have ever been an impatient optimist. And I see that twenty-one months in fetters has not changed you!" The same week they were busy making decisions about their future, the British Civil Commissioner, Mr. Crawfurd, arrived to talk to Adoniram. He was going south to choose a site for the British headquarters of Tennasserim territory and asked Adoniram to accompany him and help make the choice.

Ann remained at the mission house and began working on plans for the months ahead while Judson accompanied Crawfurd on a quick trip south. Arriving in Tennasserim territory, the two men quickly determined to set up British headquarters at Amherst, which was located on the Andaman Sea and had the advantage of a promising harbor. Adoniram prayed a prayer of dedication for the new headquarters and hurried back to Rangoon and his dear love.

An enthusiastic Ann was returning things to order at the mission house, while loving to watch Maria make new discoveries and charm the flock of converts and visitors who came calling. She was a wonder in Rangoon, with her shining fair hair, big blue eyes, and winsome smile. Ann wrote to a friend in England, recounting a bit of the past two years and describing their upcoming plans. She explained what they projected for the resettling of the mission: "*I am at times so amazed to find we still exist and are certainly out of the hand of tyranny, that it seems as though a miracle had been wrought to effect it. Twice in the midst of our sufferings I was reduced by sickness beyond all hope, but almost without human agency, restored again to health. Oh! How much we owe to that kind Being who has mingled mercy with all our afflictions.*

Ann then related their plans for living in the lower part of Burma:

> *We are now preparing to remove to Amherst, a new town lately built by the English Government. It will be quite full of Burmans. There we intend to establish the Mission, and shall have as many schools under our direction as funds will allow. Most of the Christians go with us. Our faithful Maung Ing stood by us in all our afflictions at Ava, and we intend rewarding him by making him master of one of the schools, for which he is well-qualified. Mah Men Lay is as firm as ever; she will also be employed in the schools.*

Adoniram returned in just ten days, and he described with excitement what the situation would be like in Amherst. The British were planning to create a new city out of the jungle, and there missionaries would have perfect freedom to share the gospel message in every way they could. It looked more and more like they had made the only logical decision. Rangoon would not only be under the despotic control of the malicious Bagyidaw, but the city itself was in shambles following the battles conducted here. A famine followed the devastation of war, and beasts of prey were already roaming at will. Tigers infested the suburbs of Rangoon and boldly carried off cattle and even people. Ann shuddered to think what might happen to them should a tiger wander into the mission gardens.

Several of the band of believers went ahead to Amherst to get settled in, and Ann and Adoniram were soon to follow. Mr. J was determined to take the dear old zayat with them; hence, he and several of the men dismantled it piece by piece and packed it for shipment to its new location in the south.

By now it was June, and exciting news came from Calcutta. The Wades were planning to go to Amherst, and a newly appointed couple, George and Sarah Boardman, were accompanying them. It was an exhilarating time, with a joyous sense of new beginnings. Ann and Adoniram, along with Maria and several of the believers who had returned to Rangoon, set sail on June 29 for Amherst.

Then came word of a new development that brought renewed hope for religious liberty across the land. Commissioner Crawfurd was appointed envoy to the court of Bagyidaw and planned to go to Ava to effect a commercial treaty. He sorely needed Judson's help both as negotiator and translator, and held out to him the lure that a religious freedom clause might be written into the new agreement.

Adoniram's first response was a flat no. He did not want to leave Ann and his precious child again, nor the new and hopeful rebirth of the mission. He still had vivid memories of his agonizing times of separation, far away from his dear one. But Ann encouraged him to go, stressing the value of religious liberty as a guarantee. "Mr. J," she insisted, "you will be back in just two or three months. The religious liberty clause would be of lasting good, both for us and for the other missionaries who will come." Most reluctantly, Adoniram agreed to go, finally convinced that *this* separation would definitely be a relatively short one.

Just days later, the family of three stood together at the front door of their temporary house in Amherst, which the commissioner had kindly loaned them while their own was being built. Adoniram took Maria into his loving arms one last time and gave her a long hug. The little family had a parting prayer, and Adoniram kissed Ann a loving good-bye. Heading off for the docks, Adoniram waved as he stepped on board the small vessel taking them upstream in the direction of Ava. Hopes ran high.

Ann was continuing to gain strength and beginning to feel like her old self again. Determined not to spend time brooding during her husband's absence, she set to work and within two months had erected a bamboo house and two schoolhouses. In one schoolhouse, she had already collected a group of young scholars for Maung Ing, and she would teach girls in the other. Mah Men Lay was excited to be part of the staff of teachers, and they shared a wonderful sense of hope and optimism.

Every Sunday the group of believers who had accompanied the Judsons met for services, and Ann conducted the worship with joy and thanksgiving. She wrote to Mr. J, *"After all our sufferings and afflictions, I cannot but hope that God has mercy and a blessing in store for us. Let us strive to obtain it by our prayers and holy life."* It thrilled her to see the believers growing in their faith and participating as well as leading in worship. They loved singing, and their favorite hymn was the beautiful one written by their honored Teacher Yoodthan, "I Long to Reach My Golden Shore." Each time they sang those words that vividly pictured heaven, Ann would think of just how close to those "golden shores" she and Mr. J had sailed so many times these past two years in Ava.

Along with the joy that those hymns brought to Ann came nostalgic memories of the grand old hymns of the faith sung back in Bradford. To thirty-six-year-old Ann, those memories seemed a lifetime away. Her eyes would still fill with tears just thinking about sitting in her regular pew at the parish church, Mama and Papa and the family all there, singing praises together. Yet not for a moment did she want to be any place other than where God had placed her. Ann would wonder yet again if this might be just a bit of that "present yourselves a living sacrifice" over which she had pondered many a night.

Ann wrote Mr. J regularly, never sure if the letters would reach him but wanting to commune with him anyway, telling him about daily progress in the thriving little mission in Amherst. On September 14 she wrote:

> *I have this day moved into the new house, and for the first time since we were broken up at Ava, feel myself at home. The house is large and convenient, and if you were here, I should feel quite happy. The native population is increasing*

very fast, and things wear a favourable aspect. Maung Ing's school has commenced with ten scholars and more are expected. Poor little Maria is still feeble. I sometimes hope she is getting better; then again she declines to her former weakness. When I ask her where Papa is, she always starts up and points towards the sea. Pray take care of yourself, particularly as it regards the intermittent fever at Ava. May God preserve and bless you and restore you in safety to your new and old home, is the prayer of your affectionate Ann.

It was the last letter he would receive from his beloved Ann. In October Maria was taken with a fever, and as her faithful mother cared for her, often far into the night, Ann herself was struck with a high fever. It was a return of the deadly spotted fever (meningitis). The British doctor came at once and was most attentive. In a few days, Ann felt a bit stronger. But soon the fever struck again, and the doctor grew increasingly worried. For nearly two weeks, her fever raged. Then Ann seemed to improve as it slowly abated. The commandant found the kind wife of a British officer who cared for Maria and remained in the home. Even as the doctor was hopeful that recovery was near, the fever returned for the third time. Ann realized all too clearly that her strength was drastically waning and, looking at the physician, calmly told him, "I am not afraid to die."

Sunday, October 22, her pain seemed to subside, and Ann repeated over and over, "The teacher is long in coming, and the new missionaries are long in coming." Then repeatedly she looked around and reached for Maria, saying, "Take care of my baby; take care of my child. I must die alone and leave my little one, but as it is the will of God, I acquiesce in his will." In just above a whisper, she added, "I am not afraid of death." Mah Men Lay and Mah Doke came and were in great distress at the condition of their beloved Mah Yoodthan.

The band of believers gathered in sorrow at the new mission house, recently built with such high hopes. They remained with Ann, weeping in helpless anguish and unable to do anything to prevent her life from slipping away. As she grew increasingly weak, Ann said quietly, "Tell the teacher that the disease was most violent, and I could not write him." It seemed to tax all her strength just to form words, and she concluded, "Tell him how I suffered and died."

By Tuesday, October 24, Ann was no longer speaking. At eight o'clock that quiet autumn evening, she slowly opened her eyes, whispered one soft phrase in Burmese, and breathed her last. There awaited for Ann Judson an eternal crown of glory, for she had reached her Golden Shore.

Epilogue
1826-1827

EXACTLY A MONTH AFTER ANN'S DEATH, ADONIRAM JUDSON received a black-trimmed letter written in an unfamiliar hand. In the custom of the day, letters of condolence were trimmed in black, so Adoniram knew at once this correspondence meant someone had died. Immediately his mind raced to little Maria, who had been struggling to regain some strength when he had left Amherst four months earlier. Judson was stunned when he opened the envelope and read the first few lines from Captain Fenwick, assistant superintendent of Amherst. Numb with shock, his hands shaking, the words were seared on his mind and heart:

> *My dear Sir, to one who has suffered so much and with such exemplary fortitude, there needs but little preface to tell the tale of distress. It were cruel indeed to torture you with doubt and suspense. To sum up the unhappy tidings in a few words—Mrs. Judson is no more.*

Adoniram's entire world was gone. His heart, his dear love, the one who had gone to any length to save *his* life—was gone forever. In that moment of overwhelming grief, he sank to the floor in anguish. The news was too awful to comprehend. The other part of him was gone.

Because of Ann, he had been able to survive two years of torture, deadly illness, prison, and near starvation. But this experience was vastly worse for Adoniram. Every morning when he awoke and realized it wasn't just a nightmare, but all too real, the agonizing pain of her loss hit him again.

To compound the sorrow, his only earthly link with Ann, their little Maria, lost her hold on life six months to the day after her mama died. Maria was buried beside her mother under the *hopia* (hope) tree, just yards from where they had landed at Amherst so full of anticipation less than a year before. After Ann's death, Adoniram wrote several times to his mother-in-law, Rebecca Hasseltine, sharing with her information about the last months of her "Honey's" life, knowing that the two of them understood in a special way the unique gifts of the woman so dear to both. Adoniram sent Rebecca a poem he had written in tribute to Ann, calling it, "The Solitary Lament." In one stanza he expressed his grief by writing, "*O, bitter cup which God has given! Where can relief be found? Anon I lift my eyes to heaven, Anon in tears they're drowned.*"

The next eight years became Judson's "dark night of the soul." He continued to be a leading voice in the mission as more missionaries arrived to reinforce the work, but with Ann's death, the darkness nearly overwhelmed him. By January 31, 1834, however, through sheer dogged determination, Judson managed to complete the translation of the entire Bible into Burmese, and as he knelt to dedicate it to God, he sensed in a very real way the presence of Ann. Without doubt, she was the driving force behind its completion, and her selfless devotion and sheer determination to keep him alive were the reasons the translation had become a reality. At about this same time, his emotions, so long immobile, seemed to revive again, and he began once more to participate in the life of the mission.

Adoniram Judson went on to marry twice more, each marriage a happy one, which says much about the fundamental largeness of his soul. Nonetheless, there was no doubt that Ann was an intrinsic part of his heart and spirit, and he spoke freely about his love for her to his second wife, Sarah, and to Emily, the third. In a letter he wrote to his wife Emily in 1846, he spoke of the particular joy there would be one glad day in heaven when he, Ann, Sarah, and Emily all rejoiced together around the throne of grace.

Ann would surely have rejoiced to see what God did in Burma in the years that followed. Her Mr. J had ever declared that he could "die happy" if he could see the Bible in the heart language of the people, a healthy little church, and a hundred believers. When Adoniram Judson died in 1850, there was indeed the Bible in the language of the people (still widely in use nearly two hundred years later), one hundred churches, and more than eight thousand believers. And now, even into the new millennium, Burma has one of the largest populations of Baptists on earth.

Ann's Legacy

The legacy of America's first woman missionary remains powerful more than two hundred years after her death. The depth of her faith, courage, and commitment to Christ withstood the challenge of unimaginable suffering and emerged unequivocally triumphant. Several adjectives were used to describe Ann in her growing-up years: *determined, headstrong, impulsive, persuasive, courageous, and inquisitive,* to name a few. That strength of character and depth of faith were tested in the crucible of great suffering and emerged triumphant. Each became a part of the unique contributions she made toward forging a missions consciousness in America.

Ann had no pattern to follow. She was the first missionary woman and as such set an incredibly high standard for the thousands who have followed in subsequent generations. She was uniquely gifted and singularly committed to her missions calling. For Ann, as for Adoniram, it was a "mission for life." Historians have often referred to Ann Hasseltine Judson as "the woman of the century" in nineteenth-century America. Without doubt, her fidelity and commitment have continued to set her apart. Ann mastered an extremely difficult language and not only translated the first catechism and various portions of Scripture into Burmese but also the first portions of the Bible into Siamese. She was *the* pioneer missionary school teacher and an author of excellence. While spending nine short months in the United States attempting to recover from life-threatening liver ailments, she managed to write a book about the mission to the Burmese Empire that galvanized Baptists in the United States into missions involvement. She was uniquely gifted and singular in commitment to her missions calling.

Historians have heaped on Ann Judson countless words of praise for leading the way for women to respond to God's call to "go and tell the nations." Dana Robert, a well-known missiologist, described her as "an evangelist, school teacher, pioneer Bible translator and savior of her husband Adoniram." Another theologian and historian, James Hill, saw Ann as Adoniram Judson's "good genius," a woman of consummate tact and inventiveness who showed heroic resolution in the very face of death. Hill commented that Ann did all this while remaining wholly unaware of being heroic. Without question, Ann made possible the extraordinary contribution that Adoniram Judson made to the evangelization of Burma.

Ann Judson was a risk taker. Who else but the intrepid Ann would leave the security of family, home, and country two hundred years ago to plant her life on foreign soil? Ann was also unquestionably her "own woman," assertive in a time when that trait was rarely noted or admired in women. She saved her husband's life during the war years in Ava and Aungbinle, not one time but three times. Historian Harriet Conant referred often to the "majestic consistency" of her practical good sense, many skills, and peerless fidelity. Historian Stacy Warburton told of how Ann's effervescent, joyous, and loving personality attracted Adoniram to her and made them such effective partners in ministry.

Ann Judson's life and death caught the imagination of a generation. Primarily due to her many letters, history has a clear idea of some of the atrocities of the prison years. Her epic letter to her brother-in-law, Elnathan, after their release from Ava, is a masterpiece of understatement. Ann and Adoniram endured the seemingly unendurable because of their view of this life as merely a preparation for eternity. The unfathomable depth of her faith and commitment are matched only by the incredible drama of what happened during the last years of her life.

The eminent Baptist historian Francis Wayland called Ann Judson "one of the most remarkable women of her age." The British government considered themselves wholly in her debt and credited her accordingly in a tribute published in a Calcutta paper after the war: "Mrs. Judson was the author of those eloquent and forcible appeals to the Government, which prepared them by degrees for submission to terms of peace, never expected by any, who knew the hauteur and inflexible pride of the Burman court."

Fellow missionary Henry Gouger, whose life was permanently impacted by the influence of Ann and Adoniram Judson, said of her:

> *The overflowings of grateful feelings, compel me to add a tribute of public thanks to that amiable and humane female, who, though living at a distance of two miles from our prison, without any means of conveyance, and very feeble in health, forgot her own comfort and infirmity, and almost every day visited us, sought out and administered to our wants. While we were all left by the Government destitute of food, she, with unwearied perseverance, by some means or other, obtained us a constant supply.*

Gouger continued praising the courage and kindness of Ann and concluded, "*When the unfeeling avarice of our keepers confined us inside, or made our feet fast in the stocks, she, like a ministering Angel, never ceased on her applications to the Government for a respite from our galling oppressions.*"

The *Calcutta Review* wrote with the highest of praise for Ann:

> *The prison of Aungbinle, though the name be not euphonious, merits an immortality of renown, for never on earth was witnessed a more truly heroic example of the unconquerable strength of a Christian lady's love and fortitude, than was exhibited at Aungbinle by Ann Judson. What the mother and wife must have endured, we will not endeavor to depict.*

A fitting tribute to Ann Judson was penned by Adoniram Brown Judson, Adoniram's first son to reach adulthood. In later life, he served as an eminent surgeon in New York and wrote of what he had heard his father tell of the matchless Ann. Dr. Judson recalled the letter his father had written to Ann on New Year's Day, 1811, in which he talked of their next New Year's greeting, a greeting that might be exchanged in the "uncouth dialect of Hindustan or Burma." Adoniram Brown Judson wrote, *"Little did they think, that in a few short years her life was to end in the desolation of a Burmese hut, with no friend near but heathen converts, and that her last word would be a sigh in the strange language that both had learned to love. Such was to be the ending of one of the most heroic lives ever laid on the altar of sacred duty."*

In New York City's famous Riverside Church are stone carvings commemorating historical figures whose lives have exemplified some aspect of Christ's life. Among the sixty-three so honored, only eight are Americans, and only four of the entire number are women. Only one couple is honored: Ann and Adoniram Judson. We have very few portraits of Ann, but her memory is indelibly imprinted in thousands of lives, both in America and in Burma. Her remarkable life remains a profound influence. What better word to sum up the life of Ann Judson than the word Adoniram used to describe her in an 1846 letter: *incomparable.*

In 1830 Adoniram Judson journeyed up the Irrawaddy with thousands of tracts. Repeatedly people would come to him and plead, "Teacher, give us a writing." They would look earnestly into his eyes and inquire, "Are you Jesus Christ's man?" Every morning when starting a new day, I endeavor to ask myself, "Am I Jesus Christ's woman?" God grant that, without fail, each of us, each day, be "Jesus Christ's person."

The Rest of the Story

IN AN OBSCURE VERTICAL FILE IN THE ARCHIVES OF THE AMERICAN Baptist Historical Society, a remarkable account was discovered, an account that brilliantly illuminates the eternal impact of Ann Hasseltine Judson. Nearly a hundred and fifty years ago, an unusual event occurred in the remote jungles of southern Burma.

In the generation after Ann and Adoniram Judson, a missionary couple named Lovell and Murilla Ingalls joined the Baptist mission in Burma and worked in several areas. Rev. Ingalls died after a few years, but his wife continued her ministry for an amazing forty-six more years. Much of her work was itinerant mission endeavors in the jungles of southern Burma, often in areas that were nearly inaccessible.

On one particular day she had made her way to a village where she had never before been. As was her custom, she told the story of God's message of love, beginning with Creation, traveling through the Old Testament, and then telling of the birth of Christ, his life, his death for humanity's sins on the cross, and his glorious resurrection. In the crowd that day was an elderly man visiting from another, even more remote village. After Mrs. Ingalls's message, he hurried to her side, and with eager eyes pleaded with her to come to his village. Mrs. Ingalls asked, "Where do you live, sir?" The man described the location of his village, and Murilla explained that on this trip she was scheduled to visit villages in another direction. However, she promised that on her next mission journey, she would definitely include *his* village.

Murilla Ingalls kept her promise, and a few months later headed in the direction of the elderly man's distant village. News of her impending arrival traveled ahead of her, and all of the local population gathered to hear the visitor's stories. For many in that remote area of the jungle, she was the first white person they had ever seen. The village welcomed her and gathered around the largest house in the village. The verandah of the house, up on stilts for protection from flooding, was long and commodious enough to hold many people. Others of the village clustered all around its base. The crowd grew and grew, listening raptly as Murilla began with the creation of the world and traced the history of God's people all the way to the birth of Christ.

When Mrs. Ingalls told of Christ's sacrifice on the cross for the sins of all who trusted him, she suddenly heard a quavering voice call out from the far end of the verandah. "That's it! That's it! That's the rest of it!" the voice called out in excitement, and a frail little woman stood up and began pushing her way through the crowd. Making her way to Murilla as quickly as she could, her face was alight with eagerness. "Mother," asked Mrs. Ingalls when the woman reached her, "What do you mean, 'That's the rest of it?' "

Her face glowing, the elderly villager explained, "Long, long ago, when I was very young, I lived in Ava. You see, my husband was one of the emperor's courtiers. During part of the time, there was a white foreigner, a beautiful lady who was destitute and in great anxiety about her husband. He was lying in chains in the death prison," the venerable old woman reminisced. "My heart pitied her and I used to give her rice and eggs, and she would tell me about her God, and how he had provided a way of salvation from our sins. But later," she continued, "my husband fell under the emperor's displeasure and we fled to the river. We took a little boat and hastened down the Irrawaddy. After many days, we finally dared to land and hide away in this jungle." She then fervently declared, "I never forgot the white lady and what she said about the one true God who created all things, but I could not remember *just* how we could get rid of our sins. Now you have told the part that I had forgotten—and that is the 'rest of it'!"

Murilla Ingalls heard the story in amazement. The man who had invited her to this village was the son of this woman. The Lord had remembered this lady's kindness to "Ann of Ava" and had permitted her to hear the rest of the story. She believed, as did her son, and they were joyfully baptized. Not long after Mrs. Ingall's visit, the elderly woman joined Ann Judson in glory. Without doubt, the legacy of the remarkable Ann Hasseltine Judson continues to live on, in remote villages and nearby cities, not just in Burma but wherever the name of Christ is proclaimed.

What Happened to Them?

KING BAGYIDAW

Bagyidaw was the seventh king of the Konbaung dynasty in Burma. He was on the throne during the first Anglo-Burmese War, which lasted from 1824 until 1826. It was the longest and most expensive war in British India history. The stress of war caused Bagyidaw to become a recluse, and his power devolved to his empress and her brother. His brother, Crown Prince Tharrawaddy, forced Bagyidaw to abdicate in 1837 and put to death Bagyidaw's wife and her brother. He then placed Bagyidaw under house arrest and claimed the throne for himself. Bagyidaw became insane and died in 1846.

EMILY VON SOMERON

Emily lived with her relatives in India after her years with Ann and Adoniram. She grew up to be an outstanding teacher. Family lore says that through the years, certain grand hymns of the faith invariably brought her to tears as she remembered the life and influence of her beloved Miss Ann.

HENRY GOUGER

Henry Gouger lived many years after his imprisonment at Ava and Aungbinle, and in 1860 he wrote an illuminating account of those long months in two death prisons. Thanks to Gouger, many details of those harrowing months have been preserved, along with his account of the heroics of Ann Judson and his great and lasting admiration for the couple who influenced his life and faith. His book, published in 1860, is titled *A Personal Narrative of Two Years' Imprisonment in Burmah*.

KOO-CHIL

The Judsons' Bengali cook had come from Calcutta to Burma with Ann Judson in 1823 and became key in helping them survive. Koo-chil was devoted for life to Ann Judson. His resourcefulness kept Ann and baby Maria alive during the dreadful deprivations of Aungbinle prison. Koo-chil often wept when telling about the horrors of Aungbinle and the suffering he witnessed there. He was devastated by Ann's death but faithfully continued to serve Adoniram for the rest of his own life. In his later years, he married a Burman Christian woman and courageously left his childhood religion and accepted Christ. It was a special day of rejoicing for Adoniram when he was privileged to baptize the loyal Koo-chil.

MAH MEN LAY

Mah Men Lay, beloved friend of Ann Judson and the first female convert in Burma, lived only about one year after Ann's death. Her contributions to the early years of ministry in the small band of believers were significant and impacted many lives, both the students she taught and the women she led to Christ. She died in September 1827. During her last weeks, when Men Lay was failing rapidly, she continued to express her joy and faith. Mah Men Lay's favorite topic those final days was heaven, and she spoke repeatedly about the joy that was going to be hers in entering heaven and meeting her dear Mah Yoodthan there. During the final week of her life, she declared, *"But first of all, I shall hasten to where my Savior sits and fall down and worship him, for his great love in sending the teacher to show me the way to heaven."*

MARY AND ABBY

Mary and Abby, the two young Burman daughters of Maung Shwa-bay, who lived through the Ava and Aungbinle days with Ann, went to Amherst to live with their father and continue in the mission school. Abby was never strong after the deprivations during the many months of Adoniram's imprisonment and died in February 1827. Mary lived, however, and several years after the war, Adoniram had the joy of baptizing her.

MAUNG ING

The faithful Maung Ing was a man of firsts. He was one of the first converts and was instrumental in keeping the Judsons alive. Maung Ing became the first Burman preacher to be commissioned as a "home missionary." He preached as, he made an eight-month trip south to Tavoy and Mergui, where he preached the gospel to all he met—in the streets, in homes, and in zayats. Maung Ing printed out some Christian ideas on a banner and suspended it in front of his house. This appears to have been the very first use of visual aids in religious work.

MAUNG NAU

Maung Nau, the first Burman believer, died during the war years, triumphant in his faith. He is still honored two hundred years later in churches all over Burma as the trailblazer.

MAUNG SHWA-GNONG

The brilliant scholar so closely tuned to Adoniram Judson's own heart preached faithfully in Burma's interior during the war years. In December 1826, Adoniram learned that Shwa-gnong had died of cholera.

DR. JONATHAN PRICE

The horrors of imprisonment deeply affected Jonathan Price. However, he chose to continue working for the Burmese government. His Burmese wife died giving birth to a child. Price contracted tuberculosis, which claimed his life in 1829.

ADDITIONAL HISTORICAL INFORMATION

The events that took place in Burma after the death of Ann Judson are covered in detail in my book *Bless God and Take Courage*. The book follows the legacy of Ann and Adoniram Judson and the history of Baptists and of missions in Burma after the Anglo-Burmese war.

The missionary society mentioned by Luther Rice to Ann Judson at the 1823 Triennial Convention meeting in Boston is the first society in America to give an offering when the Triennial was founded in 1814. The Wadmalow-Edisto Female Mite Society was founded by Hephzibah Jenkins Townsend in 1810, and their first offering in support of the Judsons was $44.00. The story of this founding mother is in the book *Her Way: The Remarkable Story of Hephzibah Jenkins Townsend* by Rosalie Hall Hunt.

There are no family records of Ann's brother, Joseph, having an opportunity to visit with Ann while she was in America, but it is very likely. Joseph married Chloe Whipple, the daughter of a neighbor in Bradford, after Ann and Adoniram had gone to Burma. Joseph and Chloe moved to South Carolina where he became a prosperous businessman. Records from the late 1800s indicate that the couch on which Ann rested to recover from her liver disease belonged to Joseph and was later passed to his son J. A. Hasseltine (who had been given the name Adoniram Judson Hasseltine). The couch was loaned to the national Woman's Missionary Union, located at that time in Baltimore, Maryland. There is no record of its present location.

According to *The Judson Centennial Celebrations in Burma* (1914, p. 126), the prison at Let Ma Yoon was 30 by 40 feet in area, 6 feet high at the sides, and 12 feet high in the center. The magnificent tamarind tree, some twenty feet in circumference, is said to be over five hundred years old. It was still standing in 2017.

CHAPTER SOURCES

Chapter One

Earl D. Campbell and Frederick W. Richardson, *The Hasseltine Genealogy*, self-published, 1997.

Rosalie Hall Hunt, *Bless God and Take Courage: The Judson History and Legacy* (Valley Forge, PA: Judson Press, 2005), 19–20.

James D. Knowles, *Memoir of Mrs. Ann H. Judson, Late Missionary to Burma*, first ed. (Boston: Lincoln and Edmunds, 1829), 9–12.

Chapter Two

Hunt, *Bless God and Take Courage*, 18–20.

Jean Sarah Pond, *Bradford Academy: A New England School* (Bradford, MA: Bradford Academy Association, 1930), 38–58.

Chapter Three

Hunt, *Bless God and Take Courage*, 22–23.

Sharon James, *My Heart in His Hands* (Durham, England: Evangelical Press, 1961), 17–21.

Pond, *Bradford Academy*, 50–80.

Arabella Stuart Willson, *The Three Mrs. Judsons* (Missionary Series), ed. Gary W. Long (Springfield, MO: Particular Baptist Press, 1999), 3–6.

Chapter Four

Hunt, *Bless God and Take Courage*, 21–23.

Knowles, *Memoir of Mrs. Ann H. Judson*, 12–25.

Willson, *The Three Mrs. Judsons*, 3–6.

Chapter Five

Courtney Anderson, *To the Golden Shore*, first ed. (Boston: Brown and Company, 1956), 25–31.

Hunt, *Bless God and Take Courage*, 1–18.

Edward Judson, *The Life of Adoniram Judson* (Boston: American Baptist Publication Society, 1883), 1–15.

Chapter Six

Anderson, *To the Golden Shore*, 31.

Hunt, *Bless God and Take Courage*, 7–17, 354.

Adoniram Judson, personal journal, 1788–1849.

Stacy R. Warburton, *Eastward: The Story of Adoniram Judson* (New York: Round Table Press, 1937), 1–19.

Chapter Seven
Gordon Langley Hall, *Golden Boats to Burmah* (Philadelphia: Macrae Smith Co.,
    1961), 26–29.
Hunt, *Bless God and Take Courage*, 14–18, 22–24.
Judson, *The Life of Adoniram Judson*, 16–25.
Knowles, *Memoir of Mrs. Ann H. Judson*, 33–34.

Chapter Eight
Hunt, *Bless God and Take Courage*, 25–26.
Knowles, *Memoir of Mrs. Ann H. Judson*, 35–36, 40, 42.

Chapter Nine
Hall, *Golden Boats to Burmah*, 30–39.
Ethel Daniels Hubbard, *Ann of Ava* (New York: Books for Libraries Press, 1913),
    30–34.
Hunt, *Bless God and Take Courage*, 26–30.
Judson, *The Life of Adoniram Judson*, 20–35, 562.
Francis Wayland, *A Memoir of the Life and Labors of the Rev. Adoniram Judson*,
    2 vols. (Boston: Phillips, Sampson and Company, 1853), 39–92.

Chapter Ten
"A Portrait of Adoniram Judson" (Salem, MA: Essex Institute Historical
    Collections, Vol. CV—1969), 296–299.
Hall, *Golden Boats to Burmah*, 41–45.
Hubbard, *Ann of Ava*, 34.
Hunt, *Bless God and Take Courage*, 29–34.
"Missionary Letter," *The Vehicle* or *Madison and Cayuga Christian Magazine*, no.
    11 (August 1814, vol. 1), 79–81.
Wayland, *A Memoir of the Life and Labors of the Rev. Adoniram Judson*, 35–40.

Chapter Eleven
"A Portrait of Adoniram Judson," 297–299.
Hall, *Golden Boats to Burmah*, 44–50.
Hubbard, *Ann of Ava*, 33–34.
Hunt, *Bless God and Take Courage*, 31–33.
James, *My Heart in His Hands*, 42–43.
Judson, *The Life of Adoniram Judson*, 34–35.
Wayland, *A Memoir of the Life and Labors of the Rev. Adoniram Judson*, 93.

Chapter Twelve
"A Portrait of Adoniram Judson," 301–302.
Hall, *Golden Boats to Burmah*, 56–61.
Cecil B. Hartley, *The Three Mrs. Judsons: The Celebrated Female Missionaries*
    (Philadelphia: G. G. Evans, 1860), 35–37.

Hunt, *Bless God and Take Courage*, 34–35.
Knowles, *Memoir of Mrs. Ann H. Judson*, 44–52.
Judson, *The Life of Adoniram Judson*, 37–55.

Chapter Thirteen
Hall, *Golden Boats to Burmah*, 66–71.
Hubbard, *Ann of Ava*, 48–52.
Hunt, *Bless God and Take Courage*, 37–43.
Knowles, *Memoir of Mrs. Ann H. Judson*, 63–75.

Chapter Fourteen
Hall, *Golden Boats to Burmah*, 76–79.
Hubbard, *Ann of Ava*, 61–65.
Hunt, *Bless God and Take Courage*, 47–48.
Knowles, *Memoir of Mrs. Ann H. Judson*, 84–86.
Judson, *The Life of Adoniram Judson*, 64.
Wayland, *A Memoir of the Life and Labors of the Rev. Adoniram Judson*, 117.

Chapter Fifteen
Hubbard, *Ann of Ava*, 61–79.
Hunt, *Bless God and Take Courage*, 48–51.
James, *My Heart in His Hands*, 66–69.
Judson, *The Life of Adoniram Judson*, 47–57.
Wayland, *A Memoir of the Life and Labors of the Rev. Adoniram Judson*, 118.

Chapter Sixteen
Hall, *Golden Boats to Burmah*, 83–93.
Hubbard, *Ann of Ava*, 77, 80–84, 89–90.
Hunt, *Bless God and Take Courage*, 51–54, 57–60.
Knowles, *Memoir of Mrs. Ann H. Judson*, 103–109, 111.

Chapter Seventeen
Anderson, *To the Golden*, 170–178.
Hubbard, *Ann of Ava*, 80–91.
Hunt, *Bless God and Take Courage*, 53–60, 373.
James, *My Heart in His Hands*, 74–81.
Judson, *The Life of Adoniram Judson*, 84.
Leonard, Bill J., *Baptist Ways: A History* (Valley Forge, PA: Judson Press, 2003), 274–276.
Wayland, *A Memoir of the Life and Labors of the Rev. Adoniram Judson*, 170

Chapter Eighteen
Hall, *Golden Boats to Burmah*, 94–102.
Hubbard, *Ann of Ava*, 94–97, 101, 104–109.

Hunt, *Bless God and Take Courage*, 60–65.
Knowles, *Memoir of Mrs. Ann H. Judson*, 120–122.
Wayland, *A Memoir of the Life and Labors of the Rev. Adoniram Judson*, 165–172.

Chapter Nineteen
Hall, *Golden Boats to Burmah*, 95–110.
Hunt, *Bless God and Take Courage*, 60–65.
Judson, *The Life of Adoniram Judson*, 96–98.

Chapter Twenty
American Baptist Missionary Magazine, 1814, in archives of American Baptist
      Historical Society, 411.
Hall, *Golden Boats to Burmah*, 110–118.
Hubbard, *Ann of Ava*, 110–128.
Hunt, *Bless God and Take Courage*, 64–68.

Chapter Twenty-One
Hall, *Golden Boats to Burmah*, 113–124.
Hubbard, *Ann of Ava*, 113–128.
Hunt, *Bless God and Take Courage*, 65–72.
James, *My Heart in His Hands*, 95–99, 103–107.

Chapter Twenty-Two
Hall, *Golden Boats to Burmah*, 123–127.
Hunt, *Bless God and Take Courage*, 71–72, 77–78.
Knowles, *Memoir of Mrs. Ann H. Judson*, 142.
"A Letter from Mr. Judson to Dr. Baldwin," *American Baptist Missionary Mag-
      azine*, 1820, 435.

Chapter Twenty-Three
Hall, *Golden Boats to Burmah*, 123–152.
Hubbard, *Ann of Ava*, 133–135.
Hunt, *Bless God and Take Courage*, 77–78.
Knowles, *Memoir of Mrs. Ann H. Judson*, 159–212.

Chapter Twenty-Four
American Baptist Missionary Magazine, 1814, 254.
Anderson, *To the Golden Shore*, 266.
Hall, *Golden Boats to Burmah*, 157–165.
Hartley, *The Three Mrs. Judsons*, 99–105.
Hubbard, *Ann of Ava*, 129–131.
Hunt, *Bless God and Take Courage*, 82, 84–87.
Knowles, *Memoir of Mrs. Ann H. Judson*, 180.

Chapter Twenty-Five
Hall, *Golden Boats to Burmah,* 115–117, 167, 176.
Hartley, *The Three Mrs. Judsons,* 99–105.
Hubbard, *Ann of Ava,* 132–138, 141, 146–147.
James, *My Heart in His Hands,* 124.
Knowles, *Memoir of Mrs. Ann H. Judson,* 180–184.

Chapter Twenty-Six
Hall, *Golden Boats to Burmah,* 171–172.
Hubbard, *Ann of Ava,* 141–147.
Hunt, *Bless God and Take Courage,* 93–96.
Knowles, *Memoir of Mrs. Ann H. Judson,* 189.

Chapter Twenty-Seven
Hall, *Golden Boats to Burmah,* 189–198.
Hubbard, *Ann of Ava,* 150–161.
Hunt, *Bless God and Take Courage,* 98–103.
Knowles, *Memoir of Mrs. Ann H. Judson,* 213–224.
Warburton, *Eastward,* 89–93.

Chapter Twenty-Eight
Hall, *Golden Boats to Burmah,* 197–199, 203–212.
Hubbard, *Ann of Ava,* 161–183.
Hunt, *Take Bless God and Courage,* 104–117.
Judson, *The Life of Adoniram Judson,* 216.
Knowles, *Memoir of Mrs. Ann H. Judson,* 108, 161–200.

Chapter Twenty-Nine
Hall, *Golden Boats to Burmah,* 204–207.
Hubbard, *Ann of Ava,* 164–176.
Hunt, *Bless God and Take Courage,* 112, 116–117.
James, *My Heart in His Hands,* 156.

Chapter Thirty
Hall, *Golden Boats to Burmah,* 207–208, 212.
Hubbard, *Ann of Ava,* 181–182, 188–194.
Hunt, *Bless God and Take Courage,* 116–117, 124, 208.
Wayland, *A Memoir of the Life and Labors of the Rev. Adoniram Judson,* 378–379.

Chapter Thirty-One
Hall, *Golden Boats to Burmah,* 221, 224–228.
Hubbard, *Ann of Ava,* 190, 197–209.
Hunt, *Bless God and Take Courage,* 126–134.
James, *My Heart in His Hands,* 162–164.

Chapter Thirty-Two
Hall, *Golden Boats to Burmah*, 228, 233–234.
Hubbard, *Ann of Ava*, 209–216.
Hunt, *Bless God and Take Courage*, 138–143.
Judson, *The Life of Adoniram Judson*, 247–259.
Knowles, *Memoir of Mrs. Ann H. Judson*, 243, 253–259.
Warburton, *Eastward*, 108–112.

Chapter Thirty-Three
Hall, *Golden Boats to Burmah*, 232–234.
Hubbard, *Ann of Ava*, 209–224.
Hunt, *Bless God and Take Courage*, 139–149.
Warburton, *Eastward*, 111–112.

Chapter Thirty-Four
Hubbard, *Ann of Ava*, 230–231.
Hunt, *Bless God and Take Courage*, 144–149.
Wayland, *A Memoir of the Life and Labors of the Rev. Adoniram Judson*, 112–113, 316–317.

Chapter Thirty-Five
Burma Baptist Chronicles (Rangoon, Burma: University Press, 1963), 56.
Hall, *Golden Boats to Burmah*, 241.
Hubbard, *Ann of Ava*, 230.
Hunt, *Bless God and Take Courage*, 149–153.
Knowles, *Memoir of Mrs. Ann H. Judson*, 260–265.
Warburton, *Eastward*, 114.

Epilogue
Hartley, *The Three Mrs. Judsons*, 174–175.
Hunt, *Bless God and Take Courage*, 153, 157, 162, 315, 319, 349–353.
Rosalie Hall Hunt, "The Matchless Mrs. Judsons," *American Baptist Quarterly* 24 (September 2005), 198–208.
James, *My Heart in His Hands*, 191, 196–199, 201–204.
Judson, *The Life of Adoniram Judson*, 298.
Warburton, *Eastward*, 115.

What Happened to Them?
Burma Baptist Chronicles, 57–58.
Hall, *Golden Boats to Burmah*, 244–245.
Hunt, *Bless God and Take Courage*, 169.
Judson, *The Life of Adoniram Judson*, 300.

BIBLIOGRAPHY

American Baptist Missionary Magazine. Volumes dated 1814–1826. In archives of American Baptist Historical Society.

"Adoniram Judson, The Apostle of Burma." *Calcutta Review 27* (1850): 423–55.

Allen, Jonathan. "Sermon Delivered at Haverhill, February 5, 1812, on the Occasion of Two Young Ladies Being about to Embark as Wives of Messieurs Judson and Newell, Going as Missionaries to India." Haverhill, MA, 1812.

Anderson, Courtney. *To the Golden Shore.* 1st ed. Boston: Brown and Company, 1956.

Brumberg, Joan Jacobs. *Mission for Life: The Story of the Family of Adoniram Judson.* New York: The Free Press, 1980.

Burma Baptist Chronicles. Rangoon, Burma: University Press, 1963.

Campbell, Earl D., and Frederick W. Richardson. *The Hasseltine Genealogy.* Self-published, 1997.

Gouger, Henry. *A Personal Narration of Two Years' Imprisonment in Burmah.* London: John Murray, 1860.

Hall, Gordon Langley. *Golden Boats to Burmah.* Philadelphia: Macrae Smith Co., 1961.

Hartley, Cecil B. *The Three Mrs. Judsons: The Celebrated Female Missionaries.* Philadelphia: G. G. Evans, 1860.

Hubbard, Ethel Daniels. *Ann of Ava.* New York: Books for Libraries Press, 1913.

Hunt, Rosalie Hall. *Bless God and Take Courage: The Judson History and Legacy.* Valley Forge, PA: Judson Press, 2005.

Hunt, Rosalie Hall. "The Matchless Mrs. Judsons." *American Baptist Quarterly,* 24, no. 3 (September, 2005): 198–208.

James, Sharon. *My Heart in His Hands: Ann Judson of Burma.* Durham, England: Evangelical Press, 1998.

Judson, Adoniram. Personal Journal, 1788–1849, and correspondence. American Baptist Samuel Colgate Library. Rochester, NY.

Judson, Ann Hasseltine. *An Account of the American Baptist Mission to the Burman Empire, in a Series of Letters Addressed to a Gentleman in London.* Washington, DC: Mission Press, Columbian Office, 1823.

Judson Centennial Celebration in Burma, 1813–1913. Rangoon: Mission Press, 1913.

Judson, Edward. *The Life of Adoniram Judson.* Boston: American Baptist Publication Society, 1883.

Knowles, James D. *Memoir of Mrs. Ann H. Judson, Late Missionary to Burmah*. 1st ed. Boston: Lincoln and Edmunds, 1829.

"A Letter from Mr. Judson to Dr. Baldwin." *Baptist Missionary Magazine*. 1820. Archives of the American Baptist Historical Society.

Leonard, Bill J. *Baptist Ways: A History*. Valley Forge, PA: Judson Press, 2003.

Manly, Louise. *History of Judson College*. Atlanta: Foote and Davies, 1913.

"Missionary Letter," *The Vehicle* or *Madison and Cayuga Christian Magazine*, no. 11 (August 1814) 79–81.

Pond, Jean Sarah. *Bradford Academy: A New England School*. Bradford, MA: Bradford Academy Association, 1930.

"A Portrait of Adoniram Judson." Salem, MA. Essex Institute Historical Collections, vol. 105, 1969.

Robert, Dana L. *Women in Mission: A Social History of Their Thought and Practice*. Macon, GA: Mercer University Press, 1996.

Warburton, Stacy R. *Eastward: The Story of Adoniram Judson*. New York: Round Table Press, 1937.

Wayland, Francis. *A Memoir of the Life and Labors of the Rev. Adoniram Judson*. 2 vols. Boston: Phillips, Sampson and Company, 1853.

Willson, Arabella Stuart. *The Three Mrs. Judsons*. Missionary Series. Edited by Gary W. Long. Springfield, MO: Particular Baptist Press, 1999.

Wyeth, Walter N. *Ann H. Judson: A Memorial*. Cincinnati: privately published, 1888.

INDEX

310